Belief Transformations

# RENNER Studies on New Religions

*General Editor*
Armin W. Geertz, Department of the Study of Religion, University of Aarhus

*Editorial Board*
Johannes Aagaard, Department of Systematic Theology, Center for New Religious Studies, University of Aarhus
Steffen Johannessen, Department of Danish, Modern Languages and Religious Studies, The Royal Danish School of Educational Studies, Copenhagen
Helle Meldgaard, Department of Systematic Theology, Center for New Religious Studies, University of Aarhus
Ole Riis, Department of the Study of Religion, University of Aarhus
Mikael Rothstein, Institute of the History of Religions, Department of the History of Religions, University of Copenhagen
Margit Warburg, Institute of the History of Religions, Department of the Sociology of Religion, University of Copenhagen

RENNER Studies on New Religions is an initiative supported by the Danish Research Council for the Humanities. The series was established to publish books on new religions and alternative spiritual movements from a wide range of perspectives. It will include works of original theory, empirical research, and edited collections that address current topics, but will generally focus on the situation in Europe.
The books will appeal to an international readership of scholars, students, and professionals in the study of religion, theology, the arts, and the social sciences. And it is hoped that this series will provide a proper context for scientific exchange between these often competing disciplines.

# BELIEF TRANSFORMATIONS

Some Aspects of the Relation Between Science and Religion in Transcendental Meditation (TM) and the International Society for Krishna Consciousness (ISKCON)

---

*Mikael Rothstein*

AARHUS UNIVERSITY PRESS

Copyright: Aarhus University Press, 1996
Printed in England by Cambridge University Press
ISBN 87 7288 421 5

Published with the financial support of the Danish Research Council for the Humanities

AARHUS UNIVERSITY PRESS
University of Aarhus
DK-8000 Aarhus C
Fax (+45) 8619 8433

73 Lime Walk
Headington, Oxford OX3 7AD
Fax (+44) 1865 750 079

Box 511
Oakville, Conn. 06779
Fax (+1) 680 945 9468

ANSI/NISO
Z39.48-1992

All rights reserved. No part of this book may be reproduced, stored, or transmitted, without the permission of the publisher or an authorized licensing agency.

# Acknowledgements

The apologetical hostility towards TM and ISKCON is strong and it was satisfactory to see that my informants, tiffs taken into consideration, had confidence in the project of comparative religion. I am aware of the ethical and psychological challenge that goes along with fieldwork, and I am grateful to those individuals who have given me their trust. The Institute of the History of Religions, University of Copenhagen, and the Research Network on New Religions (RENNER) have supported this book financially for which I am grateful. Finally I wish to express my thanks to my colleague Jørgen Podemann Sørensen for help and inspiration over the years.

This book is a slightly revised version of my Ph.D. thesis from 1993.


Mikael Rothstein
Albertslund
December 1995

# Contents

1. Introduction — 13
2. Transcendental Meditation (TM): An Outline — 25
3. TM and Syncretism — 35
4. The Development of TM's Belief System and the Historical Self-Esteem of the Movement — 62
5. TM: Science as Hierophany — 80
6. Concluding TM: Syncretism as Strategy and Religious Innovation — 98
7. The International Society for Krishna Consciousness (ISCKON): An Outline — 107
8. ISCKON and Syncretism — 115
9. ISCKON and Evolutionary Theory — 144
10. TM and ISCKON: Basic Differences — 166
11. Disputes Between TM and ISCKON — 184
12. Conclusion — 192

Notes — 201

Bibliography — 216

Index — 227

# Preface

In the field of comparative religion all religions are suitable for analysis. For the discipline no religion, religious phenomenon, or religious expression is too odd or too exotic to be studied. Scholarly attention to the most recent religions of the western world, however, are rather limited in comparative religion. Whereas only a few studies on new religions and new religious movements have been produced by scholars of comparative religion, sociologists of religion are very much occupied with the phenomenon. This means that studies in the belief systems and ritual practices of the new religions are relatively few in numbers. By now we know a lot about the sociological aspects but not enough about the religious contents of the new religions. Nor have the historical roots of the new religions always been taken into consideration. Of course the sociological studies relate to the beliefs, rituals and history of the group or groups implied, but very often a deeper understanding could be developed if the analysis concentrated even more on theology, ritual practice and the process of historical change within religious traditions. This, in my opinion, is the obligation of scholars of comparative religion, and this is what shall be pursued here concerning *Transcendental Meditation* (TM) and *The International Society for Krishna Consciousness* (ISKCON).

### A Note on Sources

My data is international as well as local (Danish). Almost everything in print is distributed internationally, and even when local Danish newsletters and other print material are considered it is clear that the religious content hardly differs substantially from international publications. My informants, however, are almost exclusively local, a fact that makes the character and value of the material derived from my fieldwork less ambiguous. My work involves two levels of research: The religious beliefs and official interpretations are analysed through internationally distributed, officially authoritative books, magazines, and other publications, while the receptions of these beliefs are (primarily) studied locally in Denmark. In this sense the present study concerns the relation between science and religion in Danish ISKCON and Danish TM. As the belief systems of the two religious groups, according to the internationally distributed materials are the same everywhere, the analysis nevertheless has a bearing on the two in general.

It is of course important to note that Danish members, with a background in the Protestant Western world, may be inclined to interpret their (new) religious understanding in a way different from fellow-believers elsewhere in the world. For instance, we cannot ignore the fact that the diversity of ethnicity among the members of ISKCON occasionally leads to conflict because the various sub-populations of the group interpret certain religious notions and ethical demands differently (Burr 1984, 235 f.). Nor should we ignore the fact that TM and ISKCON in Denmark are small and in many ways insignificant religions. TM numbers at the most 300 core members, ISKCON around 50. Elsewhere in the world the number of members is numerically larger, although the figures in terms of percentage of the population may be the same. What I am about to present, therefore, is a study of common (international) beliefs within the groups, but the applications of these beliefs are (primarily) analysed locally.

**Literary Sources**

Most studies in contemporary new religions are primarily sociological. The empirical data therefore are usually somewhat different from the material on which this volume is based. This difference raises some methodological problems of principle interest. While the sociological approach primarily relies on fieldwork and statistics, the approach of the historian of religions will just as much focus on various kinds of texts. I am not suggesting that sociologists are unaware of the literary sources, nor that texts are of no significance to sociologists. My point is that sociological analysis in this field in general is interested in aspects that are enlightened through other sources than those in print. In order to clarify my empirical base, which is mostly based on printed materials, I shall briefly describe the texts and comment on their nature and use.

ISKCON as well as TM are religions of letters. Both are based on divine revelations which appear in textual form, and exegetical or theological writings are of immense importance to both groups. This does not mean, however, that all members of the groups are equally engaged in text studies. Some are not. The general picture, though, indicates that the believers (those we may term core-members) in general are well read and well acquainted with the literary foundation of their religions.

There are at least three levels of texts to be considered: 1. Original sacred texts, 2. Modern commentaries and supplements to these original sacred texts and 3. Texts with no formal religious status, although reflecting the religious beliefs of the groups.

Given the occasional character of the last category, it is difficult to define these texts unambiguously. In 'texts with no formal religious status' I include mail-outs, internal pamphlets, religious magazines, newsletters, and so on. At first glance this bulk of materials may seem unimportant, but this is not the case. The religious beliefs and their sociological manifestations are significantly expressed in these kinds of texts. In the case of TM a careful hermeneutical reading of all available texts, including those of no formal religious status, helped sociologist Eric Woodrum describe the belief system of this group (Woodrum 1975). As a matter of fact the popular texts distributed by TM and ISKCON serve as important guides to the actual beliefs of the groups. What we find here are expressions of beliefs and organizational strategies that have survived several layers of interpretation and consideration. The texts in category 1 and 2 have been read, discussed, interpreted, and related to all aspects of the believer's lives, and in the texts in category 3 they find indirect expression. In other words the diffuse texts in category 3 are a distillation of a (more or less) official religious canon embodied in categories 1 and 2.[1]

As they appear I will distinguish between texts of actual and formal significance. This does not imply that the original texts in category 1 and 2 are of less value than those in category 3. It only means that they occupy the believer's attention in other ways than texts that are more easily read and understood. This difference between texts and the way they are perceived and used relate, of course, to the general question of differentiation in small religious groups.[2] Only a minor sub-population, the nucleus or elite of the group, is aware of the entire tradition and its literary foundation, whereas the majority of those participating in the group's activities will be less interested.

In TM and ISKCON the texts in category 1 are traditional Hindu scriptures. The two groups do not cover the same texts, and the scriptures shared by them are, according to theological affiliation, read in very different ways (as in the case of the *Bhagavad Gita*; see chapter 11). While ISKCON in principle is able to use TM's classical texts such as the Bhagavad Gita and the *Vedas*, TM shows no interest in the *Puranas*, the *Mahabharatha* or the multitude of hagiographies on *Vaisnava*-saints that are so dear to ISKCON. Hence ISKCON embraces all traditional *sruti* as well as *smriti* scriptures, while TM almost exclusively restricts itself to the Bhagavad Gita and the Vedas in the religious argumentation. While the classical texts are of utmost relevance, the modern expositions of these texts are even more important. Commentaries, translations and theological elaboration regarding the ancient scriptures are referred to in category 2. In ISKCON as well as TM the *guru*'s translations and commentaries are the main reference.

**Fieldwork**

Apart from interviews with members of TM, my fieldwork since 1988 has been that of the 'participant observer'. I have attended meetings, meditation sessions, lectures and so on over the years, and I have tried to keep up with the written materials published by TM in Denmark as well as internationally. Unfortunately TM has become sceptical of my work since 1993. Members of the group consider it a problem to be designated a religious group, and therefore my writings on the subject run counter to their official policy. This is not the case with ISKCON which I have regularly visited since 1990. My work with ISKCON has been structured in much the same way as with TM: interviews and participant observation. I have interviewed a sample of 11 individuals in TM and 12 in ISKCON. Apart from the more prominent members, my informants remain anonymous.

CHAPTER 1

# Introduction

If there is inconsistency between the sacred texts and modern science, the sacred books have to be rewritten.
(The Dalai Lama[1])

In 1985 Derek Stanesby wrote:

Today natural science rules as queen over all and is commonly accepted as the supreme source of all knowledge. The table has turned. Contemporary religious thinkers now tend to take the authority of science for granted and they try to match their theology to the prevailing western scientific tradition. (Stanesby 1985, 2)

Previously, in the early days of science, the scientific thinkers tried to match their ideas to the religious dogmas in order to establish them as facts. Indeed, in the Middle Ages, the theology of the Church was considered 'Queen of the Sciences'. During the 17th Century's intellectual revolution, heavily promoted by the theories of Copernicus, the scientific world view gradually developed and became divided from religion. It is evident, however, that the religious view of life and being was never totally suppressed, and even today most people allow religious thought to assert some influence over their minds, thus leaving space for metaphysical or religious speculations in a situation of scientific supremacy.

Comparing the situation of the pre-secularized society to that of today, a remarkable structural resemblance is seen. In the 17th Century, when the foundation of modern science was laid, science had to justify itself through the theology and mythology of the religious establishment. Today religion faces the same challenge: It very often has to justify itself through the contemporary dominating system of understanding which is science, or at least to prove itself worthy of attention by arguing against science. The religions cannot ignore what we might term 'the secular myth of science', and frequently modern religious movements will align with science by using scientific language (Ellwood and Partin 1988, 14).

This book focuses on the relations between religion and science in two new religions of the contemporary western world, namely the *International Society for Krishna Consciousness* (ISKCON) and *Transcendental Meditation* (TM), the former being a modern representative of the *Gaudia-Vaisnava (Bhakti)* tradition of the Bengal mystic and religious philosopher Caitanya Mahabrabhu (1486-1533), whereas the latter is linked with the monistic *Advaita-Vedanta* tradition of another prominent religious innovator of India, Sankara (788-820). Both groups will be introduced more comprehensively in separate chapters (2 and 7). Each group represents distinct examples of new religions in the West, and each in its own way relates to the dominating feature of the modern, secularized world, namely science. Both religions, however, are of Hindu origin, a fact which has to be taken into consideration whenever their relationship to science is discussed. Science in the modern sense of the word, as pointed out by professor of philosophy Holmes Rolston, arose in the western world, and one can hardly understand the emergence and nature of scientific thought separated from the foundation of Western culture, namely Christianity and Aristotelian and Platonic philosophy:

Science arose in the West, with logical connections to monotheism. God rationally orders a good creation, disenchants it, forbids polytheism, animism, and nature worship. God sets humans in dominion over nature and calls them into a historical covenant. Such beliefs can grow scientific, especially when combined with Platonic and Aristotelian philosophies, which value rational thought. The early scientists hoped to 'think God's thoughts after him', and science and theism, even in warfare, have since managed to coexist in kinship. Even those who hold that science has now displaced religion may find that monotheism was an effective, necessary preparatory stage. (Rolston 1987, 258)

Considering that the dialogue between science and religion has been going on for centuries in the West, which is not the case in India, we can understand that the material and problems presented here in some respects are new. Both religions are, although originated in India, rooted in the West, and their interest in science — being positive or negative — is closely linked to their present cultural setting. Consequently this book does not deal with the relationship between science and Hinduism. Rather the theme is the relationship between science and two specific western religious groups of Indian origin. None of these groups represent mainstream Hindu thought, and none of them can claim a genuine recognition in India at this moment, although in some respects a closer contact is about to be established. On the other hand, of course, the origin and cultural heritage of both groups are important to our survey, as the present appearances of the groups are determined by a mixture of their Eastern and Western elements.

How do two different new religions react towards science? What are the consequences once religious notions are confronted with secularized, scientific points of view? Do the specific religious ideas of the religions influence their attitudes towards science, and if so why and how? These are some of the questions posed, and hopefully answered, in the following. As the religions at stake in certain fundamental ways are very different from one another, no single answer is given. Rather two characteristic examples of how the meeting between science and religion may turn out are described.

The different attitudes that will appear relate to well-known aspects of Indian religious history, namely the theological antagonism between the monistic Advaita-Vedanta school and the theistic Bhakti traditions. The divergent opinions are many, and the details are multitudinous. The central theological question; whether 'the ultimate truth' should be interpreted either as the non-personal divine (*Brahman*) or as a personal god (*Vishnu, Krishna, Rama* etc.), has been intensively debated over the centuries, and among the most recent representatives of the two traditions the question is still relevant. This theme could be studied extensively within the framework of the traditional material focusing on the different interpretations of for example, the *Vedanta-Sutra*, where the monism of Sankara opposes the theism of Ramanuja, Madhva, Nimbarka and others. Here, however, I shall concentrate on the arguments put forward by two modern Hindu or Hindu-inspired religious groups, both established in the Western world within the last thirty five years. One of them is linked with the theistic Bhakti-tradition while the other rests on a monistic perspective. As indicated above the analysis is limited to one specific theme: The divergent attitudes towards modern science, as expressed by TM and ISKCON.

The present theological disagreements between the two groups only occasionally lead to actual confrontations. In general, ISKCON and TM exist separately with no formalized contact whatsoever. It is true that ISKCON very intensively argues against the Advaita-Vedanta philosophy, and it is true that groups like TM indirectly are mentioned, but direct references are only made exceptionally (see chapter 11). In the case of TM the antagonisms are constantly modified. Nevertheless, the beliefs of TM clearly show that the theistic dogmas of the Bhakti traditions are considered inferior to the absolute monism taught in the Advaita-Vedanta. Consequently, in the analysis of their relationship to modern science I shall concentrate on the belief systems and the differences between the two. In this perspective, and contrary to most studies in contemporary new religious movements, I shall focus on historical and comparative issues rather than on sociology. As some sociological aspects seem to influence the predispositions of both groups, the sociological aspect, however, will not be completely ignored. Although an account of the historical development of the antagonisms between the Advaita-Vedanta philosophy and the Bhakti tradition is not attempted, this account, I hope, will cast new light upon how the two traditions conduct themselves in the modern, secularized world. The basic assumption is that the religions, when related to modern scientific thought, react differently and either form a synthesis or engage in combat with the modern scientific world view according to the nature of their religious ideas, thus forming new or consolidating traditional belief systems. The implications of this subject, and the strategy of the analysis, are further developed below.

The attitude towards modern science as the focal point has been chosen for several reasons. The main interest is on the one hand the creation or development of religious ideas when these occur, and on the other the rejection of or misgivings towards religious innovation or change. Traditionally rooted religious groups like ISKCON and TM were forced to respond to the challenge of modern science, once the founders of the groups inaugurated their missionary work in the West. In the case of TM the confrontation with modern science has led to religious creativity in terms of innovation and syncretism, while the case of ISKCON shows an example of strengthened religious identity through a more or less consistent rejection of the new. No matter how the meeting between science and religion has developed, something has happened which reveals to us aspects concerning the development of religious belief systems and mythologies and the way in which they are communicated in general, and in the exemplified religions in particular. In this case the particular is emphasized in favour of the general, and I shall argue that the traditional (or original) beliefs of the religions in question, by their nature, determine the groups' attitudes towards scientific thought in modern society.

With the conception of science in focus, the analysis concentrates on one of the most recent developments in the history of the world's religions, namely the confrontation with secularized cosmologies. Science, no doubt, is the dominant system of meaning and explanation in the so-called post-Christian, secularized western world, but one can only to a certain extent compare science to religion, and I shall by no means engage in a detailed discussion on definitions. The aim is not to clarify the ontological or epistemological status of science or scientific thought, neither to define the borderline between religion and science. Such philosophical tasks are generally outside the scope of comparative religion. Here it suffices to mention that science and religion are contrasting systems, at least in Protestant Western societies. It is, however, important to acknowledge that science, taken in the broadest sense of the word, is a comprehensive system which forms a substantial reference to most peoples' understanding of their life and world, and that a common ground between science and religion is after all identifiable, especially if we consider the questions posed by both. At the bottom line religion and science alike are engaged in a quest for facts and truths. Therefore the relation between science and religion, for the purpose of analysis, will be treated within the framework of the concept of syncretism thus methodologically being paralleled to the actual religions.[2] This is not to say that science is religion, nor religious. What interests us is the fact that science and religion, referring to 'different cognitive spheres' (Acquaviva 1979, 177), each in their own way form a coherent system of understanding and an interpretation of the world.

18   Introduction

Religious and secular cosmologies are not identical, but they stand on a common ground which makes it possible to study their interaction in the perspective of syncretism.

**Syncretism**

Syncretism is normally understood to be the process of two or more religious systems growing into one another, thus forming a new religious body, but, as mentioned by historian of religions Carsten Colpe, no comprehensive discussion of the concept of syncretism is apparent among contemporary scholars (Colpe 1987, 218-19).[3] One particularly important problem seems to be that the nature of religious interaction or integration vary a lot. Sometimes two (or more) belief systems are completely integrated into one another (e.g. the Afro-Brasilian cults which involve Catholicism and West-African religion), and sometimes syncretism may constitute a situation of religious partnership with no consistent merging (e.g. Shinto and Buddhism in Japan). As we shall see the first aspect of the phenomenon is considered here.

According to Colpe (in a summary of how the concept of syncretism is usually understood) syncretism may serve as an explanatory category in a specific context. It may also, he states, be looked upon as a method for describing and categorizing religious and cultural phenomena. Colpe also points to two basic manifestations of syncretism or syncretistic phenomena: Syncretism may constitute either relations between complex wholes or relations between particular components. Finally, he emphasizes that the concept of syncretism can be used to describe either a state or a process. Above all it is considered a tool for interpretation (Colpe 1987, 219). At this point we may add that this 'positive' aspect of the concept corresponds to a 'negative' aspect: 'Syncretism' as a cultural phenomenon corresponds to 'no syncretism'. By this I imply the fact that religious identity and the construction of religious meaning sometimes are the results of conscious concentration on one tradition in opposition to others. A religious body may well consolidate itself by deliberately disregarding other religious constructions, thus fertilizing what is significant to itself while ignoring foreign religious concepts and social systems. In doing so, however, the officialy disregarded religious traditions are in fact being considered. In order to isolate one religion (or religious system) from another, both religions (or religious systems) must be recognized one way or another. Hence the 'negative' syncretism suggested here is nothing but yet another way of perceiving what inevitably occurs, namely the confrontation of different cultures and religions and what follows thereof in terms of cultural and religious change. Consequently examples of deliberate avoidance of inter-religious or inter-cultural influence may also be studied through theories of syncretism. In the following both perspectives are implied.

As religious belief systems are dynamic, it seems futile to focus on the final product of the syncretistic process. At best we are able to define a religion's *status quo*. We shall never be able to define the end of a religious development unless the religion dies out. On the other hand, for the purpose of definition, this may be a useful strategy after all. Following historian of religions Helmer Ringgren we may ask: 'What is the result of syncretism. What is it like? How does it function?' (Ringgren 1969, 12). Ringgren himself suggests some possibilities:

> It [syncretism] may become an artificial product without many followers, at best an eclectic philosophy, but not a functioning religion. But it may also function and become a real religion, if it meets the need of a number of people. One might say, perhaps, that when the final product becomes functional, it is no longer syncretism in the narrow sense of the word. It all depends on whether you look at the phenomenon from a historical or a functional point of view. It is questionable, whether any follower of a syncretistic religion experiences his faith as a mixture of elements from two or more religions. (Ringgren 1969, 12-13)

Ringgren's account raises some crucial questions. Firstly, I find it hard to distinguish between 'artificial' and 'real' religion. Obviously Ringgren sees the problem of artificial or real in relation to the question of function, but he does not take into consideration that small, heretic groups may function very well and constitute any given element belonging to the phenomenon of religion, as in the case of many new religions of the modern as well as ancient world.[4] Hence in the following, any religious construction, whether syncretistic or not, will be acknowledged as genuine religion.

20  Introduction

Secondly, Ringgren indicates that syncretism is no longer a relevant notion whenever the final product becomes functional, thus favouring the functional point of view over the historical. In doing so he concentrates on the present or final state of a given religious development, thereby risking the loss of important historical dimensions. Further this approach seems to exclude any closer look into the mechanisms which constitute the syncretistic belief system, functional or not. It seems as if Ringgren's initial questions are out of tune with the phenomenon he is dealing with. Syncretism is not something that can be isolated from religion. The phenomenon is a part of the dynamic character of religion (and human culture in general). It is only for the purpose of analysis that syncretism stands out in this analysis. Further it should be emphasized that syncretism is probably better understood if we recognize the phenomenon as something natural and totally expectable. The merging of cultures and religions will always take place when cultures and religions meet. Only rare examples of isolated groups express a development without interferences from other cultures or religions. Syncretism may be a dimension in a process of acculturation or it may be introduced in order to emphasize the universality of certain religious notions. Above all syncretistic developments are deliberately promoted, or at least are quite clear to the minds of the individuals or groups involved. It would be wrong to assume that new religious paradigms arise from nothing or from the unconscious of the cultures. Consequently any state of a religion has to be understood as a transitional phase in an ongoing development, a fact highly identifiable in the present material. In favour of this notion, historian of religions Armin W. Geertz quotes Robert D. Baird (1971) who says:

Historically speaking, to say that 'Christianity' or the 'mystery religions' or 'Hinduism' are syncretistic is not to say anything that distinguishes them from anything else. (Geertz 1992, 179)

Baird, according to Geertz, holds that the term 'syncretism' runs counter to the historical method, as any development or change is part of the historical process. Geertz carries the argument further:

To insist on using the term [syncretism] to characterize certain religions implies that they have brought together elements that are conflicting and illegitimate. It is indeed a pejorative term. Besides the implicit theological and/or ethnocentric value judgement of this attitude, the term diverts the attention from one of the central aspects of religion, namely that it serves as a creative mechanism for producing and reproducing unity, meaning, and meaningful relationships even in the face of inconsistencies. (Geertz 1992, 179)

It is correct, I believe, to consider syncretistic developments as an integral part of the history of two or more religions. On the other hand, it is appropriate to sort out that specific aspect of the historical process in order to analyse more precisely how a syncretistic process takes place. This means that no religions are 'syncretistic' contrary to others, but it also means that syncretistic phenomena may be focused on in the otherwise historical or phenomenological study of any religion. Obviously this discussion relates to the ongoing debate on tradition and change. Although at this point only few historians of religions have contributed, this debate reflects the growing awareness of the complicated relations between traditional religious notions and innovations occurring within the limits of the same religious tradition. It is my suggestion that the novel elements may in fact be looked upon as part of the established tradition (TM), and that misgivings towards syncretism may lead to deliberate action against any merging (ISKCON).[5] Colpe's and especially Ringgren's discussions of syncretism concentrate on definitions and actually lead us nowhere. What we need is neither definitions, nor classifications. What interests is the phenomenon of syncretism, and what we need, therefore, is a strategy that will allow us to ascertain how the dynamic process of religious and cultural coalescence takes place. Otherwise we shall end up with several descriptive types of syncretistic belief systems, with no understanding of why and how the process takes place. It is my intention here to consider the susceptibility to syncretistic development in the religious basis of TM and ISKCON: Why are syncretistic developments with science allowed in TM's case and rejected in that of ISKCON? Why are religious notions sometimes brought into harmony with science, and why is religion at other times looked upon as completely antagonistic to science? What are the preconditions that allow Advaita-Vedanta and TM to embrace modern science, and what are the preconditions that prevent *Vaisnava-Bhakti* and ISKCON to do the same?

The primary strategies are 1. To look into the 'common grounds', that is the analogies and homologies of or conflicts between the involved systems of understanding, 2. To discuss the new languages, new symbols and new modes of expression that emerge as a result of the encounter whether positive or negative. In this way I hope to be able to characterize how, more precisely, science is positively understood in TM's belief system and negatively interpreted in ISKCON.

As mentioned above, it is not my intention to discuss the influence of science on new religions in general. No doubt this subject is relevant to the comparative study of religions, but any generalization requires monographical studies as the empirical background. Far too often the comparative analysis of new religious movements has failed to take detailed monographical studies into consideration. My intention, therefore, is to present two semi-monographical studies in a comparative perspective. By analyzing two sociologically different groups with different world-views, two types of reactions towards modern science will be treated, and by choosing TM and ISKCON, an old theological discussion can be related to the present situation. Accordingly the starting point of this work departs from two fundamentally different situations. From the perspectives of two opposing poles, the intention is to analyse the premises and functions of syncretism between science and religion when this phenomenon occurs, and to explore the reasons why when it does not.

As it appears, I find no difficulty in discussing the relation between science and religion in terms of syncretism. However the timeliness of this combination has frequently been questioned, for instance by biologist Henri Atlan. Atlan claims science and religion to represent two different modes of rationality with different characteristics. If one tries to combine them, one will not end up with a synthesis, but instead both approaches will be lost, he says. In this sense his point of view contradicts the arguments that allow the relation between science and religion to be studied within the concept of syncretism. In order to demonstrate his point, Atlan gives the legend of the unicorn as an illustration: If the existence of the unicorn could be scientifically determined, the unicorn as a unicorn will disappear (Atlan 1986).

Although I feel comfortable with Atlan's thesis on the relation between religion and science, I believe his ideas have missed a very central point. Atlan's understanding of the problem is purely philosophical. He seems to neglect the fact that religion (or mysticism as he prefers to concentrate on) always exists within a cultural setting, and that other aspects apart from the mere philosophical are of great importance. My recognition of the occasional successful marriage between science and religion is not based on any philosophical conviction. My acknowledgement of the possibility of combining the two is solely based on the outsider's observation of religious groups (or religious persons) to whom the synthesis apparently is a reality (TM), or by whom the possibility of syncretism between science and religion is considered a real threat (ISKCON) — no matter what philosophical arguments opposing their views we may advance. Further the recognition of science as a system which partly is comparable to religion is supported by the material represented by TM and ISKCON alike. In both cases science is interpreted as a system (or various systems) of meaning, and the religious reactions are developed accordingly: Science is either seen as a potentially benevolent system with which one (i.e. the religion) can form some kind of cooperation (in the case of TM), or (as in the case of ISKCON) a fundamentally malevolent system that leads away from the religious truth. In either case it is recognized that science tries to establish facts about life and death and time and space, as do the religions, but, as one will understand, the opinions vary on whether science has any success at all.[6]

It should be obvious by now that the opinion of science itself (i.e. the opinions of the scientists behind the modern scientific world view), is only of secondary relevance in this connection. Of course the reaction towards the religious enveloping or rejection of science is of interest, but not for our purpose. Our primary interest is in the religious groups and their interpretation, reinterpretation, use or rejection of modern science. On the other hand the groups themselves very often involve scientists in their argumentations. Therefore, some statements by scientists will be referred to as we procede. It should be made clear that this is for the purpose of analysing the religions and not the self esteem and world view of the scientific community.

Further it may seem confusing that some of the prominent exponents of the belief systems in both religious groups are graduated and highly qualified scientists. But this is the case.

The exposition starts with brief monographical descriptions of TM and ISKCON, followed by the analysis of TM's relation to science. An analysis of ISKCON's relation to science follows, and the exposition ends with a general conclusion.

Please note: In order to make the text readable, comparisons between the two groups have primarily been placed in the section dealing with ISKCON. When the readers have read thus far, they will be acquainted with TM's case and should be able to understand the differences (or similarities). On the other hand they might be confused if ISKCON's example was introduced for comparison in the TM section before the description of ISKCON had been completed. Likewise most of the theoretical considerations have been developed in the first (TM) section. Also note that although comparisons between TM and ISKCON are attempted, the concrete data with regard to the problems discussed here require a more comprehensive account of TM than of ISKCON. Consequently the TM part occupies more space than the part dealing with ISKCON.

CHAPTER 2

# Transcendental Meditation (TM): An Introductory Outline

Apart from the publications of the organization itself, several monographical books deal with *Transcendental Meditation* (TM) and its founder *Maharishi Mahesh Yogi*, but none of them is written by scholars of the humanities or social sciences. On the contrary these books are written by devoted members of TM and more specifically they are classified as sources for the study of TM along with the movement's official publications (examples are Forem 1984, Olson 1979). A few books have been written by ex-members, but they are biased as well. Scholarly descriptions and interpretations are primarily found in literature on sociology of religions, usually although not always for comparative purposes. In terms of sociology TM has been classified as a dimension of the Human Potential Movement (Stone 1976, 93, Bellah 1976, 346), as a 'world-affirming' religion (Wallis 1984, 21) and as a religious group offering to 'release' people from conditions obstructing the realization of their full potential (Beckford 1985, 89). In addition to these classifications, TM clearly forms a part of the broader New Age Movement (somewhat similar to the Human Potential Movement). Further, I know of two theses focusing on sociological themes, but neither one has been published (Woodrum 1975, Rose 1976). Consequently no single work stands out as the central monograph. Considering that TM has been one of the largest and most publicly discussed religious movements during the last thirty years it is remarkable that no major monograph has been published.[1]

## History: Transcendental Meditation and its Founder

Maharishi Mahesh Yogi, the founder and leader of TM (originally *Mahesh Prasad Varma*), was born October 18, 1911 in Uttar Kashi, India. Around 1941 he graduated from the University of Allahabad with a major in physics. While other sources are less specific about his education, it is always emphasized that it concerned physics (Flor 1968, 22, Russell 1978, 25), although his followers will always describe his educational background as that of a scientist. Shortly before his graduation he asked the renowned *guru*, the Shankarasharya of Jyothir Math, *Swami Brahmananda Saraswati* (1869-1953) to accept him as his disciple, but Maharishi[2] was told to complete his education first. From 1943 to the death of his Master, Maharishi, according to TM (Forem 1984, 208), was Swami Brahmananda Saraswati's closest disciple. Opinions vary regarding Maharishi's formal status in the *Sanyas*-order of the monastery of Jyothir Math. Some sources indicate that he was never properly initiated into the order (Melton 1986, 187) while others (Maharishi 1965, 8) maintain that he is in direct succession after Brahmananda Saraswati, and thus linked with the greatest exponent of monistic Hinduism, namely *Sankara* (788-820), the founder of Jyothir Math and three corresponding monasteries in India. If so Maharishi received his initiation at the age of 34. What we know for certain is that Maharishi lived according to monastic principles for 12 or 13 years, and that he apparently upheld the basic elements of that lifestyle once he commenced his mission abroad (Hinnells 1991, 247-48). He was never appointed successor of his own guru (Flor 1968 contains a picture of Maharishi paying his respect to the current Shankaracharya), but the Shankaracharya-institution over the years has remained benevolent to TM, although no formalized recognition or recommendation has been forwarded (Maharishi 1986). According to TM, Maharishi was told to carry on the visions of his Master[3] and was explicitly told to bring the knowledge and use of transcendental meditation (at that time called something else) to every living soul. According to TM, this was exactly what he did when he faced the world, and eventually established the organizing predecessor to TM (*The Spiritual Regeneration Movement* (SRM)) in 1958.

Apart from any lack of official recognition or formal initiation it seems clear that Maharishi has passed on the essence of Brahmananda Saraswati's teaching, but we may well suppose that modifications and adjustments were introduced from the very beginning.[4] However, the esoteric dimension of TM will probably prevent us from finding out exactly how and why, and the TM related materials are of no direct use for the study of Brahmananda Saraswati's life and teaching. Above all, TM will be considered here as a religion in its own right.

Today, as ever before, Maharishi appears as the infallible Master. It is very difficult to determine whether Maharishi himself is involved in current strategies and matters of organizing, but he is undauntedly credited for every achievement and every new thought within TM. His writings, his speeches and his picture dominate the bulk of informative material produced by TM. Maharishi is by all means a guru, and to his closest followers an embodiment of the divine. Indeed devotion to the Master is looked upon as a necessary condition for enlightenment (a concept which at the same time involves soteriological notions), although attempts to intellectually understand his teaching is urged as well.

**Beliefs**

TM refers to its belief system as the *Science of Creative Intelligence* or SCI. Contrary to many other religions TM has not produced a single volume or a series of books which officially describe the belief system. Therefore, no single publication covers the entire set of beliefs and far less the ritual aspects of TM. This situation is primarily due to two things, namely the dynamic character of the SCI and the fact that 'The Perennial Philosophy' is to be 'lived', rather than studied in books. SCI is ever expanding and ever increasing. For the purpose of academic analysis this means that we cannot refer to any single text as *the* authoritative account.

SCI is defined as embracing all the experience and knowledge of the nature, range, growth and application of creative intelligence. 'Creative Intelligence', then, is the 'single and branching flow of energy and directedness in the universe, a concept similar to the Absolute or simply the Divine' (Melton 1986, 189). SCI rests primarily on the monistic philosophy of Sankara, the Advaita-Vedanta, but secondly involves *Sankya*-philosophical aspects. With primary reference to the *Vedas*, the *Bhagavad Gita* and the *Upanishads*, TM teaches that 'The Absolute' is an unmanifest field of infinite pure energy and intelligence, and that Man is able to relate himself directly to this field.

Modern science forms the other important dimension of SCI. Two scientific aspects are present, one which is cosmological and another which primarily relates to medicine and physiology. The cosmological aspect involves a range of modern scientific notions and theories (primarily in the field of physics and mathematics) which TM takes to prove the validity of the religious cosmology of Advaita-Vedanta. At an early stage in his missionary work Maharishi introduced science as a corresponding 'mythology' to his religious teaching, and today (as we shall see) science has merged with religion and formed a new synthesis, a new religious belief system. The medical and physiological aspect of SCI serves to demonstrate the usefulness of transcendental meditation, the main activity of the organization of the same name. As indicated in the brief quotation below, the technique of transcendental meditation, according to TM, will improve what is not good, make perfect what is only good, and consolidate what is perfect. In terms of bodily and physical health, TM asserts that this has been proven through a long range of experiments performed by unbiased doctors, biologists and so on (some have been collected in MERU Press 1977 and further volumes are in preparation). In close cooperation with *Ayurvedic* principles for diagnosis and healing, the various branches of medical science are introduced as the medical/physiological aspect of SCI (Chopra 1989, 1991).[5]

Man is considered one with the universal laws of the cosmos, and it is believed that he is fundamentally good. The anthropology of TM depicts Man as constituted by three *aspects* of existence: He has a gross body which associates with the surroundings; an inner subtle dimension of senses, mind, intellect/ego and *prana* (breath); and finally what is termed 'the transcendental'. Correspondingly Man is a composite of three different *fields* of existence: Objective, subjective and 'transcendental' existence. TM also holds that 'all knowledge' is obtainable, and that the capability of the intellectual mind is far greater than what is currently believed. TM's motto, 'Knowledge is structured in consciousness', points to this and emphasizes that the level of consciousness determines what we intellectually as well as spiritually are able to comprehend (Russell 1978, 169).

TM holds that each person is absolute 'bliss, the great power, the great reservoir of all energy, peace and happiness' (Maharishi 1968,

157), and (using a phrase common to the society in which TM works) that 'the Kingdom of Heaven' lies within each person (Maharishi 1986, 91). The knowledge of this fact, and the ability to establish contact with all levels of 'reality, manifest and unmanifest', thus fulfilling life in every respect, is established through transcendental meditation (see below).

The path towards the ultimate goals is described in terms of 'The Seven States of Consciousness'. According to Maharishi human consciousness exists on seven different levels and spiritual development is identical with progress from the gross to the subtle fields of consciousness. Waking, dreaming and deep sleep are the first three states of consciousness known to everyone. These stages correspond closely to Vedanta's description of the four *avasthas* or 'states of consciousness'. The fourth state is termed 'transcendental consciousness', which apparently is identical with the *turiya* of *Mandukya-Upanishad*. Turiya literally means 'the fourth', the super-conscious state of illumination. The designation 'transcendental' as well as 'fourth' point to this state of consciousness transcending the three familiar, ordinary states. TM explains that this state of absolute consciousness is beyond thought, causality and identification with the physical body. What we have is 'pure, unified consciousness' or 'Being'. Turiya in traditional Hindu context refers to a psychological level. From a philosophical point of view its name is Brahman, and it is only experienced in *samadhi*.

As the practice of transcendental meditation brings the meditator to this level of consciousness, enlightenment is believed to emerge during the progression of the meditation. As the meditation goes on, the awareness of transcendental consciousness stabilizes and manifests itself also when the individual is not meditating. Eventually new levels of consciousness are reached and one enters the state of 'cosmic consciousness', which is the state of liberation or enlightenment. In this (the sixth) state, contrary to transcendental consciousness, there is awareness of the outer world, and an ability to understand the absolute-relative paradox. However, Maharishi claims that further levels await ahead: The sixth state is called 'God consciousness' which involves 'a partial solution to the absolute-relative problem'. In 'Unity consciousness' (the seventh state), when even 'God' is transcended, the ultimate reality is fully understood and any paradoxical relation between absolute and relative is resolved (Campbell 1974. Mainly Ch.7).[6]

Apart from its mystical aspect, the philosophy is also directed towards everyday life:

The Science of Creative Intelligence, says Maharishi Mahesh Yogi, offers every man 'sound physical and mental health, greater ability in action, a greater capacity to think clearly, increased efficiency in work and more loving and rewarding relationships with others'. (Forem 1984, title page)

This aspect is very important. TM's outward agitation almost exclusively points to effects such as those mentioned in this quotation and, as described below, the majority of the meditators identify with such goals rather than mysticism.

Apparently, although avoided in TM's publications, the core notion is that Man, or rather his soul (*Atman*), and 'The Absolute' (*Brahman*) are intimately interrelated, or simply that Atman and Brahman are one. The difference only appears under the influence of Maya. Hence SCI basically describes the relation between the divine in Man and the cosmic divine. Exactly how this relation is, and exactly how to overcome the separation, was, according to TM, rediscovered by Brahmananda Saraswati during his reclusion in the Himalayas for approximately sixty years. When he was eventually persuaded to accept the holy throne of the Shankaracharya of Jyothir Math (at the age of 72 in 1941), he was able to bring back a knowledge otherwise lost to Man. In a cyclical process, according to Maharishi the 'perennial philosophy' is lost due to misinterpretation but again recovered by a *rishi*. Most recently this rishi was Brahmananda Saraswati. In the traditionally shaped part of TM's mythology it is said that Krishna, five thousand years ago, brought the knowledge, but everything he taught was lost again. Two thousand years later Buddha appeared with essentially the same message, but his followers distorted it, and it was lost again. Later on Shankara restored 'the Vedic wisdom' and, established it as a dimension in people's everyday life. But even if he established his four seats of learning (the four *Maths*) the 'perennial truth' was lost once more (Maharishi 1979, 9-17).

Nothing indicates that TM at this instance will let the knowledge vanish again. TM is systematically storing (on videotapes) Maharishi's interpretations and explanations, his guidance in questions of any kind and his instructions regarding the meditation as well as initiation rituals, in order to preserve the infallible guru's words for time to come. In that perspective TM's millennial nature also reveals itself. TM is aiming at a perfect society inhabited by perfect individuals. 'The Seven Objectives of Maharishi's World Plan' announced on January 8, 1972 give an impression of how TM is planning things to develop: 1. (Individual) To develop the full potential of the individual), 2. (Government) To improve governmental achievements, 3. (Education) To realize the highest ideal of education. 4. (Social) To eliminate the age-old problem of crime and all behaviour that bring unhappiness to the family of man, 5. (Environment) To maximize the intelligent use of the environment, 6. (Economy) To achieve the economic goals of mankind in this generation and 7. (Spiritual) To achieve the spiritual goals of mankind in this generation. At this stage of the cosmic evolution 'The Age of Enlightenment', which, according to TM dawned in 1975, prevails and mankind is blessed with extraordinarily good possibilities of achieving enlightenment.

**Rituals: The Aim of meditation in TM**

The practice of transcendental meditation, said to be 'the practical aspect of SCI', is the most important ritual activity in TM. Based on Hindu notions of sacred sounds (*mantras*) the meditation technique is described as 'a means of direct perception, a direct means of getting knowledge' (Maharishi 1979, 473). As we have already seen the meditation must be understood in close coordination with the notion of the seven states of consciousness, as it is through the meditation that the spiritual development takes place. In TM's secular terminology it is said that the meditation eliminates 'stress', which is described as 'obstacles to human development'. In a religious wording the concept of stress corresponds to *karma* : Stress, TM says, causes 'future shock' (Forem 1984, 68-71) and is considered the 'cause of negative behavior' (Forem 1984, 235), and finally it is accumulated during a person's life time (Forem 1984, 57-58). The same can be said

## 32  Transcendental Meditation

about karma in a traditional context. Accordingly the meditation erases 'bad karma' and clears the path towards liberation. The meditation should be practiced for 15 to 20 minutes in the morning and evening, while sitting comfortably with the eyes closed. During meditation the meditator constantly repeats his mantra which annihilates every thought and takes the consciousness to the level of transcendence:

Turning the attention inwards takes the mind from the experience of a thought at that conscious level (B) to the finer states of the thought until the mind arrives at the source of thought (A). This inward march of the mind results in the expansion of the conscious mind (from W1 to W2).

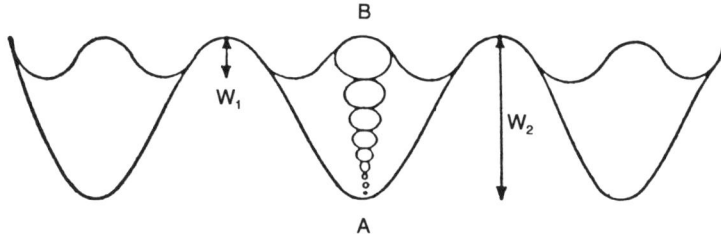

Fig. I (Maharishi 1979, 470)

Apart from ordinary TM technique a line of so called advanced techniques are offered, but above all the so-called *TM-Sidhi program* is promoted. This esoteric dimension of TM's activities, which is based on Patanjali's renowned *Yogasutra*, involves a range of para-normal phenomena including levitation. The effect is basically the same as with ordinary transcendental meditation, only the TM-Sidhi program is considered a much stronger device for spiritual fulfilment, and among inner-group members this practice has been favoured since the late 1970s (it was introduced in 1976). A precondition to the initiation into the TM-Sidhi technique is some experience with the ordinary technique. Today the TM-Sidhi program is as strongly promoted as the ordinary technique. The basic difference between the two is that through the TM-Sidhi program the individual is able to act while experiencing transcendental consciousness, which he cannot during ordinary meditation. This is why the TM-Sidhi program is much more effective, and why it will influence the collective consciousness more radically than transcendental meditation.[7]

A formal initiation is required in order to learn how to meditate. In preparation for this ritual (termed *puja*) the initiate is asked to bring flowers, fruit and a clean handkerchief as offerings in order to show respect towards the tradition. The ritual (primarily involving a recitation in Sanskrit) is conducted by a TM official, and the initiate will usually understand nothing. A closer examination of the ritual reveals the more precise nature of the initiation: The intention is to establish a certain state of consciousness during the time the mantra is passed on to the initiate so that it may work properly. The mantra will not work unless it is implanted during the correct ritual circumstances (Rothstein 1989, 60-83).

## Organization

The development of TM, apart from what has been sketched above is touched upon in Chapter 4. Here it suffices to give a brief account of the organization as it appears today.

TM is primarily based in the United States but centers are found on all continents. The national groups are autonomous but they will always refer to the mother-organization. Lifelong membership is obtained through initiation, but meditators will not hear from the organization after a year unless they register themselves as official supporters. Hence it is difficult to determine the number of practicing meditators. TM's claim is 3-4 million meditators worldwide.[8] In many respects TM's heart is the *Maharishi International University* (MIU) in Fairfield, Iowa, USA (although other centers also provide vital resources for the organization). This institution is officially credited and stands out as an excellent example of how TM officially understands itself, namely as an institution primarily occupied with scientific research and human development: TM does not regard itself as a religious movement. From the scholarly point of view this idea is unacceptable, and in the United States a federal court in New Jersey ruled accordingly. In 1978 it was established by the court that transcendental meditation was a religious practice, and hence it could not be taught in public schools (Melton 1986, 188).[9]

**Internal Differentiation**

Any analysis of TM must take the internal differentiation in the group into consideration. As the participants of TM relate to the organization in many different ways, one cannot assume the same interest nor the same conviction among those in contact with the movement. I have dealt with this problem elsewhere, and the result of this research may thus be summarized: Depending on the level of initiation, TM-members may be classified as members of the periphery or as core-members. The peripheral members only identify very loosely with the organization and usually do not regard TM's ontological system as explicitly religious. To these persons TM appears to be a dimension of the so-called *Human Potential Movement* described by sociologist Donald Stone (Stone 1976). The core members, on the contrary, explicitly interpret their engagement with the group religiously. They identify deeply with the teaching of Maharishi and with TM as an organization. The representatives of the first sub-population have only gone through the primary initiation while the members of the latter in the majority of cases are siddhas (i.e. persons initiated into the TM-Sidhi techniques) and/or TM teachers (Rothstein 1989, 60-138).[10]

CHAPTER 3

# TM and Syncretism

No doubt the integration of science into religion and vice versa in the case of TM is a syncretistic process. SCI, TM's belief system, is an equilibrium; a balancing of forces in a system. Two different systems of recognizing and understanding Life and Being have been woven together, forming the SCI, which, to the followers of Maharishi, is the ultimate and perennial expression of Reality. This combination is based on the assumption that the religious dimension is able to bestow meaning upon the non-ontological scientific dimension. In other words: At its outset SCI insists upon a certain meaning thus forcing the scientific dimension into a pattern determined by the 'knowledge of the Veda'. In this way the synthesism between the two systems is by no means equal. It is not a synthesis of partners of the same standing, but then, a syncretistic construction rarely is. As mentioned by sociologist of religion Ellwood and Partin, the alliance between new religions and science is 'quite unstable and one-sided' (Ellwood and Partin 1988, 15). The position of ISKCON vis-à-vis modern science does not suggest a corresponding interpretation. The Vaisnava-Bhakti theism does not form, nor aim at a unity with the scientific world view. Consequently, no obvious identification of science and religion is at work and no obvious syncretistic process is identifiable in the case of ISKCON.

Here, and in the following chapters, it is the intention to analyse TM's belief system as a syncretistic phenomenon, stressing the preconditions for the integration of the two components (science and religion) into one another.

In the case of TM, where science is met positively, the syncretistic process concerns the synthesis of Advaita-Vedanta/Sankya and modern science. Science cannot and shall not be regarded as religion. This fact could raise questions as to whether it is convenient to study the religious use of science as a syncretistic phenomenon. However, considering TM's actual understanding of the scientific methods and results, this hesitation seems needless. No doubt science, in a certain selection and interpretation, forms a substantial part of TM's belief system, and no real understanding of TM today is possible without recognizing this. The scientific notions are understood in the light of the monistic Hindu beliefs, and a conglomerate of the two constructions is — to TM — the most valid result. Following Colpe (Colpe 1987, 219), we may hereafter describe the belief system of TM as the result of the synthesis of 'two complex wholes' (two systems), which in its intellectual form presents itself as a system of understanding and interpretation of the world. Apart from this 'relation of complex wholes', Colpe describes also 'relations between particular components' as another syncretistic type. Regarding TM it is of great importance to observe that wholeness is always emphasized in favour of particularity whenever SCI is mentioned, as TM understands its relation to science in very broad terms. However, as we shall see, only a selection of scientific theories are in fact highlighted in SCI. In the same way certain religious (Hindu) notions are promoted while others are put to rest or only occasionally presented. We may conclude that TM's example indeed shows a syncretism between particular components. TM claims to be scientific in every respect,[1] but only a selection of true meeting-points is seen between TM's religious heritage and modern science.

The history of TM shows an evolutionary process which gradually leads to an attempted unity of science and religion. It would be wrong to say that this process is over. Since the beginning of this development, TM has adjusted its belief system to the ongoing discoveries of modern science, and nothing indicates a change in this strategy (Chapter 4). In this way the syncretism of TM is what Colpe describes in terms of a state as well as a process (Colpe 1987, 219). Talking of the historical development and the current dispositions of the movement, the dynamic concept of syncretism is very relevant, but in order to analyse the belief system as it appears right now, syncretism in TM's case should be understood as a state.

### The Personal Element

One should not overlook the importance of what Ringgren (referring to Muhammad and Rudolph Steiner) terms 'the personal element in the syncretistic process' (Ringgren 1969, 14). We have already seen that Maharishi, before he was accepted as a disciple of Brahmananda Saraswati, was told to complete his studies, and in 1942, shortly before joining his Master, he graduated from the university in Allahabad. In a speech about his efforts to bring transcendental meditation to the West, and referring to 'experiences of gods and angels', Maharishi stated the following:

It was found that those experiences can also be expressed in the languages of the West, which in modern times [is] scientific language, objective exploration of objective explanation. (Maharishi 1972)

The statement refers to the change in language as far as the belief system is concerned, a development which gradually became clear during the early part of the 1960s. What is of interest here is that Maharishi himself at that time was the only person in the movement with the authority to inaugurate such change. According to my informants Maharishi realized that people in the West needed a recognizable language in order to appreciate his teaching. In other words: The syncretistic process is not merely the result of the meeting of two different systems of understanding. It is just as much — and in the start of his missionary work primarily — the result of Maharishi's deliberate endeavors. Apparently his own educational background as a physicist and chemist has influenced his decisions.[2]

Carl Gustav Diehl makes some very relevant remarks with regard to this by commenting on 'the field where religions meet in the experience of individuals':

A meeting does take place in the sense that religious elements are confronted in the mind of a person but the result is, from the point of view of religions, status quo. The person who at the encounter does not come over will remain in his old religious tradition, and he who does come over enters into a new religious context which does not change through the encounter. (Diehl 1969, 144)

Diehl is focusing on the result of missionary work, and indeed Maharishi's interest in science is a part of his and TM's missionary strategy. Applied to TM and Maharishi this means that the merging of Advaita-Vedanta philosophy and modern science, at its outset, is the result of a single person's efforts and creativity: Originally the idea of combining religion and science was Maharishi's, and the introductory work in order to establish this combination as being meaningful was conducted by him alone. At the same time, however, there is no reason to believe that Maharishi's efforts to bring together science and religion are anything but strategic. An informant told me that the 'language of science is almost as sweet to Maharishi's ears as the language of the Vedas, because they both describe the Absolute'.[3] But the endeavours to unite science and the Advaita-Vedanta remain of importance to TM only. According to Diehl 'the religions' will not react when a syncretistic meeting takes place in the mind of a person. Regarding the present example, it is correct that neither science nor Hinduism has been influenced by Maharishi's construction of the SCI. Hinduism and science at large know nothing about SCI. It is true, however that many individuals of 'scientific' (i.e. Western, non-Hindu) upbringing have recognized what they see as the genius of Maharishi and the uniqueness of the SCI. But such persons (namely the inner-members of the TM-movement) do not represent their traditions at large. Attention should also be given to the fact that most of TM's leading figures are people from the West. Only a few persons of Indian origin are heading TM departments. In accordance with this, only a minor part of the initiated members of the TM movement are Hindus/Indians. TM's Ph.D.'s and TM's Indian *pandits* alike must be seen as individuals partaking in Maharishi's syncretistic process.

Diehl also comments on the eclecticism very often implied in syncretism:

In their looking for bearing in life thoughts and elements from different religions or differently emphasized in different religions may mix and form new concepts or even a new outlook, which the individual believes is in congruence with his 'established' religion. (Diehl 1969, 144-45)

What Diehl points to is the dynamic character of the syncretistic process; that religions — or rather religious persons and groups — are able to accommodate to one another through elaborations, reinterpretations and so forth. The striking feature is what Diehl calls 'congruence with the established religion'. In TM we are able to recognize two different aspects of such a congruence. Focusing on Maharishi (and thus the originator of SCI) Advaita-Vedanta is the 'established religion' and modern science the new component that has been introduced into the belief system. To the vast majority of his followers, Advaita-Vedanta, on the contrary, is the novel aspect in the syncretistic structure while science may be compared to 'established religion'. The quotation above (Maharishi 1972) shows how Maharishi used what he found to be a scientific congruence with his established religion. TM's agitation today focuses on science as the traditional and 'established', and presents Advaita-Vedanta as something new to our culture, something that is in congruence with science.[4]

For many years Maharishi has claimed that all he says, as science matures, will be scientifically verified (Maharishi 1968, 22f.). To TM this is a dogma of ultimate importance because it ensures victory over the doubtful on the basis of scientific proof. It was indeed this dogma that was considered proved when the scientific theory of the GUTs (to which we shall return p. 52) was interpreted as a recognition of what TM had said for a long time. But even this event cannot be regarded as syncretistic in the sense of a meeting between two religions or two belief systems. It is, I believe, the efforts of the few intellectual competent guardians of the SCI which makes the combination possible. It is not the meditators as such and certainly not a 'culture' or 'religion' that merges with something else. Further, as pointed to above, the merging restricts itself to selected elements of the religious as well as scientific world views. As we shall see, this does not mean that SCI proves meaningful only to those who have promoted it. Once established the SCI has complied with the interest of many individuals.

On this basis we can identify a structure of 'syncretistic articulation' as an element in the general articulation of the movement's ideology to its members. Historically the process started with Maharishi's personal findings which led to the formulation of the syncretistic belief system towards 1970. Today the task is taken further by a core of assistants, mainly highly graduated individuals whose academic careers are by now with the MIU. These persons share Maharishi's academic background, but they are, contrary to

Maharishi, almost exclusively westerners with no original affiliation with Hinduism. Their task, therefore, is to incorporate Maharishi's religious teachings into the framework of physics, mathematics, chemistry, astronomy, medical science and so on, and so they do.[5] It is primarily through their formulations that the local TM teachers around the world get their education, and it is beyond doubt that the reasoning and the angles and tactics of argumentation used by all inner-members of the movement, are inspired by the writings of the MIU staff. This does not interfere with Maharishi remaining the superior ideal and guardian of the belief system and the eternal symbol of Truth. Considering that the same individuals are behind almost all of TM's scientific publications, and considering that the staff at MIU forms TM's intellectual elite with special interest in developing the belief system, it can be concluded that a rather small group of individuals actually carry out the adjustment between science and religion.[6] Some of TM's core-members definitely experience an intense identification between science and the Advaita-Vedanta because they understand the arguments and are able to follow the detailed and complex religio-scientific expositions. This group, of course, consists primarily of the staff of MIU. The result of their creative process of understanding and formulation is only secondly presented to the TM teachers and subsequently to any member of the organization or any interested person.

As it appears there are good reasons to focus on individuals in terms of understanding the syncretistic process. In TM, syncretism is not the result of group-mechanisms. Single individuals have formulated a coherent description of reality, and offered their insight to others. Solid sources tell of how the label SCI was deliberately chosen to render TM a marketable commodity in an academic setting. In an interview one of Maharishi's closest associates during the 1960s, Jerry Jarvis, said:

In the fall of 1969 the Associated Students of Stanford university (ASSU) nominated me the ASSU professor for that year. In this capacity we were able to present a course of our choice. Rather than call the course 'The Principle and Practice of Transcendental Meditation', which didn't sound very academic, we called it 'The Science of Creative Intelligence'. The Admissions Office gave us 25 enrollment cards, thinking that would be enough, but at the first meeting of the new course over 300 students came!...

It was a great experience to teach the Science of Creative Intelligence (SCI) in the context of an academically accredited course. This course in SCI is what really developed the interest of the academic community in Maharishi's teaching. (Forem 1984, 216)

Wallis, referring to Scott (1978, 217), has a similar case. According to Scott the sociologist of religions, Robert Bellah, had a conversation with an official of MIU who explained that TM's secularized image was developed for public relations reasons. Further Wallis (through Scott) quotes a lecture given by one of TM's leaders during the 1970s, Charles Lutes, who said:

The popularization of the movement in non-spiritual terms was strictly for the purpose of gaining the attention of people who wouldn't have paid the movement much mind if it had been put in spiritual terms. (Wallis 1984, 35)

It is not wrong to say that the average meditator merely follows a strategy recommended by the leaders of the movement. As the SCI is highly intellectual and actually very hard to comprehend for those with no scientific background, this could be expected. It is, however, very important to understand that the individual in fact sees the syncretistic belief system as meaningful. One source, a middle-aged woman attending TM-seminars during 1990, told me that she was unable to understand the details of the SCI, but that the main aspects were perfectly clear to her. Discussing the matter she asked me whether I had been able to understand everything my teacher of physics told me in school (which I had not!), in order to demonstrate that a perfect understanding is not a precondition for a general acknowledgement. Other sources responded likewise to my questions. During an introductory class a young man asked the TM teacher who lectured, how certain mathematical equations could possibly be compared with stanzas from *Rig Veda*. Receiving a very detailed answer the young man shook his head and said:

I'm afraid I'm unable to understand all this. I was never good at mathematics, but I think I understand the principle. By the way, of course deep spiritual thoughts cannot be interpreted in simple mathematics. It has to be complicated to correspond to spiritual truth. This I understand.[7]

42  *TM and Syncretism*

This statement was very much welcomed by the lecturing TM teacher, as it made the whole construction of SCI legitimate, even if, from an intellectual point of view, it was unintelligible to the audience. Here, as always, it was emphasized that the intellectual understanding was of no absolute importance as long as the meditation was correctly performed.

Following the sociological model describing various levels of affiliation in religious groups developed by sociologist of religion James A. Beckford (Beckford 1985, 81-84), it is possible to show how the belief system is channelled through the various levels. The 'devotees' and the 'adepts', forming the inner-movement in Beckford's model, are the important link between a movement's international elite, (especially the ideologists and theorists at the MIU), and the larger group of 'clients' (in this case those partly or occasionally in touch with the TM organization, although daily practising the meditation). The members of the inner-movement will very often focus their religious attention on Hindu religion and Maharishi's person, although they are well aware of the scientific dimensions of the belief system. In other words: Even if TM's leaders promote the scientific image, a more genuine (traditional) religious affiliation with Hinduism is seen in the inner-movement. While channelling the belief system to the 'clients', however, the scientific image is highlighted. Consequently we are left with a very confused picture. How come that the inner-group is less interested in science when at the same time the elite promotes this aspect? The answer, I believe, relates to strategies of mission more than anything. In order to attract people, TM presents itself as scientific, but to those who are already engaged as inner-members, this self-understanding is only partial. Through their conduct of various Hindu rituals, their close identification with Maharishi and their compassionate interest in Hindu scriptures, members of the inner-movement tend to prefer 'the original' or 'Vedic' as it is termed, formulation. This does not mean that they reject the scientific image. They certainly do not. It only points to the fact that to inner-group members a scientific world description is not enough. To them TM works as a religion in every sense of the word, and dimensions such as ethics, art, literature, social life, rituals and so on are of equal importance to the intellectual description of reality. To the 'clients', however, the involvement with TM remains a well defined element in an eclectic way of life, and no social or cultural dimensions (except for the meditation itself) are searched for within the TM organization. All they need is a good reason to meditate, and to many the scientific interpretation offers the explanation.

The scientific dimension of the belief system was introduced in order to obtain legitimation, and by now it is evident that this strategy was a success. The meditators may not understand all of what they are told (some positively do not), but their religious life is supported by the very same structure of understanding that upholds the surrounding society, namely science, and this is the important thing. In this way the syncretistic phenomenon is important to the group at large, but it remains a fact that only few meditators are able to understand the logic of the SCI.

From a sociological point of view the balance between the notions of the religious group and the surrounding milieu is of great importance. Indeed, as pointed out by sociologist of religion William Simms Bainbridge, it is likely that a religious movement's success depends on its ability to incorporate current idioms into its belief system and ritual practice. In one case this theory is used to predict a future success for Scientology (Bainbridge 1987). On the one hand, Bainbridge says (drawing upon a theory originally proposed by another sociologist of religion Rodney Stark), Scientology has no discernible cultural continuity with the Judeo-Christian tradition (on which society at large depends) — a fact which makes success unlikely according to the theory — but on the other hand Scientology claims cultural continuity with science, that is 'the modern rival of Christianity in defining reality', a fact that theoretically gives the group a prominent basis in contemporary society. Further, Scientology grew out of the popular science fiction subculture (its founder Ron Hubbard was a popular science fiction writer), a fact that gives the group another basis. As Bainbridge sees it this is the strength of Scientology:

Among Scientology's strengths are its several links to science and technology and thus to the crucial cultural forces of our century. Born in science fiction, it can draw on this storehouse of novel ideas and on the vast popularity that this literature recently achieved. While new cosmological ideas of world ensemble and anthropic principle have as yet achieved little popularity, they provide a profound basis for development of Scientological doctrines in directions that would make them highly respectable and attractive to intellectual elites. (Bainbridge 1987, 74)

Actually Bainbridge suggests that 'some religion very much like Scientology will be a major force in the future of our civilization' (Bainbridge 1987, 75). If there is anything true in these speculations, the relative success of TM (and Scientology that originated at the same time) could be at least partly explained. Neither TM nor Scientology reveal any relationship with the Judeo-Christian tradition which, on the other hand, forms the religious basis of the society where both religions primarily exist. For sure no cultural continuity in terms of religion can be found. It is true that TM (as well as Scientology) have made some attempts to gain respectability through the Judeo-Christian tradition, but the alliances sought in that direction are few, insignificant and unimportant in comparison to TM's persistent proposals to the scientific community. If the prediction of Bainbridge is correct, the 'lack of Christianity' in TM should be a disadvantage to the group, but at the same time, the strong identification with science should act as a major advantage.

There are, though, one or two problems related to this line of argumentation. Firstly, not all new religious groups with a Christian background enjoy success. Secondly, one cannot ignore that many new religions have developed on the basis of a criticism of Christianity. In the case of TM it is interesting to observe that many inner-members express their gratitude to Maharishi for having shown them 'another path'. Officially they will most likely stick to the argument of the universality of the meditation technique, but in private conversations one will frequently meet statements like this:

We have totally forgotten our real abilities. In ancient times, I think, people were much more aware of the spiritual realities. I think the [Christian] Church holds a great responsibility. It sort of forced people to reject and forget. It is a shell with no life in it. To me it was very refreshing and very surprising to learn of the Veda. I do not see how Christianity shall ever again gain influence in spiritual matters.[8]

Many New Age groups relate themselves to Christianity, but only very rarely to a Christian doctrine recognizable to mainstream Christians. The traditional Theosophical identification of Jesus as the coming *Maitreya*, for instance, and its placing of the New Testament's Christ as one of the *Mahatmas* of the 'Great White Lodge', is of course, in some way, a further development of the Christian tradition, but the paths followed are very far away from what Christianity normally is taken to be. This makes the broad New Age movement a standing argument against Bainbridge's thesis. Harmony with the existing religious tradition may be advantageous, but the opposite situation also seems to be potentially fruitful. The New Age movement, of which TM in certain ways is a part, has established contact to a great variety of people, and numerically counts surprisingly many individuals (Melton et al. 1991), but the contact to the Christian tradition in the traditional sense is very limited.

On the other hand Bainbridge's theory seems to be supported by the way TM is seeking intercourse with science. It has already been established that SCI originally was developed in order to align with a dominating segment of modern society, and the future may very well show that the longevity of TM depended on its intense occupation with science (i.e. if TM survives). As a matter of fact TM would have no reference to Western ways and notions without its scientific image. In my opinion it is most likely that TM's relative success depends on its use of science which is the only cognitive linkage to the general world view of the modern Western world.

TM seems to be a mixture of conflicting structures. It does not attempt an understanding with the traditional religious basis of society, at least not whole-heartedly, but it does whatever is necessary to appear trustworthy in the eyes of the scientific community. Even if TM never communicates its inducements we may safely conclude that science, considering the values of contemporary society, is considered a safer partner than Christianity. One concrete example of this point of view is the fact that TM officially merges with scientists and scientific subjects, while only informal relations to Christianity exists, mainly thanks to single individuals' private relations.[9]

46  TM and Syncretism

Leaving the question of recognition and missionary visions, I now turn to TM's belief system in order to determine how more precisely the syncretism between science and religion is established.

## Religion and Science in the SCI

One of TM's most prominent monographers (like most of those who have written about TM, a dedicated disciple of Maharishi's himself), Jack Forem, describes SCI in the following words:

[It is] derived from a combination of Western scientific methods of objective investigation and the ancient wisdom of subjective development proclaimed in the Vedas. It draws together knowledge of the nature, origin, development, range and application of creative intelligence in individual life and throughout creation, from the structure of the atoms to the motion of the stars. (Forem 1984, 6)

Such descriptions rest upon earlier official announcements from TM like the following:

The Western scientific approach to knowledge is based on the non-variability of the objective means of observation. The Eastern approach to knowledge is based on the non-variability of the subjective means of observation. Speaking of the East, we know that there is a level of consciousness called rithambhara pragyan which is non-variable in its nature, and therefore, on that level, the knowledge of an object never changes but remains authentic and truly scientific for all time. Western science has continued to contribute to the advancement of civilization because good minds in he West have persistently applied to objective methods of gaining knowledge, whereas Eastern civilization has not continued to contribute to the advancement of civilization because good minds in the East have not persistently applied the subjective methodology of gaining knowledge.... The Science of Creative Intelligence is the glorious meeting ground for Eastern and Western ideals of gaining knowledge. Through this science all men everywhere will enjoy the highest achievements in life in the fullness of all glories, material and spiritual. (Creative Intelligence s.a., 2)

One observes how Maharishi is balancing between the faults and benefits of the East and West respectively. Western science is described as an outward system which has led to the 'advancement of civilization' due to the persistent efforts of 'good minds'. The contribution of the East, a science of consciousness, on the other hand, has not achieved its potential since good minds of the East have not 'persistently applied the subjective methodology of gaining knowledge'. The last statement refers to the idea that the knowledge of the perennial truth, that is the object of the 'Eastern approach to knowledge', was lost to mankind until the spiritual undertakings of Brahmananda Saraswati (Maharishi 1979, 9-17). While Western science made progress on the outer level, the spiritual development of mankind was ignored. Only since the development of SCI (due to Brahmananda Saraswati and Maharishi), has humanity had the opportunity to gain perfect knowledge because both aspects are incorporated into the same body.

The text reveals that Maharishi from the beginning was impressed by the achievements of Western culture, and that he was also conscious of how to bring Eastern and Western notions together. The text also points to the strategy that has been with TM all along: TM does not disregard Western culture. On the contrary the intellectual discourse of Western science is looked upon as impressive and necessary. By introducing 'Eastern science' in terms of Advaita-Vedanta, TM aims to complete the achievements of the West (and indeed the rest of the world). As indirectly expressed in Maharishi's text, it is believed that nothing can ultimately develop unless it is supported by 'the Creative Intelligence' which is reached through transcendental meditation.

But how are the components of SCI brought into harmony?

The monistic theology of Advaita-Vedanta (in TM especially based on the non-theistic Upanishads, the first six chapters of the Bhagavad-Gita and the Vedas) and the element of atheistic Sankhya-philosophy, are the primary preconditions to the marriage between religion and science within TM. The power ruling the universe — Brahman — is above all interpreted as *nirguna* — of no definable quality. Brahman is talked of as 'the Eternal', 'Imperishable Absolute', 'the Supreme Nondual' or *'sat-chit-ananda'* ('Pure Being, consciousness, bliss') (Maharishi 1965, 1979). It is there, but we cannot depict it or measure its nature in any way. Brahman is frequently described through negation; 'not this, nor this...', and only through mystical union is a direct perception considered possible. All the gods of the relative realm are termed *saguna*, indicating a manifestation of a certain aspect of the non-personal divine. That which is Brahman reveals itself primarily through the sacred writings, preferably the Vedas (Maharishi 1965, especially 35f.). Hence 'The Veda' or 'Ved',[10] is often put at the centre of TM's displays and argumentations. As mentioned in Chapter 11, TM only indirectly supports contemplation on the personal manifestation of the divine, and it is only for the purpose of explaining the sovereignty of the unmanifested divine (Brahman) that the personal manifestation (God/*Ishwara*) is mentioned (Maharishi 1968, 265-94).

From a structural point of view, we may consider this notion of the divine quite in harmony with the concept of natural forces within science. The natural forces such as gravity and electromagnetism cannot be directly perceived (although the existence of gravity for example is obvious!), but whenever submitted to scientific analysis any phenomenon will reveal how the natural forces — like Brahman in Hinduism — constitute the basis of its existence. In both cases absolute all-pervading forces are considered the foundation of the universe. Hence TM equates the process of scientific investigation to the practice of transcendental meditation. The meditation itself is rendered into a 'technology', which, according to TM, 'is the most important tool for all future scientific research' (MIU Press 1988, 7, Modern Science 1988, iii) because it is through meditation that Man can most directly understand the Universe.

A compatibility between Indian philosophy and Western science is not only a TM dogma. In his 'critical survey' into the relations between science and religion, professor of philosophy Holmes Rolston considers some of the philosophical, metaphysical and religious notions which go along with the idea of Brahman. Among other things Rolston asks in what sense nature is descriptively explained as a derivation of Brahman (Rolston 1987, 260). The notions considered by Rolston are primarily *samsara, avidya* (ignorance), *prakrti* ('nature') , *maya* (illusion) and *parinama* (evolution/creation), all of which are present in Advaita-Vedanta or Sankhya. Discussing the implications of the various notions, and relating them to the scientific understanding of the world, Rolston says:

Certain elements here are congenial with scientific descriptions. All natural items use common tectonic materials, manifestations of a simple primordial energy. Apparently substantial matter dissolves into a fluxing wave set that at microscopic levels loses its pictureability and becomes (in Hindu vocabulary) 'formless and undifferentiated'. If one does go back to the big bang, all 'name and form' collapses in the incredible energies of the primordial state, when the universe was collapsed into nothingness, which was also the consummate greatness.
... Brahman is the spaceless, timeless matrix for the particle play. Brahman is the infinite potential, the superposition of quantum states, from which there bubble up in random play [here Rolston refers to the concept of lila] the material states of our native levels. The entropic and negentropic tendencies in phenomena can be demythologized from Shiva, the destroyer, and Vishnu, the creator, aspects of Brahman. (Rolston 1987, 261)

What Rolston points to is some kind of common ground of science and religion (or more precisely science and certain Hindu notions), some principles of great functional likeness or even of the same 'substance'. Rolston refers to scientific theories about 'the Big Bang', quantum mechanistics and entropy and finds structural parallels. TM centres on other theories but perceives the same kind of similarity.

While Rolston considers Hindu notions in a broader sense, others have specifically touched upon Sankara (who, of course, is of direct relevance in TM's case). Let us, by quoting historian of religions Frederick Copleston, see how Sankara, hypothetically, would consider science, even if our considerations in this respect remain considerations. According to Copleston, scientific knowledge and method (had it existed at that time) could be accommodated within the framework of Sankara's philosophy. Copleston says he would not regard science as the only way of obtaining knowledge about the world, and concerning his soteriological notions (the liberation of the soul from the sphere of time and change) he would not attach ultimate value to science. However:

At the same time he could quite recognize the pragmatic value of science not only in regard to its technological application but also in regard to the conceptual mastery which it provides over the world of plurality. ... it would be possible for him to recognize the role of science within this world, without thereby being compelled to abandon his metaphysics. (Copleston 1980, 73)

The important point has already been made clear: Certain structural and functional parallels between science and Advaita-Vedanta/ Sankhya are recognizable, and in principle, following Copleston, TM is liable to regard science in much the same way as Sankara hypothetically would have done. Sankara did not know of modern science and therefore never bothered. Maharishi is facing a scientifically oriented world and therefore focuses his attention on science. The syncretism between science and religion in TM is a historical phenomenon in the sense that it only occurs because TM finds itself in a certain place at a certain time where science dominates. If, however, the preconditions to such a development had not been present — if TM's religious and philosophical basis had been differently shaped — then clearly TM would have acted in another way.

In principle it is the same phenomenon Carsten Colpe points to (although with no strong determination) in his article on syncretism and secularization. Talking of the meeting between indigenous peoples' religions and Christianity he says:

If we disregard names of spirits, places, persons and gods, which generally are taken from one or the other tradition and only in sophisticated exceptions are coined artificially, and just look to structures and essences, we have to ascertain a complete amalgamation. In mythologies which are concerned with gods, heroes, tricksters, and ancestors, combination is the more frequent form in which syncretism becomes concrete. The Christian Trinity has room for one or two Christian or native figures, and analogously the same holds true for Christian figures in families or clans of native gods; in the mythical prehistories of the tribes or clans the roles of biblical and native actors can be combined or the actors just added to each other, and the same can be established in the eschatological posthistories. (Colpe 1977, 164-65)

This phenomenon is well known, for instance in the Afro-American religions of Brazil where Catholic saints are identified with the Orixas of the Yoruba in terms of common functions or appearances (Bastide 1978). TM has no ancestors and no personal gods to introduce to science, but neither has science anything to equal such entities. Instead TM has a row of metaphysical notions and principles which, in TM's interpretation, are comparable to scientific models and theories of the universe. In this sense the similarity between Colpe's example, or the example from Brazil, and TM is a matter of structure. The pattern and the function seems to be the same. This has already been described, but in the following chapters the discussion will go into more details.

TM prefers very complicated scientific models for identification. The idea is clearly that the level of complexity in the scientific parallels functions as a stronger evidence than more comprehensible examples. Indeed some of TM's public announcements are totally unintelligible to ordinary people with no expert knowledge of physics (Fig. II). On the other hand it would be wrong to identify the complexity of TM's scientific writings as manipulating maneuvers. There is no reason to doubt that the dedicated members of the organization, and those who actually produce the scientific materials, are convinced of the profound religious meaning of the complicated calculations and equations. The attention is only drawn to the complicated nature of the materials in order to describe how SCI usually is articulated.[11]

Only rarely a more simple use of science is seen. Maharishi for example outlines how the unmanifested impersonal takes the form of the manifested realm, by introducing the example of hydrogen and oxygen:

Remaining as hydrogen and oxygen, the substance takes on different qualities and appears as vapour, water and ice. Similarly, the omnipresent impersonal almighty Being, while remaining as the absolute, manifests into different qualities of forms and phenomena of creation. (Maharishi 1968, 266)[12]

According to TM sources, the Vedic knowledge cannot be rendered into scientific language unless the most recent and most speculative theories are introduced. Only at this point has science matured to a degree where a genuine comparison between scientific results and 'Vedic knowledge' is possible, they claim. Accordingly TM refutes any critique. A TM representative said:

SCI may be incomprehensible to many people, but there is no other way to explain things. Even if Being is simple to reach through meditation, it is very hard to explain what it is in ordinary or scientific language. If you make the equations more simple, they become scientifically meaningless.[13]

## 52  TM and Syncretism

This problem of communicating the belief system is very hard to overcome: The details are hard to understand, but the only alternative formulation is that of the traditional Advaita-Vedanta. Hence, if TM wants to explain its notions to a Western audience, it has to use the complicated language of modern science.

Now let us consider some examples of how SCI is promoted. The first example is rather simple, the second somewhat less comprehensible to most people. Each example, however, points to the same conclusion, and apart from the more or less complicated setting, the structure of the texts and pictures is the same.

### Example One

Since 1988[14] TM has intensively worked to demonstrate the parallels between quantum physics and transcendental meditation.[15] The arguments are derived from a rather recent, but also speculative, set of scientific theories concerning a so-called Unified Field which, according to the physicists behind the theories, is the source of all laws of nature. These theories (known as 'Grand Unification Theories' or simply GUTs) claim all the natural forces (electromagnetism, weak interaction, strong interaction and gravity) and particles of nature to be united in 'Superunification' (Morris 1990, 59-63), thus suggesting a basic unity in the cosmos. This idea that everything emerges from a common field, shares distinct features with Advaita-Vedanta's notion of Brahman as the unifying source of the entire universe. In other words, the basic assumptions in Advaita-Vedanta and the theories of 'Grand Unification', from a structural point of view, rest upon a common ground. On this basis TM has built a detailed argument which aims at demonstrating how the notions of 'the Veda' and the principles of transcendental meditation are confirmed by the most recent scientific theories (there are iconographic as well as textual approaches to this matter. We shall return to the pictures below). On the back of one of the more prominent and intellectual publications in this respect, the publishers write:

Exploration of the Unified Field of all the laws of nature is at the forefront of contemporary scientific research. This journal is devoted to research on the Unified Field and its applications for the benefit of mankind. It draws upon a new technology for investigating the Unified Field that combines the approach of modern science and ancient Vedic Science as brought to light by Maharishi Mahesh Yogi.

Modern science has arrived at an increasingly comprehensive and unified understanding of the laws of nature. Most recently, theoretical physics has identified a unified structure of natural law on the most fundamental distance scale of nature. In super-symmetric quantum field theories, this boundless and all-pervading 'Unified Field' is described as the self-interacting, self sufficient, and infinitely dynamic source of the physical world. All the force and matter fields that comprise the universe have their basis in it and sequentially emerge from it through a self-interacting dynamics by which this Unified Field gives rise to all diversity. In discovering the Unified Field, physics has glimpsed the unified structure of the entire universe.

The following paragraph relates specifically to TM's religious, or rather mythological, heritage and reads:

This account of the Unified Field from modern physics correlates precisely with the experience of a self-sufficient, self-interacting, and infinitely dynamic field of consciousness delineated by the founders of the Vedic tradition in the Himalayas many thousand years ago. These ancient seers discovered the capacity of the human mind to become consciously identified with this universal and unbounded field of pure intelligence at the foundation of nature, and they delineated the self-interacting dynamics by which it gives rise to all diversity in nature.

At this point the text turns to the special achievements by Maharishi and his organization:

Maharishi has revitalized and reinterpreted this ancient tradition in the form of a modern systematic science, known as Maharishi's Vedic Science. He has also made available a technology, called the Maharishi Technology of the Unified Field, by which anyone can effectively investigate the Unified Field of all laws of nature on the level of direct experience of consciousness. The integrated science linking modern science and Vedic science, also founded by Maharishi, is known as the Science of Creative Intelligence. (Modern Science and Vedic Science 1988)

According to TM the SCI deals with the analysis and understanding of nature or the entire cosmos. 'Nature' is compared to 'Absolute Truth', 'the Absolute', 'Creative Intelligence' and consequently, but only rarely in the words of TM itself, Brahman or the divine. In the same way TM says that human consciousness rests upon a fundamental state of awareness which is 'transcendental consciousness'. According to TM this level of existence can be directly experienced through transcendental meditation. During the experience of transcendental consciousness, 'Being' or 'Pure Intelligence' — which is the same as Brahman — is perceived with no limitation and any paradox between relative and absolute dissolves (Campbell 1973, 111). TM, therefore, sees the GUTs as a mirror of 'nature's sequential functioning', which in turn 'mirrors the sequential, self-referral, self-interacting flow of the Veda":

The Bhagavad Gita describes the dynamism of natural law within its own unmanifest nature in the words *prakritim svam avashtabhya visrijami punah punah* — 'Curving onto my own nature, I create again and again'. This self-referral functioning on nature is described by unified quantum field theories (1984) in terms of 'spontaneous sequential symmetry breaking', the phenomenon whereby the Unified Field creates the entire manifest universe from within its own self-referral (non-linear) dynamics. It is this process in nature that, unseen, is creating a Unified Field based perfect civilization from the embodiment of the Unified Field, the embodiment of the totality of pure knowledge, Maharishi. (Maharishi 1986, 1)

The Veda is itself the foundation of the universe (nature), which to the academic mind, according to TM's interpretation, finds a modern expression in the theory of the Unified Field. SCI, then, combines the two dimensions, Veda and academic science, and reestablishes an insight into the mechanisms of the universe which is more than merely descriptive. SCI, like its straightforward religious predecessors but contrary to ordinary science, also directs people and tells them how to behave in order to fulfil their lives, physically as well as spiritually. To TM, SCI is as genuine and normative as the original Veda.

Thus the intellectual process of modern physics is paralleled to the process of transcendental meditation. In both cases Reality in some mode is experienced. In physics through intellect. In meditation through 'our own inner divinity, our consciousness'.

The figure below shows one of TM's typical descriptions of the relation between the GUTs and transcendental meditation.

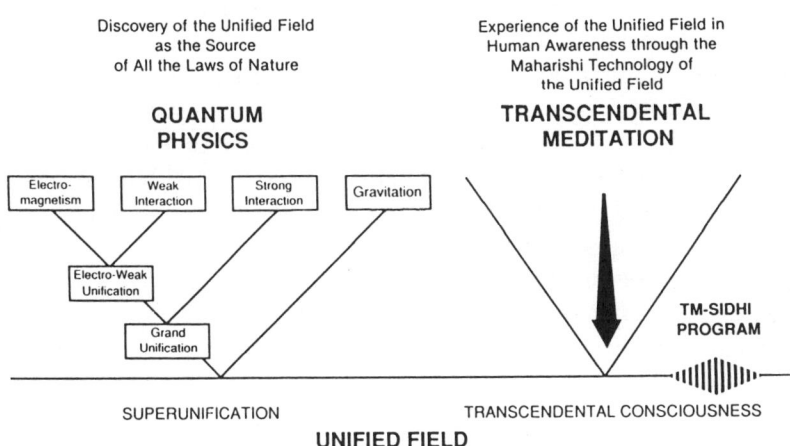

*Fig. II* (MIU Press 1988, 7)

From an iconographic point of view it is seen that both aspects of cognition (quantum physics and transcendental meditation) are depicted in the same way, as triangles or funnels, through which all knowledge or all forces are condensed into the same point, namely 'superunification' or 'transcendental consciousness'. The scientific theory, which in itself bears no meaning, becomes meaningful through this identification, and the theories of the Unified Field not only support TM's claims, they also become an integral part of TM's understanding of the world. The syncretistic process, therefore, is not loyal to the self-esteem of the natural sciences since the identification of 'superunification' as transcendental consciousness forces religious meaning upon an otherwise secular scientific theory.

**Example Two**

This example is taken from an article in MIU's 'Modern Science and Vedic Science' (1989, 142-43) by MIU psychologist Professor Michael Dilbeck. The table (fig. III) depicts the relations between physics, mathematics, and physiology in terms of the first verse of the Rig Veda and involves a wide range of recent scientific theories. The structure of the table speaks for itself: The stanzas of the first verse of the sacred text correspond to scientific principles or theories in three different fields of learning. The structure of the table itself suggests that knowledge in its totality is contained within the verse, and that modern science by now is gradually — and through different paths — approaching the same knowledge.

Any deeper exploration into the scientific details is beyond my ability. Our main interest, though, is not the reasonableness of TM's design, but rather the fact that the design has been made, that it was possible. Again we must focus on the structural aspects. In TM's interpretation the religious language of Rig Veda covers the same phenomena as the technical languages of modern science. No ordinary reading would result in a rendering such as the one proposed by TM, but then, TM's reading is not ordinary. The interpretation, according to TM's internal logic, rests upon the wholly developed consciousness of Maharishi, and thus more than ordinary intelligent reasoning lies behind. Like SCI in general, this isolated aspect has only come forth because Maharishi's spiritual knowledge and ability to interpret what modern physics is pointing to, have become known to others. The staff of MIU, who is behind this publication, is directly inspired and led by Maharishi, and it is never kept a secret that without Maharishi's knowledge and guiding light, such an undertaking would not have been possible (Modern Science 1989, iv). The syncretistic process therefore involves Maharishi's person as the central figure. He is the direct precondition for this interpretation. On this basis it is obvious that TM's interpretation is based on a recognition of 'the Veda' and Maharishi as ultimate authorities. It is a specific interpretation of the sacred text, which focuses on common features that allows the minute identification with science.

## Tradition and Renewal

Recently, commenting on 'tradition and change' Armin Geertz has turned the focus from change to persistence, claiming persistence and change to be aspects of the same social phenomenon, namely, 'tradition' (Geertz 1992, 23):

> In order for a tradition to remain viable, it must be resilient on the one hand and malleable on the other. It must change in order to retain meaning in the face of changing social and political circumstances. It must draw on the central narrative to account for change. It must objectify and symbolize agents of change whether foreign peoples or ideas, internal mechanisms or factional interests, in order to identify and ultimately assimilate these agents in terms of indigenous theory. (Geertz 1992, 23-24)

This is precisely what TM has done, or at least aimed at. Maharishi's ambition to adapt his teaching to modern, Western standards led to the incorporation of science into his traditional religious monism. The cultural and social conditions surrounding Maharishi himself and his teaching was fundamentally twisted once he left India. He found himself to be in a situation where he would either remain traditional but unnoticed, or become untraditional and known. Although choosing the latter possibility he, in TM's view, never left his roots and never compromised his teaching. It was prolonged in a way so that it could reach people in the West, and any current change is indeed looked upon as a continuous development along the original path. The language for communicating the message has been broadened, but the message itself, according to TM, remains unchanged. Even if TM's construction of a synthesis between science and religion only appears to be logical and inevitable to the believers themselves, it is obvious that this creative syncretistic process rests upon tradition. What TM has done is the result of the possibilities already contained within Maharishi's religious outset, and, focusing on Maharishi, the result of the possibilities from his educational

## TABLE 2
## ANALYSIS OF KEY THEORIES FROM PHYSICS, MATHEMATICS, AND PHYSIOLOGY

| | ऋचो अक्षरे<br>RICHO AKSHARE<br>The verses of the Ved exist in the collapse of fullness (the kshara of 'A')... | परमे व्योमन्<br>PARAME VYOMAN<br>...in the transcendental field. | यस्मिन्देवा<br>YASMIN DEVA<br>In which reside all the devas, the impulses of creative intelligence, the laws of nature... | अधि विश्वे निषेदुः<br>ADHIVISHVE NISHEDUH<br>...responsible for the whole manifest universe. |
|---|---|---|---|---|
| **Physics — Superstring Theory** | In heterotic superstring theory, force and matter fields are generated by spontaneous compactification (collapse) onto a Calabi-Yau space or orbifold, leading to the topological breaking of an internal gauge symmetry down to a grand unified subgroup. | As the dynamics of the superstring field appear only at the Planck scale, they are effectively unmanifest. At observable distance scales, the dynamics of natural law are approximately described by an ordinary super-symmetric quantum field theory of point-like particles. | All the fundamental particles and forces arise as the massless modes of vibration of the underlying superstring field. The gravity superfield and the gauge superfields result from the direct product of the left-moving modes and solitons with right-moving modes. | The gravity, gauge, and matter superfields together span the five fundamental categories of quantum fields responsible for the whole manifest universe; the spin-2 graviton, the spin-3/2 gravitino, the spin-1 force fields, the spin-1/2 matter fields, and the spin-0 sparticles. |
| **Mathematics — Set Theory** | The principles of set theory describe the progressive unfoldment of greater and greater infinite totalities starting from the null set. This process of generating sets is based upon the collapse of a finite or infinite totality of sets to a point value—a single element of a new set. | The infinite totalities and processes described by set theory transcend the boundaries of the finite localized expressions of nature in space and time and must be located in the infinite, unbounded field of consciousness. | The principles of set theory embody both the organizing power that creates the mathematical universe from the null set as well as the organizing power that structures mathematical knowledge, on the basis of logical analysis of collections of objects. | The organizing power embodied in the axioms of set theory is capable of generating all known mathematics — all mathematical structures can be located in the set theory universe, and all proofs can be validated on the basis of the principles of set theory. |
| **Physiology — Molecular Genetics** | Principle of transcription—the DNA molecule contains the totality of biological knowledge within an organism. This knowledge is expressed when a specific portion of the DNA molecule is transcribed or copied into messenger RNA through the process of complementary base pairing. | DNA stands for the transcendental in the field of physiology in that it is metabolically non-active and stable in itself, and yet it is the basis for the regulation of the metabolic pathways and activities of the organism. | The most fundamental physiological value of information is available in the physical structure of the codon, a sequence of three nucleotides in messenger RNA. The sequence of each codon and their specific arrangement in messenger RNA is specified by the information contained within the functional units of DNA, the genes. | The genes, by determining the specific sequence of codons in messenger RNA, are responsible for generating structural and functional proteins in every cell of the organism. These proteins both act as essential components for many anatomical structures and regulate basic physiological activity. |

*Fig. III*

## IN TERMS OF THE RICHO AKSHARE VERSE OF THE RIG-VED

| यस्तन्न वेद् | किमृचा करिष्यति | य इत्तद्विदुस् | त इमे समासते ॥ |
|---|---|---|---|
| YASTANNA VEDA | KIMRICHA KARISHYATI | YA ITTADVIDUS | TA IME SAMASATE. |
| He whose awareness is not open to this field . . . | . . . what can the verses accomplish for him? | Those who know this level of reality . . . | . . . are established in evenness, wholeness of life. |
| Before superstring theory, quantum gravity was beset by apparently insurmountable problems resulting from severe ultraviolet divergencies. In superstring theories, the massive string modes provide an effective high-frequency cut-off, rendering the theory free of divergencies. | In previous unified field theories based on extended supergravity, the spin-1 and spin-1/2 components of the N=8 gauge supermultiplet are apparently too few to account for the rich structure of elementary particles and forces at the electro-weak and grand unified scales. | Theorists acquainted with the internal gauge structure of the heterotic string and its spontaneous compactification to four dimensions can explain the emergence of an entire grandunified family of gauge forces along with complete chiral generations of quarks and leptons. | Superstring theory presents a profound holistic vision, in which all the diversified aspects of natural law are not separate from the unified field itself. All the fundamental particles and forces are modes of vibration of the self-interacting unified superstring field. |
| Without the knowledge of set theory, rigorous mathematics would be restricted to finitistic arguments and constructions—mathematical procedures that can comprehend, relate, and manipulate only a finite number of distinct elements at one time. | Restricted to finitistic methods, most of modern mathematics could not have been developed—including the fields of analysis and topology. Fields such as these require the transcendental concepts of set theory to formulate their most fundamental principles (axioms). | All branches of modern mathematics employ the language of set theory to express their basic concepts and principles, and systematically employ the principles of set theory to analyse in an exact way both finite and infinite collections of elements. | By providing a common language and a common criterion of right knowledge for all areas of mathematics, set theory provides a foundation for a grand unification of mathematics in which all mathematical knowledge and activity are integrated in a single, coherent whole. |
| Defects in the transcription process, due to an insufficient or faulty transfer of information from DNA to messenger RNA, disallows the knowledge contained in DNA to be properly utilized and leads to the formation of an RNA with an incorrect sequence of nucleotides. | Defects in the transcription process which result in the formation of a faulty protein cause the organizing power inherent in that protein to be either not properly expressed, or expressed in such a manner as to distort and even disrupt normal physiological activity. | The proper transcription of messenger RNA ensures that the sequence of nucleotides in the DNA is copied through the process of complementary base pairing in the correct corresponding sequence of nucleotides in messenger RNA, thus enabling the complete information in DNA to be properly expressed. | The proper transcription of messenger RNA enables correct information from DNA to be utilized for the construction of properly functioning proteins — the essential organizers and regulators of balanced biochemical activity. This provides the essential basis for effective and integrated physiological activity. |

background as a physicist. The development, therefore, corresponds to TM's own linear historical vision which places the organization as a logical consequence of an ongoing loss and rediscovery of the Vedic gnosis as well as the meditation technique. Most directly this is expressed in Maharishi's earlier writings:

The whole complex of the universe is so designed that all must evolve — angels, man, animals, birds, insects — and all must forge ahead on the highway of evolution and must reach the ultimate destiny in God Consciousness... Therefore, according to the Divine Plan, comes the Spiritual Regeneration Movement.[16]... Here comes a process suited for the present time. (Maharishi 1968b, 143)

Likewise in Maharishi's commentary on the Bhagavad Gita. Towards the end of the preface it reads:

India is a country where Truth matters most and Indians are a people to whom God matters most. Indian soil has witnessed many times the revival of life's true philosophy. The people of India have never hesitated to return once more to the right path whenever it was convincingly pointed out to them that their way of life had taken a wrong course. This receptiveness to Truth of the Indian people has always been a source of inspiration and a signal of hope to all movements aiming at the revival of true life and living. (Maharishi 1979, 16-17)

The most recent of the movements Maharishi mentions is, of course, TM; and the Indian people — so we learn from the full context — are no longer the only population towards whom 'Truth' is articulated.

This analysis focuses on the development of the belief system. From a sociological point of view, however, it is necessary to stress again that only Maharishi himself and a minor group of leading members of TM, are in fact rooted in Hinduism, while the vast majority of those developing and articulating the SCI today are of Western origin. 'Tradition' in TM's case therefore involves the phenomenon of Westerners adopting Hindu concepts as a part of their own heritage (as we shall see a similar phenomenon can be identified in ISKCON).

In the following chapter, the development of TM's belief system will be discussed more intensively, and I shall primarily focus on how TM undauntedly claims SCI to describe an absolute, cosmic Reality. The chapter demonstrates how the same religious structures are identifiable at every stage of TM's history, even within TM's scientific image.

CHAPTER 4

# The Development of TM's Belief System and the Historical Self-Esteem of the Movement

During the last three or four decades TM has undergone significant changes and passed through different periods with different characteristics. In order to describe and analyse the development of TM's belief system, and determine how and when science was introduced as a means for religious expression, it is necessary to look closer into this development. In the previous chapter I have already discussed aspects with relation to TM's general development, but here I shall focus the attention on the historical dimension. This discussion leads to a specific analysis of TM's most recent development which is contained in Chapter 5.

It was on December 31st 1957 Maharishi 'was inspired' to establish the *Spiritual Regeneration Movement* (SRM) to 'spiritually regenerate mankind' (Maharishi 1986, 6), and therefore the year 1957 is celebrated as the inaugural year of Maharishi's movement, now known as TM. Two years before, in 1955, he had left Uttar Kashi in the Himalayas where he had lived in reclusion, observing a vow of silence since the death of Brahmananda Saraswati in 1953, and begun his mission in the city of Rameshvaram in the state of Kerala in South India. According to TM 'a faint impulse, so gentle, so tender, [that] came so naturally', made him approach the world again: Rameshvaram...Rameshvaram (the name of the city) was repeatedly mentioned in Maharishi's mind:

> It was the impulse of nature itself that moved Maharishi in 1955 to leave his secluded life in Uttar Kashi and travel to southern India, with no other thought or plan in his mind than simply to follow the whisper of nature, 'Rameshvaram'. But in this innocent move was contained the blueprint of a new age and a new civilization, just as the sprouting of a seed has all the vitality to expand and produce the fruit, season after season. (Maharishi 1986, 1)

According to TM Maharishi made a point of visiting temples and shrines wherever he went on his way to Rameshvaram, and during a stay in a temple of *Kanyakumari* he first received 'the inspiration to give the blessing of the Himalayas — the eternal wisdom of life contained in the Bhagavad Gita — to the people of South India' (Maharishi 1986, 189). On a later occasion when he visited the temple of *Guruvayur Krishna* in Kerala the same inspiration came to him, but this time it was from 'the embodiment of the Absolute, Lord Krishna' (Maharishi 1986, 189).

At this early phase of his mission, Maharishi had already developed his belief system. According to TM's reflections concerning the earliest stage of Maharishi's work, his 'philosophy' was wholly developed when he left his recluse in the Himalayas.[1] At that stage, however, it only existed in his mind in the sense that he had never educated pupils or even given lectures. The belief system was not formulated in language, nor spoken nor in print. Somehow it had to be articulated: When Maharishi, following 'nature's impulse', approached a temple in Rameshvaram a man came up and asked him if he gave lectures. Maharishi answered no, but confirmed that he had given up his vow of silence. In his own words he 'never thought of lecturing'. Nevertheless, according to TM, the man arranged a series of seven lectures and imparted Maharishi to his plans:

I replied, 'I will give you the titles in one week'. So it was strange. I had no option, and it just came like a very natural flow. I never thought of lecturing. So I dictated him seven topics, not knowing what I did say. Speaking had been such a foreign thing. I said 'leave a copy with me'. (Maharishi 1972, no page)

The most important references to the period (1952-57) is given in TM's official history of the movement written in 1985 (Maharishi 1986, 177-202). Here it is described how the press caught the story of a *yogi* from the North who spontaneously gave a series of lectures, and how Maharishi, due to the efforts of the delighted people of Rameshvaram, travelled throughout Kerala and initiated people and taught them how to meditate (Maharishi 1986, 193). According to the same source, six months after Maharishi's arrival, the devotees of Brahmananda Saraswati and Maharishi in Kerala arranged a 'Spiritual Development Conference' in honor of the two. The devotees arranged a *yajna*, a ritual to 'invoke the blessing of God' in the city of Cochin from October 23 to 26, 1955 where 'spiritual leaders, leaders from all walks of life, and devotees of Guru Dev for all over India attended' (Maharishi 1986, 193). It is also explicitly mentioned that an astrologer was consulted in order to determine when and how Maharishi's knowledge would be most successfully brought to the rest of the world (Maharishi 1986, 194). After leaving Kerala, Maharishi travelled throughout India for about two years where 'hundreds, sometimes thousands of the local people came to hear [his] wisdom and be instructed in the technique of Transcendental Meditation' (Maharishi 1986, 199).

TM's reflections on this period describe Maharishi as the true inheritor of Brahmananda Saraswati's position. He did not become the new Shankaracharya, but he did become his own guru's tool in the process of spiritual regeneration. It is said that the TM Movement began in 'Infinite Silence' on a spiritual level according to Vedic principles (Maharishi 1986, 177-79). For our purpose it is relevant to observe that Maharishi's activities in this period (1953-58) — according to the sources that have been at my disposal — were contained within an entirely Indian/Hindu milieu. We must not forget that Maharishi had some scientific training before he joined his guru, but it is significant that no external (Western/scientific) influence upon Maharishi is seen in the first phase of his activities. The sources may be weak at this particular point, but from what we know, nothing seems to indicate any scientific influence at this early stage.

As far as I know, only one publication with relation to Maharishi appeared prior to 1958, namely a book entitled 'Beacon Light of the Himalayas' (a title referring to Maharishi's person) which was to commemorate the Spiritual Development Conference in Cochin (I have not managed to obtain the book). Apparently this book was produced by some of Maharishi's followers, not by himself. Hence it is very difficult to know what Maharishi actually said. TM's historical outlining is not too clear at this point: There are a lot of quotations, but most of them cite what Maharishi has said in later years, recalling how it all started (Maharishi 1986). Even so, one important thing is mentioned, namely that a group of devotees of Brahmananda Saraswati in the town of Alleppey started an organization called *Adhyatmic Vikas Mandal* after a discourse where

Maharishi 'elucidated the true meaning of spiritual development' (*adhyatmic vikas*) (Maharishi 1986, 194). Considering that founders of this organization were devotees of the former Shankaracharya, it is reasonable to believe that they have considered Maharishi's teaching authoritative. Although we cannot ignore possible alternative explanations such as a demand for renewal, it seems that Maharishi was capable of representing his own guru's ideals in such a way that traditional devotees of Brahmananda Saraswati (and hence followers of the Advaita-Vedanta religion) accepted him. In other words, it seems as if Maharishi's teaching was quite traditional. Further there is nothing special about the way he was received and treated: The charismatic guru is a well established institution in the Hindu context. Maharishi's classical appearance in this respect is documented in many photographs. Exclusively Indians and no Westerners are seen in the pictures from this period (1952-58) (Maharishi 1986, 31-57).

Sociologist Eric Woodrum, from a sociological point of view, has described how TM gradually left its explicitly religious origin and entered a phase of intended secularization, by dividing the history of the group into three phases. His phases, however, do not cover the earliest years of Maharishi's religious carrier (1953-58) where, as we have seen above, the foundation of TM was laid. On the other hand, what Woodrum is interested in is the TM movement, and no actual movement existed prior to 1958.

Above all Woodrum describes TM's development as a shift from 'Other-worldly religion' to 'This-worldly religion'. The first phase in his system, covering the years 1959-65, he calls 'the Spiritual-Mystical Period':

...when TM was interpreted as the most important component of a holistic program for spiritual evolution, non-attachment to the relative, material realm, eventually leading to liberation from the cycle of rebirth, and attainment of nirvana [sic]. (Woodrum 1977, 39)

In this period straightforward religious publications such as 'Love and God' (1965, Maharishi 1965) and 'Science of Being and Art of Living' (1963, Maharishi 1968) appeared, and Maharishi was admired as a genuine representative of an old religious tradition. No reformulation of the classic beliefs was seen, neither in content nor in terminology.

Woodrum's period, beginning in 1959, marks Maharishi's arrival to the West. According to another sociologist, Donna Sue Rose, Maharishi had travelled to Kuala Lumpur in Malaysia by May 1958 as the first stop on his first World Tour. In August he was in Singapore, and then he went to Hong Kong. After half a year of missionary work in South East Asia 'he realized that at his rate of progress it would take him over two hundred years to reach all the world's population'. Therefore he decided that he had to go to 'the most developed country', namely the USA, because he believed people there to be more 'in the habit of adopting new things', contrary to people in Malaysia, Singapore and Hong Kong where he started his missionary activities outside India (Rose 1976, 50). TM's own historical account talks about the USA as the 'most creative country' (Maharishi 1986, 275), and it is said that people in the States responded with great warmth and appreciation and that Maharishi had an 'enthralled' audience at every lecture (Maharishi 1986, 275). People in the States, TM says, 'felt blessed in his presence' (Maharishi 1986, 241). At this point Maharishi terms his followers 'the family of good disciples of Shri Guru Deva' (i.e. Brahmananda Saraswati) (Maharishi 1986, 234), and although he approached the West there is no sign that he would give up his traditional style.

Maharishi's first years in the West have been described by some of his followers. With great enthusiasm and humour Helena Olson, for instance, tells about how Maharishi stayed with the Olson family just after arriving in the United States in 1959. The followers were few, and good personal relations existed between the individuals. Maharishi was considered a personal friend, and there was no organization apart from what was established more or less *ad hoc* by the same devoted meditators. In Olson's book Maharishi is described as a holy man from India, a 'Master from the Himalayas' (Olson 1979, 23). One of the things that is frequently mentioned is Maharishi's astonishment at the ways of 1959 Americans. For instance he became embarrassed when accommodated in a teenager's gaudily decorated room (Olson 1979, 41) and he was amazed to discover how easily the phone was used (Olson 1979, 97). He had a 'shrine room' prepared where he lived, and in the first 'Meditation House' another shrine room was arranged (Olson 1979, 118). According to Olson, Maharishi was quite explicit concerning Hindu religious notions. *Karma, samsara*, reincarnation, purification and unity with the divine are mentioned in many speeches (Olson 1979, 141f.). Apparently no transformation into scientific language was introduced at this point, but in the mid 1960s Maharishi discovered that 'the spiritual experience of transcendence' could be described as 'impulses of creative intelligence'. In 1972, commenting on what made him develop the scientific language Maharishi said (as already quoted on p. 37) that:

It was found [in the mid 1960s] that those experiences can also be expressed in the language of the West, which in modern times [is] scientific language, objective exploration of objective explanation. (Maharishi 1972, no page)

Maharishi is not explicit about when this discovery was made, but it must have been just prior to the next phase suggested by Woodrum (1965-69) which Woodrum terms the 'Voguish, Self-Sufficiency Period'. Maharishi's important work 'The Science of Being and Art of Living', originally published in 1963, did contain predictions that science eventually would be able to confirm the 'Vedic knowledge', but no actual attempt was made. During this period, Woodrum rightly says TM experienced a considerable growth, and was to some degree identified with the ideals of the 'counterculture', a fact which shows a development towards Western modes and ideals, although those of a subculture with no general influence. The scientific presentation which was supposed to establish SCI as a trustworthy system in the eyes of the Western establishment, was not introduced to the public with any determination until later. Characterizing the period between 1965 and 1969 Woodrum says:

The traditional Hindu understanding of the goals and effects of TM were significantly modified. The goal of 'cosmic consciousness' was described in terms of bliss, energy, and peace without references to the loss of the individual ego or the serious implications of non-attachment to the relative, material realm. (Woodrum 1977, 40 f.)

It was during this period that TM strove to align itself with persons

68  *The Development of TM*

or groups with ambitions of changing society. TM wanted to change things, and apparently the leaders of the movement thought that this was most successfully done through cooperation with people who had equal ambitions. In this period TM primarily agitated in campuses, and a special branch of the organization (at that time SRM) was set up in 1965, namely the Students International Meditation Society (SIMS) (Forem 1984, 210). Further TM made positive contact to various notabilities in the so-called counterculture (musicians, actors etc.) (Maharishi 1968, back cover). Most remarkably for our purpose is the shift in language. The terminology from the earlier period was softened, and strictly religious words were substituted by alternative terms with no direct reference to religious beliefs. Apart from the examples mentioned by Woodrum, quite importantly the concept of 'stress' as an alternative to karma (see p. 31) was introduced.

Jack Forem's book 'Transcendental Meditation' (Forem 1984), originally published in 1974, touches upon the development of TM in the period between 1965 and 1969, but no information is given concerning the development of the belief system. Written in 1974, his description of the movement's history primarily consists of considerations about the past (1965-69), and as a matter of fact there is only little material covering this period in TM's current publications. Apparently the 'counterculture' years are only of little interest to TM today. However, something interesting may come up when the next volume of TM's official history appears (it has been awaited since 1986).[2]

The success during the 'counterculture' period was limited. Towards the end of 1968, according to professor of philosophy Jacob Needleman, Maharishi returned to India, rather disappointed by the low rate of initiations in the USA (Needleman 1972, 131-32). During his ten years of missionary activities in the USA, Maharishi and TM had, according to sociologists of religion William Simms Bainbridge and Daniel H. Jackson, performed a total of 15,300 initiations, a number far below the intended ten percent of the population (Bainbridge and Jackson 1981, 144). This indicates that the history of TM, as experienced by Maharishi himself, was not a purely positive and progressive process (although this is what contemporary leaders of the organization and the published material suggests) and a change of image might have been a necessary strategy.³ The short period of four years, where counterculture ideals were promoted in terms of 'communal living', 'peace' and 'love', however, was never to influence TM at large.

Some years before, as we have seen, Maharishi had gradually begun to discuss the possibility of a scientific identification of his belief system, and in 1969 (as already mentioned) one of his closest associates, Jerry Jarvis, introduced the Science of Creative Intelligence (SCI) to the American public (Forem 1984, 216). It seems as if Maharishi withheld the 'scientific strategy' in favour of the 'counterculture strategy' from 1966-69. Since 1970 the focus has shifted accordingly. Until 1970 (since the mid 1960s) TM aligned primarily with students and counterculture youth, but after 1970 the ambition has primarily been to introduce TM and SCI to academics, businessmen and educators at all levels. Woodrum, therefore, correctly begins his final phase in 1970, and apparently he maintains this as the last in his most recent article on TM from 1985. According to Woodrum in this period, 'The Secular, Popular Religious Phase', TM emphasizes: 'the practical physiological, material, and social benefits of TM for conventional persons, with almost no other-worldly references' (Woodrum 1977, 41). It was from 1970-85 TM most intensively strove to prove its claims concerning the meditation through physiological, neurological and psychological experimentation (Bloomfield et. al. 1977). More important, this also was the period when TM established its scientific image and did (as we have already seen) whatever possible to be recognized as a non-religious organization. Among the most important features of this development was the establishment of MIU and, of course, the rendering of the belief system into scientific terminology.

Woodrum is not the only one who has made this observation. A similar development is described by Robert McCutchan:

Publications dating from the late fifties are overtly religious and spiritual. Other early publications such as Love and God, Commentary on the Bhagavad Gita, The Science of Being and Art of Living, are overtly Hindu and religious. After about 1970, however, the movement focused entirely (at least in terms of its public phase) on the scientific verification of psychological, physical, and social benefits of TM. None of the more recent publications even mentions God, much less Hindu cosmology. Simply one could say that the Hindu cosmology remained, but expressed in more 'sanitized' language. *God* became cosmic creative intelligence; *atman* became the pure field of creative intelligence within, *karma* became the law of action and reaction; *brahman* became the ground state of physics. (McCutchan 1977, 146)[4]

The language changes, but the object remains the same. McCutchan's text very clearly points to the structural correspondence between Advaita-Vedanta and science. The phrase 'Creative Intelligence', which McCutchan quotes, has no scientific meaning, but 'the law of action and reaction' and 'the ground state of physics' are somewhat intelligible to scientific thinking. Comparing the different words used at different times we can conclude that Brahman (Maharishi 1963 and 1965), 'bliss' (Goldhaber 1976), and 'the ground state of physics' or (referring to the previous chapter) 'The Unified Field' (MIU Press 1988) in fact refer to the same.[5] In the same way it is possible to compare TM's texts (not only words or expressions) from different periods. The following example from the late 1970s regarding 'Brain Wave Coherence and Cosmic Consciousness' ('a glimpse of life lived from the field of all possibilities'), presents a description and interpretation of an EEG analysis of meditators:

## Finding:

Witnessing was positively correlated ($r = .64$, $p < .01$) with the total alpha (8-12 Hz) EEG coherence between the four electrode placements, and was less strongly but significantly correlated with coherence in the theta (4-8 Hz, $r = .41$) and beta (12-25 Hz, $r = .45$) frequency bands...Subjects with the clearest experiences of transcendental consciousness also reported the strongest signs of stabilization of pure awareness ($r = .77$, $p < .001$).

## Interpretation:

Cosmic consciousness arises through the regular practice of the Transcendental Meditation technique which stabilizes pure awareness or transcendental consciousness ... In this state of perfect mind-body co-ordination thoughts meet with full and harmonious co-operation of the body, resulting in powerful, fulfilling actions. (Maharishi 1978, 446-48)

During the past decades TM has changed course and strategy, and by necessity the style of the written sources has changed accordingly. What is described above, however, is fundamentally the same thing Maharishi thought of when he in 1965 poetically wrote:

How do we improve the depth of our heart?
By probing deep into the purity of our being. By exploring the finer regions of the impulse of love that murmurs in the silent chamber of our heart. By diving deep into the stillness of the unbounded, unfathomable ocean of love present within our hearts. By a simple technique of self-exploration or by what is commonly known as Transcendental Meditation. (Maharishi 1965, 21)

The first text refers to scientific findings regarding the meditation's effect. The technical data, obtained through EEG analysis, points to the fact that specific patterns of brain activity are seen during meditation. This description of changes in brain waves is interpreted as signs of higher states of consciousness appearing during meditation. The second text is not occupied with the empirical measurement of alternative states of consciousness. Here it is simply declared that such 'finer regions' exist, and that they can be reached through meditation. The scientific text aims at a verification of the meditation's effect while the traditional religious text simply states what are supposed to be facts. In this sense the two texts refer to the same things, but with different emphasis according to different goals and different strategies.

Summing up we can conclude that the outer appearance of the movement and the way the belief system is articulated varies over the years, but it seems as if no actual change has taken place with regard to the content and structure of the belief system. According to Woodrum, and apparently to McCutchan as well, TM is now as secularized as ever, a fact mainly due to the current strategy of recruitment promoted by the leaders of the organization (Woodrum 1982, 100), and the process of deliberate secularization will continue. Woodrum's conclusion, of course, is more than ten years old, but at this moment, TM's intention of developing a secularized image has certainly not declined. On the contrary the organization has intensified its secular image during the last decade. However, I seriously doubt that this means that TM *in fact* is secularized, and that SCI is a non-religious belief system. In my opinion the apparent secularization may well turn out to be something else. Consequently I shall suggest yet another phase which is closely linked with TM's discovery of the Unified Field that was placed at the top of TM's agenda in the year 1983, but, more important I shall suggest another way of seeing things.

**A New Phase?**

Maharishi proclaimed 1983 to be the 'Year of the Unified Field, The Ninth Year of The Age of Enlightenment' (Maharishi 1986, 592). At that point he formulated 'The Maharishi Technology of the Unified Field' by:

...uniting the glimpse of the Unified Field by modern science, the abundant knowledge of the Unified Field through Vedic literature, and the large body of scientific research on the Transcendental Meditation and the TM-Sidhi programme. (Maharishi 1986, 592)

1984 was proclaimed 'Year of Unified Field Based Civilization', 1985 'Year of Unified Field Based Education' and 1986 'Year of Unified Field Based Perfect Health for All Mankind'. In 1985 Maharishi inaugurated a new university, *Maharishi Vedic University* (MVU) in cooperation with 'Vedic scientists'. From 1987 onwards TM (MIU to be precise) has published the periodical 'Modern Science and Vedic Science' and various books on TM and science (e.g. MIU Press 1988, Chopra 1989, 1991, Wallace 1991), and MIU has intensified its scientific educations. In short: TM has made every effort to align with science. By now the belief system is only articulated in scientific terms to the public, while it was confined to a traditional religious (Hindu) vocabulary in its earliest stages. But how does this suggest yet another phase in TM's development? In what way does this intensified interest in science describe something new?

During Woodrum's second phase TM obviously was not interested in formulating a new, coherent cosmological language. The need for practical meditation and alternative cultural identity was favoured. In Woodrum's final phase, when science was deliberately introduced into the belief system, we see a new interest in cosmology. During this phase TM wants to establish a new language in order to explain its beliefs and ideals. This reconstruction of religious language, I believe, has culminated in recent years. TM has now entered a phase where cosmological explanations have regained their original position, although there has been a complete change in language. Science has become more than a strategic device. The language of science has become a plausible way of communicating religious meaning. If the scientific phrases were of nothing but scientific significance it would be correct to see TM as secularized indeed. However, the theory of the Unified Field is not just another scientific cosmology to TM. It is interpreted as a scientific confirmation of ancient religious truths, and therefore it refers to the same truths as the ancient religious tradition of the Advaita-Vedanta. While adopting the scientific language of the West, Maharishi never discharged the religious language of Hinduism. He merely stopped using it. The difference is very important. TM never spoke against, and never speaks against Hinduism (nor any other religion).

In his latest phase Woodrum finds TM to be without 'other-worldly' references which means that secularized, scientific notions have taken over. However, since 1983 — since the introduction of the Unified Field Theory in a TM context — the 'other-worldly' perspective has been reintroduced even if these references are made in scientific language. As we have already seen, TM's publications explicitly mention that a close correspondence exists between the scientific expressions and the Veda, and in the following chapter we shall see how members of the movement are inclined to interpret scientific models and figures as expressions of religious truths: 'The Scientific Age is Rising to be the Age of Enlightenment', TM says (Maharishi 1986, 589).

Consequently there are reasons to see the last ten years of TM's history as a period of religious reinterpretation rather than a period of intensified secularization. Due to the discovery of 'common grounds' between Advaita-Vedanta and the Unified Field Theory, science has been given a new status. It has become an expression of religious truths. Chapter 5 provides a closer examination of this development. Here it suffices to conclude that what appears to be scientific supremacy over religion in TM is in fact the opposite.

Focusing on appearance and style, science dominates religion, but regarding content or substance, religion still reigns.

**TM's Internal Perspective**

TM's self-perception and conceptions of how principles of religious truth have been and currently are articulated, is of some relevance in this connection. According to TM any change or development can be explained within the framework of the belief system. This means that the historical development described above, from TM's internal perspective, can be utilized and elaborated into meaningful phases in the movement's salvation history. For our purpose it is interesting to observe that the internal conceptions of development confirm that nothing substantially new is seen in the present articulation of the belief system.

The internal understanding of a religious philosophy is not necessarily a constructive approach to its history. However, TM's self-esteem and comprehension of history and evolution, is of great significance in this connection. We are interested in the development of beliefs and how they are articulated, and by considering TM's own understanding we are able to determine how the current belief system is understood and indeed how it fits into TM's general cosmology.

In the introduction to TM's official history the publishers (referring to the period until 1986) explain the history of 'the Dawn of the Age of Enlightenment', the millenial era inaugurated by Maharishi, as:

...the history of the senquential unfoldment of pure knowledge and its infinite organizing power from the source of pure knowledge in one individual; His Holiness Maharishi Mahesh Yogi...Every step in the growth of Maharishi's Movement has been the natural expression of the force of evolution, silently reshaping the destiny of the world through the thought and action of one moving in perfect attunement with the infinite intelligence of nature. (Maharishi 1986, 1)

From the first instance, according to this text, TM has been led by cosmic principles, and the current phase of the movement is not interpreted differently (Maharishi 1986, 2). From a sociological point of view, TM has attuned itself to the demands of the surrounding world, and in principle TM accepts this description, but the focus is, as we understand, placed somewhere else. To TM the changes in belief system and organization is more than history and sociology: According to leading members of the movement, the shape of the organization has developed concurrently with the spiritual state in the world.[6] This means that any modification and any alteration in beliefs as well as organizational matters, is connected with the concept of consciousness. This makes two levels of investigation necessary: 1. The beliefs, and 2. The organizational matters, including the image of the group. As Woodrum is primarily occupied with matters of social structure and organization, he does not deal with the historical self-esteem of the group at any length. If, however, the attention is more directly focused on TM's idea of how and why the outward development has taken place (and still does), new perspectives emerge.

TM believes Maharishi to lead the group with ultimate success (Maharishi 1986, 2). Being a *Maha-sidha* he is totally aware of the present situation in the cosmos, he knows how things were and he knows how they will be (Maharishi 1986, 2). Consequently he is able to design the belief system and the organization as appropriately as possible according to the present situation. The main dogma in this connection concerns the asserted correlation between consciousness and social life expressed in terms of the 'Maharishi Effect', which is one of TM's most important (and especially soteriological) notions. The 'Maharishi Effect' is described as a field theory of consciousness, suggesting that mental states can influence the behavior of others at a distance. It is claimed that if the square root of one percent of a given population regularly meditates (preferably through the TM-Sidhi program), then any conflict, any unease, and any negative impact on society will be impossible. The higher consciousness of those performing the meditation will affect the surroundings, and in fact the entire universe (Aron and Aron 1986).[7] In religious terms the individual and the group will integrate with the Absolute, the Creative Intelligence or simply the divine. Referring to TM's origin and the traditional religious language of the Advaita-Vedanta we are, of course, dealing with the relation between Atman and Brahman. In short this means that any shift in organizational principle or group image, as TM sees it, is due to the shifting states of consciousness permeating the world. 'Any country has the leadership it deserves',[8] TM asserts, as the state of consciousness, so it is claimed, determines the structure and arrangement of society. The same, TM explains, is true concerning TM itself. As the belief system explains the development of higher states of consciousness (individually and collectively) to be a progressive process, the state of consciousness in the world today is regarded as higher than ever since Maharishi inaugurated his mission. If we turn to a somewhat more familiar vocabulary it is obvious that the concept of karma is at stake. Through meditation 'stress' (i.e. karma) is annihilated and consciousness will expand. Individual or group — the process is the same.

Considering the 'Maharishi Effect' TM's present appearance must be regarded as ideal according to the world's present requirements. Everything is adjusted to the demands of modern society and no alternative way of promoting 'the perennial truth' is competitive. In other words: According to the religious logic of TM, the present articulation of the ancient Veda in terms of the SCI is the result of divine processes. What Rolston has termed 'demythologization' (p. 49) is to TM a divinely directed adjustment of the articulation of never changing spiritual truth. This is why the inherent meaning of the Advaita-Vedanta, according to TM, remains unchanged while the presentation of this meaning has developed into something new. In the words of a leading member of TM in Denmark: 'The traditional religious language is worn out. We need a new language, a new way of expressing things'.[9] This does not mean that something new is said, only that a new language is used. No matter what the sociological and historical facts may be, it is firmly established in TM's belief system that the changes are the result of a dynamic evolution towards higher states of consciousness, and eventually perfection during 'The Age of Enlightenment'. TM is a religion, and reality is (also) understood in non-empirical categories.

Referring to Brahmananda Saraswati, Maharishi has explained the relation between enlightened Man and 'nature', and apparently the principles he describes can be also extended to cover institutions. Every single instance in the life of a saint, he says, has a tremendously far-reaching influence. The whole of nature is involved in every expression of his life. The laws of nature are moulding every activity. Relating to this statement TM describes Maharishi as an equivalent to Brahmananda Saraswati:

> Every instance in his [i.e. any enlightened persons] life is the story of his level of consciousness — supreme enlightenment, Brahman, the eternal Veda — unfolding itself in world consciousness. This is the status of Maharishi himself, who emerged in our time as the perfect channel for nature to work out its divine plan for the spiritual regeneration of mankind. (Maharishi 1986, 2)

It is beyond doubt that this conception is imposed on every aspect conceivable: Every living being, any cultural phenomenon — including any nation or organization — is shaped according to its level of consciousness, TM says. The example of Maharishi and his fellow-saints shows perfect harmony, but to the average person or culture in general, harmony is an aim, not a reality. In the case of the TM movement itself it is believed that the existence of high-grade harmony is more likely to appear here than in society at large (Aron and Aron 1986). This, of course, is due to the fact that the meditators, according to TM, systematically are developing higher states of consciousness, as mentioned above. Taken further, this means that the TM movement (along with anything else), at any given time, is shaped according to its spiritual standard. The organizational development therefore is an outward expression of the spiritual developments in the group.

From this complex of beliefs any alteration in the TM movement can be explained. They may not correspond with sociological analysis, but focusing on the self-esteem of the TM movement we have to acknowledge that this, from the believer's viewpoint, is the only possible explanation to changes. This means that the current manifestation of TM, from an internal perspective, is natural and logical. It is recognized that the organization has changed in many ways over the years, but it is believed that the appearance at any given time has been the most suitable, and that no substantial changes with regard to the belief system and the rituals have taken place. It is often emphasized that the movement is led by Maharishi's guiding light and that everything he does is for the benefit of all:

Those around him have witnessed time and time again that everything he does is perfect for the moment and perfect for all time, perfect for the immediate environment and perfect for the entire world. (Maharishi 1986, 2)

As an intimate identification between the 'Eternal Knowledge', Maharishi's person and the organization is central to the belief system, this statement also covers points of view concerning TM at large. Most profoundly this belief was expressed to me during private communication with a TM source:

One cannot assume that Maharishi, embodying the Veda, can lead an organization in any other direction than that of the Veda itself. It would be an intellectual misconduct to assume anything else. If something is wrong with our movement we are not to blame Maharishi. We are to blame ourselves, for TM is the sum of those participating in the work of Maharishi, and most of us have only walked a tiny part of the path leading to perfection. TM [the organization] is what it can possibly be under the present circumstances.[10]

According to the sources discussed above, the articulation of the belief system started as 'nature's innocent impulse'. Prior to Maharishi's first lectures the belief system only had a 'spiritual existence' and a manifestation in the Vedas. Perhaps we could even claim that the belief system, considering its divine origin, had its pre-worldly existence, exclusively accessible to Maharishi, prior to his first public performance. What interests us the most, however, is that the belief system, according to Maharishi, was in some way wheedled out of him. It emerged at a certain time when 'nature' found it appropriate. Until Maharishi deliberately took over, and started to build up the predecessor to TM (the SRM; Spiritual Regeneration Movement), he was, according to my TM sources, led by the Absolute, Brahman, 'nature' or whatever expression one chooses (Maharishi 1986, 2). Consequently, according to the sources (Maharishi 1986, 1-2, Maharishi 1972), the very beginning of TM, rests upon a close connection with the divine.[11]

In the latest phases of the movement's development (1983 onwards) this perspective is maintained and it is believed that the present formulations of the belief system, the ritual practice and the organizational and ideological matters are as consistent with the divine as ever (Maharishi 1979, 9-17, Maharishi 1986, 1). Any attempt to understand the beliefs of TM and the development of the belief system must take this into consideration. The description of how Maharishi originally was urged to articulate his knowledge is of great importance to the believers. A certain aura surrounds the story, and we may indeed introduce 'the myth about SCI' as a useful term in this respect. It is, I believe, very important to understand that the belief system is regarded as divinely inspired or given, and that the history of the belief system accordingly is interpreted as the history of the way in which the divine unfolds itself to humanity. Again we may refer to Maharishi's description of how the 'pure knowledge' repeatedly is lost and recovered (Maharishi 1979, 9-17) and TM's statements regarding the unfoldment of SCI from the Absolute beginning with Maharishi's 'innocent move towards Ramesvaram' (Maharishi 1986, 1). To the believers these themes are forming an important narrative structure which we may safely term one of TM's basic legends.

From the very beginning the development of the belief system has been determined by tradition. This tradition, as it appears, has been viable enough to change whenever needed, and at the same time remain faithful to its basic notions and structures. It has, quoting Armin Geertz, managed to 'change in order to retain meaning in the face of changing social and political circumstances' (p. 59). Consequently I have pointed to the fact that we find TM's religious origin represented in the most recent, science-related developments of the belief system. Secondly it has been established that TM understands its belief system to be a contemporary manifestation of the eternal Veda, and that TM therefore carries the 'Vedic tradition' into the modern world. How, more precisely, this is done, and how religious meaning is contained within TM's scientific belief system is discussed in the following chapter.

CHAPTER 5

# TM: Science as Hierophany

Sociologist of religion Eric Woodrum suggests that TM has by now entered its final, secularized phase with no focus on strict religious ideas. I have already argued against this conclusion. In the following I shall pursue the discussion by introducing the theories of historian of religions Mircea Eliade concerning what he terms 'the sacred' and its manifestations. (The notion of the sacred is not favoured by all scholars. To my mind, however, the concept is often relevant for *analytical* purposes. I do *not* suggest any ontological reality when I use the term, and as one will discover, I am not unconditionally enthusiastic about Eliade's conceptualization). On this basis, and apart from analysing the belief system, I shall suggest a new characteristic of the current phase of the TM movement which, contrary to Woodrum's model, sees TM as religious indeed. Relating to the problem of syncretism, this means that TM's use of modern science is a new way of expressing religious truths, rather than an expression of secularization.[1] In this sense TM is not a symptom of secularization. More correctly it should be seen as a reaction against the loss of religion.

**The Basic Assumptions in Eliade's Hierology**

More than anyone Mircea Eliade has claimed the notion of the sacred as the central phenomenon to religion. Although avoiding a genuine definition of religion, Eliade indirectly suggests an idea of what religion is: To Eliade religion, above all, is the manifestation and the experience of the sacred. This characterization, being implicit as well as explicit, makes the history of the world's religions a process of ongoing interpretations and reformulations of the sacred in its various manifestations. These manifestations Eliade terms *hierophanies*. The hierophanies, then, he defines as expressions of some modality of the sacred, and he emphasizes the phenomenon of hierophanies to be historical events, simply because they appear in history.

Throughout Eliade's work this focus is maintained and the hierophanies are looked upon as that which constitutes religion.

An important aspect in Eliade's idea is that the sacred manifests itself in objects which are an integral part of our natural, profane world. Following Rudolph Otto, Eliade sees the sacred as something of a wholly different order, and that the sacred manifests itself in otherwise natural, profane objects is of immense relevance:

> It is impossible to overemphasize the paradox represented by every hierophany, even the most elementary. By manifesting the sacred, any object becomes *something* else, yet it continues to remain *itself*, for it continues to participate in its surrounding cosmic milieu. A *sacred* stone remains a *stone*; apparently (or, more precisely, from the profane point of view), nothing distinguishes it from all other stones. But for those to whom a stone reveals itself as sacred, its immediate reality is transmuted into a supernatural reality. In other words, for those who have a religious experience all nature is capable of revealing itself as cosmic sacrality. The cosmos in its entirety can become a hierophany. (Eliade 1987, 12)

It is my suggestion that TM's intense interest in modern science leads to yet another hierophany, in the sense that people (members of TM) see the sacred or 'sacredness' expressed in science. In other words, I find it perfectly possible to interpret the syncretistic system of SCI as a hierophany.

This idea, of course, runs counter to the usual classification of science as secular and therefore contradicts the self-esteem of TM since the scientific image forms an important part of the organization's ambition of appearing as non-religious. However, one does not necessarily have to expect congruity between such official religious claims and what from a scholarly point of view seems to be the true identity of religious groups. As we shall presently see, the idea of science as hierophany has certain advantages in the historical study of TM as a tradition.

According to Woodrum (1977, 41) TM, by now, is solely occupied with the practical, physiological, material and social benefits of the meditation. He also points to the fact that almost no 'other-worldly' references are made in the movement's literature. There are reasons for believing that Woodrum has been focusing too strongly on the outer appearance of the movement, even if he is wholly aware of the existence of two distinct sub-populations (which he terms 'average meditators' and 'inner-group'). A closer interrogation into the sub-population of core members of TM shows all the traditional hierophanies to be present. TM experiences hierophanies under all the traditional circumstances (rituals, scripture, guru, mantra etc.), but also through a medium otherwise looked upon as antagonistic to religion. That medium is science.

Modern science, of course, forms a coherent cosmology (although the inconstancy due to ongoing achievements and debate makes it more changeable than the religious cosmologies), but this is not enough to make it a hierophany. In order to be interpreted as sacred, any phenomenon or object must be meaningful. It needs an ontological bearing. And above all: It must be interpreted as antagonistic to the ordinary, secular world. To the ordinary scientific mind, however, nothing but 'natural' exists. The classical deductive method of science claims everything to be explicable within the limits of logical reasoning, and the distinction between sacred (or supernatural) and profane (natural) is without relevance. In order to comprehend such categories, a system of meaning and interpretation far beyond the borders of what we usually understand science to be, is required. In forming the SCI this is exactly what TM has developed. Relating to the terminology of Eliade, modern science is the profane 'object' in which the sacred, according to the beliefs of the TM members, manifests itself. As the following analysis will show, this makes TM's use of modern science comparable to its use of the Advaita-Vedanta which traditionally brings forth the sacred in the school of Maharishi and his predecessors.

At this point, though, it must be emphasized that my use of Eliade's theory and terminology differs from his own at one important point. Apparently Eliade restricted the hierophanies to embody natural objects and phenomena and religious objects or symbols of universal and ancient occurrence. In his phenomenology, contrary to that of other scholars such as Widengren, van der Leeuw and others, we rarely meet descriptive categories like sacrifice, prayer or priesthood. Rather, emphasis is laid on natural hierophanies. In Eliade's 'Patterns in Comparative Religion' (1983) this orientation is very clear: Sky, sun, moon, water, stone, earth and vegetation are central categories throughout the exposition. Due to the nature of these categories taken from the natural environment, Eliade's hierophanies could be termed 'natural' contrary to the otherwise 'cultural' categories mentioned above (sacrifice, prayer, priesthood etc.). It also appears that Eliade never mentions modern objects as bearers of hierophanies, and consequently his general approach may be looked upon as an escape from modernity. To my knowledge Eliade most directly attempts an analysis of the sacred in the modern world in his book 'Myths, Dreams and Mysteries' (1960), where the first chapter is entitled 'The Myths of the Modern World', and in the essay 'The Occult and the Modern World' (1976, 47-68), but also in these connections he avoids any positive evaluation of modern religious images and symbols.[2] To Eliade the modern world has ignored its intimate relation to the archaic religious symbols. Eliade wanted Man to relive the sacred, and it appears that he found nature to expose the sacred more directly than anything. This very complex mixture of creative hermeneutics, religious sentiment and intellectual brightness makes Eliade's notions hard to handle, but at the same time it makes them open for further elaboration. On the one hand Eliade claims hierophanies to manifest themselves in any given form, but digging into the hierophanies he tends to ignore the possibility of 'modern' manifestations of the sacred. In interpreting scientific theories and results as some kind of hierophanies to TM, I obviously go beyond the limits originally imagined by Eliade. Science is modern *per se*, and the tool of the natural sciences is a highly developed technology. To Eliade any historical or contemporary hierophany is a reactualization of an already existing, archetypical hierophany, and as he apparently restricts these original hierophanies to nature, he probably would not acknowledge my interpretation of science in the TM context as a modality of the sacred.[3] To my mind, however, the recognition of science as some kind of hierophany (as it appears to the believers) is inevitable in TM's example. But this example is by no means unique: The contemporary new religions, using symbols derived from the life and surroundings of modern urban people, provide us with good examples. Focusing on the development of religious canon in various new religions for instance, I have elsewhere pointed to the fact that tape recordings, videos and computer software may function as very powerful religious images, and that they clearly may be acknowledged as sacred objects. This is not due only to the religious content of these specific electronic media. The objects themselves hold religious significance once they are embodying religious meaning. In Scientology, for instance, the central religious activity depends on an electronic device which is understood to be the precondition for spiritual development and fulfilment. This device, the 'Electropsycometer', is by all means of religious significance as it symbolizes the 'Bridge to Total Freedom' just as it leads to it. The apparatus was designed and continuously improved by Scientology's founder L. Ron Hubbard, and today the electropsycometer (or 'E-meter') remains the central therapeutic and cultic object. The electronic devices, which are in the possession of all serious scientologists, are stored in special cases and carefully kept out of reach of those with no formal initiation. Function and symbolism unite in the object and make it sacred (Rothstein 1992).

Thus TM's occupation with natural science and scientific technology is, as far as I can judge, out of tune with Eliade's idea of religion, but within the reach of my own. One thing, however, may connect the two understandings. Eliade claims nature and natural objects to be the only true bearers of hierophanies, and a closer look at TM's belief system may reveal that nature in fact *is* that which constitutes the experience of the sacred in TM. The fact is that the scientific theories and models used by TM, one and all, aim at a convincing and logically meaningful description of nature. One may object that figures and formulas are no representation of nature, but from a scientific point of view this is wrong. Certain aspects of nature do not appear in a form conceivable to our senses. Our only way to describe such aspects is through the abstract language of the exact sciences such as physics, mathematics and chemistry. In so far as TM is doing, we may conclude that the object of religious interpretation undauntedly is nature, although we cannot talk of any tangible phenomenon such as a mountain, the moon or water. Rather, TM's nature hierophanies (if we allow this interpretation) are of the most spectacular kind, especially when we consider that 'nature' or even 'natural forces' in TM's terminology are synonymous with 'the Absolute' or 'the divine'. Following Eliade, we may also conclude that modern science is the profane 'object in which the sacred', according to the beliefs of the TM members, 'manifests itself'. This leaves us with a new hierophany. Through physics and mathematics, so it seems, a new way of experiencing the sacred has appeared. By returning to the theories of the Unified Field I shall give a concrete example.

## The Scientific Theory of the Unified Field as Hierophany

During the mid 1980s TM discovered what in its owns interpretation appeared to be the final scientific proof of the originality and uniqueness of the SCI. The Theory of the Unified Field (also termed 'Grand Unification Theories',GUTs) suggested by scientists outside the influence of TM in the beginning of the 1980s, was interpreted as the academic expression of the perennial truth, since long ago presented by Maharishi. The intimate identification with science had been the strategy for years, but in one respect the scientific launching of the Unified Field Theory became especially relevant: It made one of Maharishi's important predictions come true, thereby — so it was believed — setting the scene for a final breakthrough for TM. As early as 1963[4] Maharishi, referring to the theory of relativity of Albert Einstein, wrote:

If and when physical science arrives at what Einstein was trying to pinpoint by his Unified Field Theory, one element will be established as the basis of all relative creation. With the rapid pace of development of nuclear physics, the day does not seem to be far off when some theoretical physicist will succeed in establishing a Unified Field Theory. It may be given a different name but the content will establish the principle of unity in the midst of diversity, the basic unity of material existence. (Maharishi 1968, 32)

In TM's interpretation this is exactly what the modern theory of the Unified Field does (as expressed in the text further below). Quite in line with what the recent material reveals, Maharishi originally believed a Unified Field Theory to be the outset for a fundamentally new kind of Western science:

The discovery of the field of this one basis of material existence will mark the ultimate achievement in the history of development of physical science. This will serve to turn the world of physical science to the science of the mental phenomena. Theories of mind, intellect, and ego will supercede the findings of physical science. (Maharishi 1968, 32)

Further in the text Maharishi explains how such a science will gradually approach that which is the essence at all times at every level; Being — both relative and absolute — that is the ultimate reality of all that exists.

This is the situation in which TM stands today. The scientific community has, as TM sees it, confirmed what Maharishi has said for many years. It is only natural, then that the theory of the Unified Field occupies a prominent part of TM's missionary strategy.

While TM claims the Unified Field Theory to be of immense importance, the scientific community, however, shows a more reticent enthusiasm. For one thing there are several theories on the subject, and according to scientists no one knows which one is more likely to be correct, if anyone at all. Furthermore, the GUTs make predictions which have not yet been verified by scientific experiment (Morris 1990, 151).[5] However, TM claims to produce the evidence, although no external scientific acknowledgement supporting TM's suggestions has been seen:

Maharishi Technology of the Unified Field [i.e. transcendental meditation and the TM-Sidhi program] provides for the first time, the experimental methodology to verify Unified Field theories. It does so by opening the Unified Field to direct experience on the level of consciousness and by enlivening the qualities of the Unified Field — for example, creativity, dynamism, and orderliness — on the observable levels of physiology, psychology, behavior, and society.

The Maharishi Technology of the Unified Field has thus expanded the glimpse of the Unified Field provided by supersymmetric Unified Field theories of modern physics to the full vision of the total potential of the Unified Field and its practical value for human life. The credit for this historic achievement goes to:

1. Maharishi's insight into the functioning of nature
2. The availability of the complete knowledge of natural law in Vedic Science, as brought to light by Maharishi,
3. The discovery of the Unified Field by modern science, and

4. The scientific research validating the Maharishi Technology of the Unified Field   (MIU Press 1988, 6)

This may also be the place to quote one inner-member of TM in Denmark who, commenting on a mathematical model in a MIU publication on the Unified Field Theory, said: 'Well ... it may sound strange, but in fact the model is a picture of God'. He added that the depiction was of course nothing but an image, but he acknowledged that the divine could be described, and intellectually perceived, through physics (Rothstein 1989b, 65).

One interesting thing from our perspective is that TM rests its argumentation and credibility upon theories which to the surrounding (scientific) world are debatable. Why would TM risk its carefully built up scientific image by associating with speculative theories of no general recognition? Considering the consequences if the GUTs were confirmed, and considering Maharishi's expectations in this respect, TM's trust in the theories may prove understandable. According to physicist Paul Davies, the consequences of a verification of the GUTs would be of paramount importance to science:

The theory has as its goal the compelling dream of a Unified Field theory — a single field of force that incorporates within it all the forces of nature: gravity, electromagnetism and the two nuclear forces. But that is only half the story. The fundamental connection between the quantum particles and the forces that act between them implies that any theory of the forces is also a theory of the particles. It follows that a superunified theory should yield a complete description of all the quarks and leptons too, and explain why they [are organized in levels].

It is sometimes remarked that attaining this dazzling prize would represent the culmination of fundamental physics, for such a theory would be capable of explaining the behavior and structure of all matter — in a reductionist way of course. It would enable us to write down all of nature's secrets in a single quotation, a sort of master formula for the universe. Such achievement would confirm the fond belief that the universe runs according to a single, simple, breathtakingly elegant mathematical principle. The compulsion for this ultimate goal has been expressed by John Wheeler in the following terms: 'Some day a door will surely open and expose the glittering central mechanism of the world in its beauty and simplicity'. (Davies 1986, 157-58)

Even Davis' account — like Maharishi's prediction and characteristic of such a theory — leads to comparisons with the religious cosmologies and cosmographies. The GUTs are aiming at a coherent description and understanding of the universe, a fact that makes the GUTs of prime interest to TM which basically claims to possess such a description and understanding. If TM wants a scientific counterpart to the religious philosophy of Advaita-Vedanta (and this is the case), the GUTs seem to be the most obvious choice, even if the theory is merely a theory.

In 1978, years before the first GUTs were presented, TM physicist Lawrence Domash of the Maharishi European Research University (MERU) wrote: 'Physics is a very beautiful subject; it has developed a very complete picture of reality, and today is on the threshold of actually achieving the goals of science' (IAASCI 1978, 517), thus indicating the expectation of a perfection of science in the future. Ten years later, in 1988, TM accentuated the GUTs as a decisive progress in scientific thinking:

During the past decade physicists have developed a more unified understanding of the laws of nature, culminating in the recent discovery of completely Unified Field theories. These theories describe the unification of all particles and forces of nature in a single Unified Field. From the self-interacting dynamics of the Unified Field, all the laws of nature emerge to conduct the orderly evolution of the universe. (MIU Press 1988, 4)

During 1991 and 1992 this claim was intensified. In an advertisement covering two full pages in the *Independent* (Fig. IV), TM (under the headline 'The Constitution of the Universe') says:

In recent decades, modern science has systematically revealed deeper layers of order in nature, from the atomic to the nuclear and subnuclear levels of nature's functioning. This progressive exploration has culminated in the recent discovery of the Unified Field of all the laws of nature — the ultimate source of order in the universe. (The Independent 16 March 1992).

Our attention should also be drawn to TM's purposely avoiding contact with straightforward controversial scientific theories, even if they seem to fit perfectly into TM's notions. One such example is the theory of biochemist Rupert Sheldrake which, among other things, provides a new solution to the questions of evolution.

According to Sheldrake's theory all natural systems (from crystals to humanity) inherit a collective memory of their kind, some sort of inherent memory. As an example Sheldrake asks how the habit of pecking the tops of milk bottles among blue-tits spread across Europe shortly after the first example of the behavior was registered? The answer is that the collective blue-tit-memory made the behavior possible to every blue-tit, once a single blue-tit developed the ability. Thus, the theory implies a process involving action at a distance in both space and time, a phenomenon termed 'morphic resonance' by Sheldrake. Further, the theory claims, memories are not stored as material traces within our brains. Our own memories result from our 'tuning in on' ourselves in the past, Sheldrake says. On this basis evolution evolves, and on this basis strange examples of non-coordinated achievements can be explained (Sheldrake 1988).

Consequently this theory on 'formative causation' involves notions quite comparable to TM's 'collective consciousness' and the phenomenon of the 'Maharishi Effect', which, of course, is derived from religious notions of the relationship between Atman and Brahman (individual and collective self). In both cases the consciousness of the individual is linked with the collective consciousness, and any development depends on the relation between the two. Further the individual's action at a distance in time with relevance to the present situation in Sheldrake's theory points to similarities with ideas of karma. But TM has no official interest in Sheldrake, and the reason why seems clear enough: Sheldrake does not represent presentable scientific theories. He is a rebel to the established scientific community, and no matter how relevant his theories may be to TM, the organization cannot risk identification with far-fetched scientists. In accepting and promoting the GUTs, TM is balancing on the acceptable side of more or less controversial pioneer science.[6]

From Maharishi's early writings we may assume that the syncretistic process of religious Hinduism and modern science was planned and awaited. By now TM has developed the SCI with so many details and in so many ways that any thorough understanding of its scientific aspect is impossible to the non-physicist.[7] Nevertheless the scientific outlining of Maharishi's teachings appears to be a manifestation of the sacred to his followers. To use the terms of

90  TM: Science as Hierophany

Fig. IV

*and Ancient Vedic Science Reveal* ADVERTISEMENT

# TION OF THE UNIVERSE
## Harmony Displayed throughout the Universe
### SHI'S VEDIC SCIENCE, VERIFIED BY MODERN SCIENCE

Great Britain to bring their national constitution into alliance with the Constitution administration to be as efficient and as effective as the Government of Nature.

of all known laws of nature. The laws governing the self-interacting dynamics of the unified field can therefore be called the *Constitution of the Universe*—the eternal, non-changing basis of Natural Law and the ultimate source of the order and harmony displayed throughout creation.

In the unified quantum field theories of modern physics, the precise mathematical form of these fundamental laws is found in the Lagrangian of the superstring and the N=1 supergravity theories. In Maharishi's Vedic Science, these same fundamental laws—the Constitution of the Universe—are found in the eternal, self-referral dynamics of consciousness knowing itself. This eternal dynamics is embodied in the very structure of the sounds of the Rik Ved, the most fundamental aspect of the Vedic literature.

This chart reveals that the two descriptions of the self-interacting dynamics of the unified field—the Constitution of the Universe—provided by both modern science and Maharishi's Vedic Science are identical, and that these two great traditions of knowledge, objective and subjective—modern and ancient—uphold one another and together rejoice in providing for mankind the basic and timely knowledge of Natural Law which alone is competent to eliminate all problems and to raise the quality of life in society to the level of Heaven on Earth.

First, the chart displays, from the standpoint of Maharishi's Vedic Science, the self-interacting dynamics of the unified field—the Constitution of the Universe—in the structure of the Rik Ved Samhita, as brought to light by Maharishi's Apaurusheya Bhashya of the Ved (Maharishi's Commentary of Rik Ved).

According to Maharishi's Apaurusheya Bhashya, the structure of the Ved provides its own commentary—a commentary which is contained in the sequential unfoldment of the Ved itself in its various stages of expression. The knowledge of the total Ved—the complete dynamics of the unified field of consciousness and the mechanics of symmetry breaking through which the unified field sequentially creates the manifest universe—is contained in the first sukt of the Rik Ved, which is presented below.

| Ahamkar | Buddhi | Manas | Akash | Vayu | Agni | Jal | Prithvi | | Ahamkar | Buddhi | Manas | Akash | Vayu | Agni | Jal | Prithvi |
|---|---|---|---|---|---|---|---|---|---|---|---|---|---|---|---|---|
| य | ज्ञ | स्य | दे | व | मृ | त्वि | जम् | | हो | ता | रं | र | त्न | धा | त | मम् |
| YA | GYA | SYA | DE | VA | MRI | TVI | JAM | | HO | TA | RAM | RA | TNA | DHA | TA | MAM |

first pad expresses the eight Prakritis (fundamental qualities of intelligence) with respect to the knower or 'Rishi' quality of pure consciousness. The second pad expresses the eight Prakritis with respect to the process of knowing or 'Devata' (dynamism) quality of pure consciousness. The third pad expresses the eight Prakritis with respect to the known or 'Chhandas' quality of pure consciousness. Together, these three padas comprise the first richa (verse) of the Ved, which represents another complete stage in the sequential unfoldment of knowledge—i.e. one complete version of the Constitution of the Universe.

The subsequent eight lines complete the remainder of the Rik sukt—the next stage of sequential unfoldment of knowledge in the Ved. These eight lines consist of 24 padas (phrases), comprising 8x24=192 syllables. According to Maharishi's Apaurusheya Bhashya (Maharishi's Commentary of Rik Ved), these 24 padas of eight syllables elaborate the unmanifest, eight-fold structure of the 24 gaps between the syllables of the first richa (verse). Each line consists of three padas which, as in the first richa, respectively present the structure of self-interaction with respect to the Rishi (observer quality), Devata dynamism quality—process of observation), and Chhandas (observed quality) qualities of pure consciousness. Ultimately, in subsequent stages of unfoldment, these 192 syllables of the first sukt (stanza) get elaborated in the 192 suktas that comprise the first mandal (circular cyclical eternal structure) of the Rik Ved, which in turn gives rise to the rest of the Ved and the entire Vedic literature.

This perfectly orderly, eternal structure of knowledge—the Ved—has been preserved over thousands of years in the Vedic tradition of India.

The complete knowledge of the Ved and its profound significance for life has been revived and understood in a scientific framework by Maharishi Mahesh Yogi in his Vedic Science and Technology.

It is a highly significant feature of our scientific age that this complete knowledge of Natural Law provided by Maharishi's Vedic Science is now open to scientific confirmation through the unified quantum field theories of modern physics. Indeed, we see below that precisely this same mathematical structure of sequential unfoldment of the self-interacting dynamics of Natural Law is now available in the mathematical structure of the unified field found in the Lagrangian of the superstring, which represents the most complete mathematical expression of the detailed structure and dynamics of the unified field:

$$L_p^{(10)} = \frac{1}{\kappa}(\psi^i_{\frac{1}{2}}a_y\psi^i_{\frac{1}{2}} + \psi^i_{\frac{3}{2}}a_y\psi^i_{\frac{3}{2}} + \psi^i_{\frac{5}{2}}a_y\psi^i_{\frac{5}{2}} + \psi^i_{\frac{7}{2}}a_y\psi^i_{\frac{7}{2}} + \psi^i_{\frac{9}{2}}a_y\psi^i_{\frac{9}{2}} + \psi^i_{\frac{11}{2}}a_y\psi^i_{\frac{11}{2}} + \psi^i_{\frac{13}{2}}a_y\psi^i_{\frac{13}{2}})$$

$$L^{(24)} = \frac{1}{\kappa}(\bar{\psi}^i_a a_y \psi^i_a + \bar{\psi}^i_{a} a_y \psi^i_{a} + \chi^i_a a_x \chi^i_a + \chi^i_a a_x \chi^i_a + \chi^i_a a_x \chi^i_a + \chi^i_a a_x \chi^i_a + \chi^i_a a_x \chi^i_a + \chi^i_a a_x \chi^i_a$$

$$+ a^2_a a_{\mu\nu} + a^2_a a_{\mu\nu} + a^2_a a_{\mu\nu} + a^2_a a_{\mu\nu} + a^2_a a_{\mu\nu} + a^2_a a_{\mu\nu} + \omega^2_a a^2_L + \omega^2_a a^2_L$$

$$+ \bar{y}^i_a y^i_a + \bar{y}^i_a y^i_a + \bar{y}^i_a y^i_a + \bar{y}^i_a y^i_a + \bar{y}^i_a y^i_a + \bar{y}^i_a y^i_a + \bar{y}^i_a y^i_a + \bar{y}^i_a y^i_a$$

$$+ \bar{\psi}^i_a \psi^i_a + \bar{\psi}^i_a \psi^i_a + \bar{\psi}^i_a \psi^i_a + \bar{\psi}^i_a \psi^i_a + \bar{\psi}^i_a \psi^i_a + \bar{\psi}^i_a \psi^i_a + \bar{\psi}^i_a \psi^i_a + \bar{\psi}^i_a \psi^i_a$$

$$+ \bar{\eta}^i_a \eta^i_a + \bar{\eta}^i_a \eta^i_a + \bar{\eta}^i_a \eta^i_a + \bar{\eta}^i_a \eta^i_a + \bar{\eta}^i_a \eta^i_a + \bar{\eta}^i_a \eta^i_a + \bar{\eta}^i_a \eta^i_a + \bar{\eta}^i_a \eta^i_a$$

$$+ \phi^2_a a_{\mu} + \phi^2_a a_{\mu} + \phi^2_a a_{\mu} + \phi^2_a a_{\mu} + \phi^2_a a_{\mu} + \phi^2_a a_{\mu} + \phi^2_a a_{\mu} + \phi^2_a a_{\mu})$$

of description of the Constitution of the Universe—in precise correspondence with the first sukt of the Rik Ved.*

This precise mathematical correspondence between the descriptions of the detailed structure of Natural Law provided by modern science and by Maharishi's Vedic Science—both on the verbal level of nature's language and on the mathematical level of symbols—gives great confidence that the knowledge of the most fundamental level of Natural Law, the Constitution of the Universe, is now fully available to mankind.

Fortunately, Maharishi's Vedic Science and Technology provides not only detailed intellectual understanding of the Constitution of the Universe (above), but a highly practical, scientifically validated technology to apply this most fundamental and powerful level of Natural Law for the benefit of mankind. Over 500 scientific studies conducted at more than 200 universities and research institutes in 25 countries throughout the world have verified the immense practical benefits of this simple technology—

Maharishi's Transcendental Meditation and TM-Sidhi programme—to access the Constitution of the Universe and thereby develop full human potential in all areas of mind, body, and behaviour. When the Constitution of the Universe, the total potential of Natural Law on the self-referral level of individual intelligence, is fully enlivened by the attention of the conscious mind through Maharishi's Transcendental Meditation and TM-Sidhi programme—the applied technologies of Maharishi's Vedic Science—individual thought and action become spontaneously in accord with Natural Law. Once life is lived in accord with all the laws of nature governing physiological, psychological, and sociological processes, problems of ill-health and inappropriate behaviour do not arise. The individual receives the support of all the laws of nature for the fulfilment of all his desires and aspirations.

The single most profound application of Maharishi's Vedic Science and Technology is through collective practice of the TM-Sidhi programme. Group practice of the TM-Sidhi programme by as few as 7,000 citizens has been scientifically shown to create coherence in collective consciousness, to eliminate collective stress, and to raise life to be spontaneously in accord with Natural Law.

Extensive scientific research has shown that group practice of Maharishi's Transcendental Meditation and TM-Sidhi programme increases positive trends throughout society and decreases negative trends such as ill-health, crime, and other anti-social behaviour.

With this scientifically proven programme the entire population of a nation now has the chance to enjoy the full support of all the laws of nature for the fulfilment of all its goals and aspirations.

By incorporating the no-problem national constitution a clause which guarantees the establishment and maintenance of such a coherence-creating group, national law will gain the support of Natural Law, and the man-made constitution of the nation will enjoy full alliance with the eternal Constitution of the Universe.

To learn more about the Constitution of the Universe in both its theoretical and applied values please contact Dr Geoffrey Clements, Vice Chancellor, Maharishi University of Natural Law, Mentmore Towers, Leigton Buzzard, Mentmore, Bedfordshire, LU7 0QH, England.

* This same mathematical sequence of unfoldment has also been found at the N=1 supergravity and unified electroweak levels of nature's dynamics.

**Gift to the World from 1991, Maharishi's Year of Support of Nature's Government**
**Universe on 12 January 1992, Maharishi's Year of the Constitution of the Universe**

Eliade, SCI — or more precisely the scientific aspect of the belief system — is a 'modality of the sacred'.

In order to clarify this, two levels of analysis have been taken into consideration: As I have tried to show above, there are many structural similarities, and thus functional correspondences between the religious basis and the modern interpretation. This is a cosmological and cosmographic level. Secondly I pointed to a level of experience or cognition which directly incorporates the meditation experience. As indicated above, the meditation experience is regarded as a proof of the validity of the GUTs, a fact that makes the meditation technique ('The Maharishi Technology of the Unified Field') a means of scientific verification to TM. In order to understand how science becomes bearer of hierophanies, this aspect has to be taken into consideration. There are reasons for believing that the recognition of the sacred in physics and mathematics are based on the understanding of the ritual aspect, the meditation. Again we turn to Maharishi's comments on science:

> As physics continues to explore in finer strata of [these] finer particles it is bound to strike against the unmanifested aspect of existence which lies beyond the subtlest aspect of an energy particle — the field of Being. This is how science is certain to declare Being a scientific reality. It is only a matter of time. But however long it may be before physicists of some future generation declare Being to lie at the extreme limit of science, man should not remain deprived of the direct experience of that reality of existence which forms the very basis of life and whose realization glorifies life in all its aspects. (Maharishi 1966, 26-27)

Apparently Maharishi at that time regarded his religious or spiritual discourse towards reality pre-scientific. The technique of transcendental meditation (at that time designated 'transcendental deep meditation') was available for full intercourse with Being while humanity was waiting for a scientific acknowledgement of this fact. He clearly distinguishes between the knowledge of his pre-scientific religious heritage and that of a future science. The meditation technique, based on pre-scientific knowledge has already — within the conceptions developed by Maharishi and TM — proved the existence of 'Being', while science needs a considerable development to do so.

While insisting upon the scientific nature of the meditation technique, TM very directly points to the origin of SCI. Only rarely is the religious nature of the Advaita-Vedanta expressed directly, rather this system is termed 'ancient tradition', 'ancient knowledge' or 'ancient wisdom'. On the other hand there are expressions showing TM's internal awareness of the fact that the scientific nature of the belief system was introduced only when Maharishi brought it to the West: 'Maharishi has revitalized and reinterpreted this ancient tradition in the form of a modern systematic science, known as Maharishi's Vedic Science' (Maharishi 1966, 27).

At this point it is obvious that the science of TM is not scientific in the same way as science in general. As pointed out by Rose (1976, 52) TM's knowledge does not originate through the scientific method of discovery, but is found in the Veda and other sacred texts. According to TM all knowledge of existence is contained therein, in a complete and final form. As a matter of fact Maharishi has never brought forth anything virtually new. His function is rather that of the interpreter or 'enlivener'. Contrary to ordinary Western science which assumes that natural laws are knowable through systematic, repeatable investigation, SCI claims that the knowledge of the natural laws has already been discovered, and that this knowledge is expressed in the Vedas. There is nothing new to be discovered. What TM awaits and strives for is people's recognition and understanding of the already available knowledge. When TM calls the technique of transcendental meditation a scientific discipline, and claims 'Vedic knowledge' to be scientific it is because: 1. There is a systematic procedure of gaining knowledge (which is the meditation), and 2. The knowledge gained through this systematic procedure can, according to TM, be verified:

The knowledge of creative intelligence gained through direct experience in TM can be verified on the subjective level by anyone. The physiological, psychological, and sociological changes brought about through the practice of TM are systematic, repeatable, and scientifically measurable; therefore the knowledge of creative intelligence can be verified on the objective level also. The Science of Creative Intelligence and its practical application, transcendental meditation, is open to scientific investigation, because it is repeatable and lends itself to the scientific method...All the various branches of learning can test and validate the knowledge that it (SCI) offers. (Lecture 6 of the Standard SCI Course. Quoted from Rose 1976, 53)

The distinction between the intellectually formulated belief system and the experiences during meditation (which I consider a ritual practice) is of great importance. In one perspective the distance between the two seems gigantic, but in other perspectives the differences almost seem to disappear. Seen from the outside the gap between the formal logic of physics and mathematics is very different from the internal, psychological, mystical experiences. Among several differences it is important to note that scientific theories or results are derived from conscious, intellectual work, while the goal of TM's meditation-technique deliberately is to suspend any intellectual activity during meditation (Maharishi 1968, 46-52, 305-8). As it appears, however, TM regards a line of scientific theories to be congruous with the message of the Vedas, and 'the experience of the Veda' is exactly what the meditation is said to bring forth. In this way TM claims the meditation experience and the formal logic of science to form two modalities of the same absolute truth. Referring to the Veda, to the theory of the Unified Field and to transcendental meditation ('human awareness settling down') Maharishi has said:

Ved in its original script is just the whisper of the Unified Field to itself, and human awareness, settling down to its own self-referral state, very clearly recognizes its own self-interacting activity. (MVU 1985, 64)

This perspective is embodied in what TM terms 'Maharishi's Vedic Psychology'. According to this psychology, the individual who has attained 'the level of development where he or she is capable of perceiving the details of the inner dynamism of pure consciousness,... will spontaneously experience the Ved'. This phenomenon Maharishi locates within Rig-Veda itself by referring to the text (V.44.14) which in his own translation reads: 'The hymns seek out him who is awake' (Dillbeck 1989, 123). Consequently it is possible for individuals to 'experience the Ved' because the human mind essentially is 'pure consciousness' like the 'cosmic psyche'. It is self-referral and capable of comprehending its own nature which includes its relation to the 'cosmic psyche', the Absolute (Dillbeck 1989, 123). Again the analogy to the Unified Field of physics is apparent and another quotation from Maharishi emphasizes TM's idea:

The Unified Field, even though glimpsed by the objective approach of the different disciplines of modern science, is a subjective reality which is open to itself, which knows itself. (Maharishi 1985, 59)

The immediate advantage of this coordination of two very different aspects of the religious system is that the mystical experience becomes directly accessible to formal description and understanding. In comparative religion it is well known that mysticism in many ways is hard to handle, and among mystics of all times it has been a problem to formulate and pass on to others the mystical experiences which one has received or obtained. TM, however, has done a lot to overcome this paradox: Through the scientific version of the belief system, which at the same time is presented as a manifestation of the 'Ved' experienced during meditation, an intellectual explanation is available at all times. What the TM mystic will experience during meditation is one aspect of the same truth that is represented in the formal logic of physics and mathematics in terms of SCI. Thus the psychological and the intellectual levels are in tune. According to TM this structure, of course, was already in existence in ancient times when *rishis* recognized that the *shruti*-scriptures were manifestations of the same reality they themselves perceived during meditation. Today, when only one *Maha-rishi* ('Great Seer') has come forward, it is of ultimate value, that the spiritual truth — due to his endeavors — has been explained in a language which is meaningful and authoritative to modern man. As pointed out by writer on mysticism Nils Bjørn Kvastad, metaphysicians and mystics usually identify the real with the transcendent, which makes it possible to call metaphysics a science of reality, rather than a science of the transcendent (Kvastad 1980, 133). I do not feel inclined to talk of metaphysics, nor religion as scientific, but it is obvious that TM is persuing the same logic as Kvastad. TM sees the mystical experience as a confrontation with 'real reality', and the intellectual — but ontologically consistent — description of the same must be considered likewise.

If we go into details, two obvious advantages are seen. First of all, the meditator who has not yet experienced 'the Veda' directly through meditation, is presented with an image of the expected experience.[8] Through the diagrams and models of SCI he is able to

96  *TM: Science as Hierophany*

perceive the structure and the nature of the experience which lies ahead of him. Of course this will encourage a certain interpretation whenever an experience occurs, and no doubt a close correspondence between SCI and the meditation experience will be found if the matter is looked into more carefully. In one case a woman straightforwardly told me, that she was expecting 'a spiritual awareness in harmony with her theoretical knowledge' derived from an SCI course. The other advantage works the other way around. The despair and sense of loss, which is well known to mystics when the mystical experience withdraws, is also known to many meditators. To some it simply seems to be *the* problem. One man, who at an early stage of his involvement with TM had a strong mystical experience which involved the feeling of 'being one with the cosmos', explained to me that he frequently would consider SCI in order to relive his experience. I asked him why the original Sanskrit texts were of less importance than SCI, presuming that the poetic language of Rig Veda and the Bhagavad Gita would relate more directly to his experience. His answer pointed in two directions. On the one hand, he said, Rig Veda is the purest manifestation of that, which he felt during his experience. On the other hand, SCI proved far more accessible to him: 'The way things are described in SCI is more understandable, more accessible to me. It is a language with which I am familiar. The sanskrit of Rig Veda is beautiful, but I do not understand the words'.[9] Clearly the scientific dimension of SCI supports the understanding of what one experiences during meditation and consoles the meditators while they await their next spiritual breakthrough. Indeed TM wants to 'demystify mysticism' (Russell 1978, 143), a commonly heard phrase among inner-group members.

Elsewhere I have drawn parallels between TM's ideology and scholasticism of early medieval Europe (Rothstein 1989b, 61). Indeed TM, like the scholastics at their time, knows what is true, and like the scholastics TM aims at an understanding and interpretation of that truth. At this point the scientific image of TM meets its worst challenge as no ordinary science claims full knowledge of its object. Ordinary science is tentative, which TM is not. Final truth is known to TM, and the tentativeness of TM restricts itself to the realm of understanding that particular truth. In ordinary science the procedure of approaching final truth is an ongoing process, and the tentative method prevails at every level, at any given time.

CHAPTER 6

# Concluding TM: Syncretism as Strategy and Religious Innovation

What I have aimed at demonstrating is that TM's specific interpretation has become possible because tractable structural parallels exist between the notions of Advaita-Vedanta on the one hand and modern science on the other (in Chapter 10 where a comparison to ISKCON's case is attempted I shall go into further details). More than one scholar has commented on the dynamics of the Hindu religion(s), and considering TM's origin and the organization's ability to integrate foreign notions, it is not surprising that such syncretistic developments have taken place. Most impressively the dynamic character of Hinduism is identified in the so-called Neo-Hinduism. The term covers a wide range of religions and religious movements among which the *Ramakrishna Mission* established by Ramakrishna's disciple Vivekananda in 1897 (inspired by the ecumenical *World Parliament of Religions* in Chicago in 1893) was the first to gain influence in the West (Holm 1990).[1] Of other prominent examples from the first wave of Neo-Hinduism in the West, *The Vedanta Society* and Sri Aurobindo's movement can be mentioned. Today a wide range of Hindu inspired religious groups are represented in the West. TM and ISKCON are but two conspicuous examples. Both are obligingly mentioned by indologist A.L. Basham in his survey of the evolution of classical Hinduism. In order to explain the relative success of these and other similar religions in the West he writes:

Hinduism in the modern age is characterized by its adaptability. Using a foundation of classical Hindu thought and practice, Hindus of all types are adjusting to their present time and place. This flexibility and openness, while following the age-old traditions and teachings of the sages, will permit Hinduism to remain one of the world's major religious forces in the future. (Basham 1989, 115)

In very broad terms historian of religions R.N. Dandekar, commenting on a saying of Radhakrishnan, gives his opinion as to why Hinduism is able to absorb new dimensions into its religious system (or systems):

As Radhakrishnan points out, 'Hinduism is a movement, not a position; a process, not a result; a growing tradition, not a fixed revelation'. Hinduism, indeed, represents an exercise in expanding exploration. There is, accordingly, no possibility of any serious conflict arising from the confrontation of Hinduism and modernity. One need not be surprised if, in the course of time, modernity itself silently merges into Hinduism and thus becomes an organic part of the Hindu tradition. (Dandekar 1968, 86)

While TM cannot represent Hinduism at large, it is true that the dynamic character described by Basham and Dandekar is a distinctive feature of the organization. It is, however, important to understand that any development in TM — as TM itself understands it — is directed towards a deeper understanding of the perennial truth, already embodied in the Vedas. The fact that such a scholastic discourse is attractive to TM, though, probably relates to the general adaptability which is typical to the Hindu religion(s). No doubt Dandekar's 'modernity' (in this particular case science) has 'become an organic part of *a* Hindu tradition' (TM).

What TM demonstrates is that the sacred (also) manifests itself in physics and mathematics, and that intellectual or scientific insight into the secrets of creation and Being is a possibility. Considering the dynamic character of the Hindu religion(s) as described by Basham and Dendakar we may suggest that 'Hinduism' makes such interpretations possible because this religion is extraordinarily elastic. Unless we pursue an understanding of this phenomenon from the perspective of comparative religion we shall remain in the same position as that of the confused and unpleasantly affected natural scientist. In the words of physicist Paul Davies:

Many of the weird and abstract concepts thrown up by the new physics have struck deep chords with those of a mystical persuasion. Much to the bewilderment of the profession, cults have grown up around quantum physics, black holes and the theory of relativity. (Davies 1983, 874, quoted from Bainbridge 1987, 72)

### Innovative Beliefs and Traditional Ways

SCI is an innovation. The use of the belief system among the inner-group, though, seems more traditional. The millennial anticipation, the ritual practice and the congregational milieu to which the belief system belongs are in most respects in tune with traditional religious modes. This means that even if SCI offers intellectual explanations with scientific sentiments, the actual use of these explanations is embodied in a rather traditional religious setting. Hence the syncretism between science and religion has not affected the basic structures of traditional religious ways. As it appears it is only the belief system itself as it is officially presented, that deviates from traditional religious forms.

To the surrounding society religion largely depends on beliefs, and accordingly TM presents itself as non-religious through an attempted secularized belief system. The literature, organizational matters and not least the rituals of TM, however, are clearly religious. As we have seen, even the present construction of the belief system reveals its religious nature, when observed more closely. Above all SCI reveals an encompassing ontology which explains life and being, and through its careful definition and analysis of 'knowledge' and 'consciousness' it shows strong epistemological considerations. Further a well developed teleology is evident, focusing on the inherent structures of meaning in nature, and finally, with (indirect) reference to Hindu ideas of 'liberation', a soteriology is evident. These aspects of the coherent whole are finally contained within a millenial perspective which promises the fulfilment of all the belief system's potentials within a foreseeable future. SCI provides a cosmology which considers both ancient religious philosophy and modern scientific notions, thus placing the believer in a continuum stretching from ancient India to the contemporary Western, industrialized world — but at the bottom line the exegesis of the belief system is the same.

The best example of how this continuum works is Maharishi's person. In one single text Maharishi's contributions to science (most significantly the establishment of MIU) is mentioned in a great many details along with statements such as the following:

> Maharishi Mahesh Yogi is the true representative and the most outstanding student and teacher of the grand Vedic civilization. He is an institution in

himself and it would only be fair to say in the language of the Bhagavad-Gita that Maharishi is the long awaited god-sent Avatar. (A Special Supplement 1990, 10)[2]

In this way TM's various aspects seem to oppose one another, but nevertheless TM is one of the most influential and well consolidated new religions of Hindu origin. Apparently the Janus-faced nature of the movement, which allows Maharishi to be a god-sent avatar and a natural scientist at the same time, causes no disturbances to the believers.[3] Only external observers have questioned the religio-scientific construction.

## Mythological Change

As it appears, the deconstruction of myth has a parallel, namely a corresponding construction of a new mythology. As the myth never disappears, but only changes its appearance, it may be more correct to speak of mythical transition, or simply translation as suggested by historian of religions Wendy Doniger O'Flaherty. It would be wrong to say that the myth survives the translation with no loss at all, even if the process of translation is done carefully and compassionately. O'Flaherty, commenting on the mythology of the Bible, has said:

When a myth is translated, its classic component is somehow tarnished; this part of the Bible is invisibly lost to those who cannot read Hebrew or Greek and was visibly lost to many people when the King James translation was discarded. The Bible has crossed many linguistic borders in its journey from ancient Palestine to us, and a toll has been paid at every crossing. There is a loss of power in the myth when the Bible is translated from its magical language into our language; so, too, there is a loss of power in the ritual when the Latin Mass is translated into English. (O'Flaherty 1988, 41-42)

It is true that a loss of mythological power occurs during such transformations. In our material SCI is not the same as Vedic myth or notions contained within the Advaita-Vedanta and Sankhya, simply because the language is of a different kind (in this sense 'transition' seems more appropriate than 'translation'). To the believers, however, the inherent significance is unaltered. In order to comprehend the significance, the new mythological shape, however, needs 'some spark of originality to ignite it for us' as O'Flaherty puts it. It must, she says, eventually be 'reinflated' and 're-tumesced', and if the language that attempts to do so is inadequate or unexisting, the myth will not rise again (O'Flaherty 1988, 42). TM has reinflated a set of foreign and unintelligible religious notions in a way that makes these notions relevant and understandable to people in the West. If Maharishi had remained solely occupied with a traditional Indian way of describing his ideas, it is likely that no one would have bothered to listen to him. After all it is indicated in TM's publications that the turn to science was a necessary missionary strategy (Forem 1984, 216).

TM's mythology is in certain ways closely linked with language. In TM it is evident that the Sanskrit text, as well as the rendering into English of the Bhagavad Gita for instance, is of great importance. Above all, however, it is the spiritual significance of the text that occupies the minds of the TM members. The text is a manifestation of the divine reality with which one strives to align oneself through meditation. At one specific point, though, the rendering into scientific language cannot stand up to the original (Sanskrit) version(s). In the words of O'Flaherty there has been a translation from an originally 'mystical language' into our own, non-mystical language: SCI is not a mantra. The sound dimension of the classical sacred texts has no parallel in SCI. In TM, as in Hinduism in general, the sacred texts carry sacred sounds. Whenever recited, the sacred manifests itself through the words. There are various expressions of this understanding. As an example I quote from internal educational papers distributed during a course on SCI:

The precise sequence of sounds is highly significant; it is in the sequential progression of sound and silence that the true meaning and content of the Ved reside — not on the level of intellectual meaning ascribed to the Ved in the various translations.[4]

While structural parallels concerning cosmology, cosmography and iconography are seen, the sounds are left behind during the transition from Veda and Vedanta to SCI. This is why TM's inner-group (apart from their occupation with SCI) holds on to the classical texts: Only here is the divine present at all levels, and therefore only the classical texts can be used during rituals. In the initiation-puja, in inner-group congregational gatherings and during meditation/TM-Sidhi program, Sanskrit words — mantras — are used, not because they are 'old' or 'traditional', as TM usually says, but because they, contrary to modern or ordinary words, are able to transform. They 'work'.[5] The intellectual dimension of the belief system — the theoretical outlining of how and why the meditation works, of how and why cosmos works — is contained within SCI, but the magical and ritual dimension is strictly confined to its classical setting. The deconstruction and reconstruction of myth, therefore, remains on a superficial level. Not in the sense that it is vague, meaningless or an expression of manipulation. It is superficial in the sense that SCI only works at a descriptive level, while the creating, mystical and magical aspects of TM work according to *classical*, Hindu standards. TM, striving to establish itself as non-religious, cannot overcome this problem. Whenever the ideology of the movement is translated into action, it is done through the sacred language of Hinduism which is the carrier of the rituals. If we focus on that particular aspect, it is easy to recognize that SCI serves to legitimate what is in fact religious activities in secularized society, and that it serves as a missionary device. From what has been said above, however, it is equally easy to understand that SCI nevertheless *does* carry meaning in the religious sense of the word. In the following chapter we shall look closer into how this meaning is articulated and see how science in TM may be understood.

It seems reasonable to consider TM's strategy of scientism as one of the reasons why the organization is still alive in the West. Bainbridge's theory discussed in Chapter 3 may not fit each and every religion, and it may not stand up to each and every example, but it is correct that any new religion, in order to ensure its success, must hold on to something stable in the society where it strives to establish itself. TM has a solid hold on science, and science is the singular most dominating, meaning-constructing segment of modern society. But this does not mean that the scientific dimension of TM's belief system is merely a means of communicating a message and gaining recognition. As I have explained, science is just as much a means of perceiving the divine. Knowledge, as TM sees it, does not originate through scientific methods. Knowledge exists in the Vedas, or maybe we should say is available in the Vedic scriptures — or rather: 'Veda', as a cosmic principle, is 'total awareness and total knowledge'. Knowledge of all existence is contained therein, in complete and final form. Through scientific principles of discovery we simply approach this already existing knowledge in a new way, TM says (Maharishi 1986, 1).

Thus TM pays attention to ideas and formulations which are either very old or brand new. The Vedas are considered some of humanity's oldest texts, and the theories of the Unified Field or superstrings represent the latest scientific developments. As a matter of fact this double-orientation in time is well known to modern religious groups. Very often that which is ancient is considered original and unspoiled along with the newest which seems to represent the most advanced knowledge obtained by Mankind. In this way TM legitimates itself in two directions. It links itself to the glorious past, and engages at the same time in the vanguard of modern knowledge.

Further, as pointed to elsewhere, the monistic Hinduism in TM is upheld by individuals to whom that particular religious tradition is nothing innate. Their engagement with TM is due to conversion. As a matter of fact the members of TM are in principle more directly linked with science than with Hinduism, since modern science during their lifetime has been one of the most important foundations of Western society. The old-new dialectic, therefore, is rather complicated in TM. Of prime interest, however, is that monistic Hinduism among other things is accepted because it is 'ancient' and therefore considered 'original' or 'genuine', while modern science has attained its status because it is pioneering, new, systematic, logical and above all able to dig into the secrets of nature on the basis of intellectual skills and advanced technology. In this way we may conclude that the merits of modern science are intimately connected with its ability to rediscover what was already known in the ancient past. As TM sees it, science does not point forward even if it is new. It points backwards, into the realm of time and space where no distinction existed between absolute and relative, humanity and the divine. I have found no direct formulation of this in TM's materials, but it is an important conclusion: The newest scientific discoveries are recovering the oldest truths. Progression, therefore, is the same as enlivening the ancient Veda in all its aspects.

**Final Comment**

In the previous discussion I have tried to explain how science works as an integral part in TM's religious life and attempted to explain why science has been implemented. If we once again concentrate on internal perspectives we may find a final solution as to why TM has bothered so much in order to establish itself as scientific. As we shall see, the answer may be intimately linked with TM's notions of consciousness and indeed its entire cosmology.

In 1967 Maharishi said:

One should teach TM in terms of religion where religion is dominant, in terms of politics where politics dominate and of economics where that dominates. (Johnston 1980, 339)

With no hesitation we can supply: '... and science where science dominates'. The universality of the belief system and the trust in the efficacy of the meditation rituals make the presentation of TM a minor problem. The above all important thing is that people meditate no matter what understanding of the meditation they may have.

This notion has to be seen in connection with Maharishi's deliberate practice of 'relative preaching'. According to Maharishi every individual stands on different levels of consciousness, and therefore cannot understand the same. Not intellectually, nor spiritually. Indeed this is what TM's and MIU's motto says: 'Knowledge is structured in consciousness' (Russell 1978, 169). For that reason, the education of the individual has to adapt itself to the level of the pupil or neophyte. With reference to the Bhagavad Gita III, 29, Maharishi has said:

[If] the enlightened man wants to bless one who is ignorant, he should meet him on the level of his ignorance and try to lift him up from there by giving him the key to transcending, so that he may gain bliss-consciousness and experience the Reality of life. He should not tell him about the level of the realized, because it would only confuse him. (Maharishi 1979, 224).

## 106  Concluding TM

This means that the belief system must be articulated in a way that suits people's level of consciousness. At this instance the collective consciousness in the world is relatively low (although much higher than before Maharishi came forth), and people in the West cannot comprehend the Veda, TM says. What they can understand is science, and consequently there are good epistemological and soteriological reasons why the scientific image is promoted. Thanks to the dynamic character of Maharishi's monistic belief system, it has been possible to identify religious notions in the scientific materials, and therefore the core group of TM (which primarily is oriented towards a traditional religious interpretation of Life and Being), as well as the average meditators with no conscious religious sentiment, can relate to it. To the core members the scientific exposition remains a hierophany while people in the periphery, and those outside TM, because of the scientific wrapping, may regard SCI as non-religious. Hence, the strategy for recruitment and legitimation is more than simple tactics. It is also a religious innovation by which an old tradition remains viable.

We now proceed to ISKCON. A very different religion with a very different attitude towards science.

CHAPTER 7

# International Society for Krishna Consciousness (ISKCON): An Introductory Outline

The history and sociology of ISKCON has been studied on many occasions. Being one of the most visible Hindu factors of modern Western society, the movement has attracted a considerable interest from psychologists, indologists, sociologists and historians of religions. The latter have focused on the fact that ISKCON, being present in the West since 1965, represents a genuine Indian religion with roots in the Bengali Gaudia-Vaisnava Bhakti tradition of the 16th century, a tradition that apparently has met the needs of some, preferably younger, people in contemporary Western (and on a minor scale other) societies. The internal structures, the future of the movement, the historical development, the missionary work and the movement's insertion in society have, among other things, been subjected to scientific research (Bromley and Shinn 1989, Gelberg 1983, Judah 1974, Rochford 1982, Shinn 1987, Beckford 1985). Sociologists of religion have designated ISKCON a 'world rejecting' religion (Wallis 1984), and truly ISKCON opposes most modern values. ISKCON is very well aware of its position in modern Western society, not only in terms of its own religious self-interpretation, but also from the outsiders' perspective. Accordingly this group accepts scholarly interrogation, and as a matter of fact encourages scholars to study ISKCON.[1] This may explain why some of the finest studies in new, contemporary religions are dealing with ISKCON.

**History: ISKCON and its Founder**

ISKCON as an organization is young, but the religion it represents is old. To the members of the organization this is very important as they, with great determination, reject the novel religious notions posed by other — and actually new — religious groups with which ISKCON, to the minds of outsiders, is usually identified.

In 1965 the Indian *A.C. Bhaktivedenta Swami Prabhupada* (1896-1977) (born *Abhay Caran De*) arrived in the USA. Being a monk in succession after *Caitanya Mahabrabhu* (1486-1534), he represented an old tradition within theistic devotional (bhakti) Hinduism, and soon became one of its most energetic representatives in a process of revitalization. In 1922 he first met his own guru *Bhaktisiddhanta Saraswati Thakura* of the *Gaudiya Vaisnava Mission* (the son of *Bhaktivinoda Thakura*, the leader of the Gaudiya revivalist movement upon which ISKCON builds), but his formal initiation was not until 1933. At that time Prabhupada[2] was entrusted with the task of taking 'Krishna Consciousness' to the West, but until he entered the stage of *sannyasin* in 1959, he restricted his work to the production of English language material for the mission. His obligations as a family father had prevented him from initiating his mission in the West previously. Before his religious career, Prabhupada graduated from the University of Calcutta in English, philosophy and economics, and for a long time he was employed as the manager of a pharmaceutical company. Accordingly he was familiar with basic scientific principles (Hinnells 1991, 330). Contrary to the history of Maharishi Mahesh Yogi, Prabhupada's life is well documented in several biographies produced by his followers (Goswami 1980, 1983).[3]

At the age of 69, in 1965, he arrived in Boston with no money and no back-up but managed to gather a small group around himself during his first year in the United States. His followers, mainly recruited among the counterculture youth, increased their numbers during 1967 when Prabhupada moved to California. By 1970 there were 21 ISKCON centres in the United States and the mission spread to Japan, Canada and Europe. Worldwide approximately 350 centres exist today according to ISKCON's own listing,[4] and ISKCON claims a membership of 4000 initiated members and half a million lay members.[5]

**ISKCON's Belief System**

As ISKCON's beliefs are described in details elsewhere, I shall only draw a sketch of it here. The beliefs of ISKCON do not differ remarkably from the traditional Gaudia-Vaisnava theology, and nor does the ritual practice in general deviate from the traditional ideals although some modifications have been introduced in order to reach people in the West (Judah 1974, 18-45, Bromley and Shinn 1989).[6] The central and inalienable notion is that spiritual fulfilment is reached through the expression of devotional love (bhakti) towards Krishna. The belief system as mentioned, goes back to the Bengal mystic Caitanya Mahabrabhu, held by his followers to be an incarnation of the supreme god, Krishna (Prabhupada 1984). Caitanya inaugu-rated ISKCON's most important rituals, and even if Prabhupada is the most direct object for identification and the guiding light in every respect, Caitanya is behind it all.

Contrary to many other Hindu religions, including TM, ISKCON asserts that Krishna reigns above Brahman, emphasizing the personalization of the divinity as opposed to monistic notions of the impersonal divine (see Chapters 10 and 11). Krishna has and is supreme power, and he has the ability to attain any given form, including that of Vishnu and his several avataras (Prabhupada 1986, 226). Krishna comprises within himself the entire creation, but at the same time he is separated from, and greater than it (these two aspects of Krishna's nature is partly analysed in Jensen and Rothstein 1990, 261-65). Historian of religions J. Stillson Judah summarizes this aspect of ISKCON's theology thus:

Krishna, the Supreme Personality of Godhead, is characterized by the Gaudiya Vaisnavas as existing in a number of different ways besides that of his original nature. Some *Upanishads* speak of an attributeless, differenceless reality, or Absolute, which they call Brahman. The followers of Caitanya say, however that this is only one aspect of reality. The Ultimate Reality is Brahman with qualities. It is highly personalized as Krishna. Brahman is spirit in which individual living entities form a part without losing their identity. Bhaktivedanta teaches further that Brahman is the effulgence or halo of Krishna, the Brahmajyoti, which includes everything that exists. It is the complete whole and is called material nature when the effulgence is covered by *maya*, illusion or sense gratification. (Judah 1974,49)

It is characteristic that Krishna, at the same time, is a loving, caring personal god and the omnipresent ruler of the universe. It also stands out that ISKCON's cosmology in one presentation is highly speculative and philosophical, but that other dimensions of the belief system reveal a very direct and concrete mythology. This, however, is not only characteristic of ISKCON but of the entire Vaisnava theology: The supreme god, Krishna, is primarily described as the blue cowherd boy who blissfully plays his flute in the company of the *gopis* or his beloved *Radha*.

The myths about him are primarily found in the tenth chapter of the *Bhagavad Purana* which is one of ISKCON's favorite texts for devotional contemplation (Prabhupada 1972-85). It is the same Krishna, but in another aspect, we find in the Bhagavad Gita which, together with the Bhagavat Purana, is one of ISKCON's most important texts (Prabhupada 1986).

Krishna is said to dwell in the Vaikunta spiritual planetary system, and ISKCON carefully makes distinctions between the world of the 'conditioned souls' and the spiritual world of the liberated entities. Of course notions such as karma and samsara are important to ISKCON. It is believed that the soul transmigrates through millions of bodily forms on its way towards perfection (Prabhupada 1986, 104 etc.). It is only those who are ' Krishna conscious' who are liberated. Those who are not are subjected to continual reincarnation (in human or animal forms) and may at advanced stages, but still within the relative realm, reincarnate as demigods or as entities adapted to live elsewhere in this or another universe. Likewise, the universe passes through different stages, *yugas*, where the spiritual degeneration is intensified. The universe in its various stages lasts for four billion, three hundred million years. When it comes to an end all creation (including hundreds of thousands of universes) is inhaled back into the body of Vishnu (an expansion of Krishna), but reborn with Vishnu's next breath. Presently, ISKCON says, we are in the beginning of the *Kali-yuga*, the yuga of death and destruction. However, in this particular Kali-yuga, contrary to the conditions in most Kali-yugas, Krishna has shown a special mercy by entering this world in the shape of Caitanya Mahabrabhu thus inaugurating 'one sunny day' in the midst of a cold winter, as it is expressed. In other words: Human beings have received a rare opportunity to attain spiritual fulfilment even if we are in the Age of Death and Oblivion (Prabhupada 1986, 173-74 and 1984).

The soteriology of ISKCON is one of the most powerful aspects of the belief system. It is believed that the human soul lies slumbering in a material body, and that it falsely identifies with this body. The soul is overshadowed by an everyday 'material consciousness' which prevents it from realizing its full potential and eventual return to the godhead. Through various ritual practices (see below) it is the intention to awaken the soul and to supplant the 'material consciousness' with 'Krishna consciousness' which leads to liberation from *samsara*. This perspective is very clear to the believers, and the rituals are conducted accordingly.

ISKCON is a religion of letters which primarily focuses on the Puranas and the Bhagavad Gita (all Hindu scriptures which support ISKCON's theology in one way or another are taken seriously). These scriptures are held to be literary incarnations of Krishna, and the theological study of texts is an important dimension in the devotees' religious activities. Most interpretations of the sacred texts are considered false contrary to Prabhupada's commentaries which are considered ideal. Above all, however, it is said that the texts speak for themselves and that they are describing things 'as they are'. The notion of myth is not unfamiliar to ISKCON's devotees. They readily designate other religious systems as myths. Their own mythology, however, is considered actual historical realities.

Finally we may describe ISKCON's general goals by citing the statement of purposes of the 'Back to Godhead Magazine' which is one of ISKCON's most important means of communication between the devotees. The purposes of the magazine and the organization are the same:

1. To help all people distinguish more clearly between reality and illusion, spirit and matter, the eternal and the temporary.
2. To present Krishna consciousness as taught in *Bhagavad-gita* and *Srimad-Bhagavatam*.
3. To help every living being remember and serve Sri Krishna, the Personality of Godhead.
4. To offer guidance in the techniques of spiritual life.
5. To expose the faults of materialism.
6. To promote a balanced, natural way of life, informed by spiritual values.
7. To increase spiritual fellowship among all living beings, in relationship with Lord Sri Krishna.
8. To perpetuate and spread the Vedic culture.
9. To celebrate the chanting of the holy names of God through the *sankirtan* [see below] movement of Lord Sri Caitanya Mahaprabhu.[7]

## Rituals

The lives of the ISKCON devotees are governed by rituals. Being monks and nuns, the members of ISKCON subject themselves to ritual activity around the clock. Even the appearance of the believers signifies the ritual commitment. They are dressed according to Vaisnava standards wearing *dhoti* or *sari*. Males cut off their hair only leaving a wisp on top of the head as a symbol of nonattachment to the material realm. Their bodies are dedicated to Vishnu as his temple, a notion symbolically expressed through bodily paintings including the mark on the forehead of the believers.[8] There are two main ritual aspects: The devotional recitation of the sacred mantra and the worship of the deities of Krishna (in one incarnation or another). The recitation, or 'chanting' as it is commonly called, of the *maha-mantra* is of greatest significance. The well known phrase: *Hare Krishna, Hare Krishna; Krishna, Krishna, Hare, Hare; Hare Rama, Hare Rama; Rama, Rama, Hare, Hare* is supposed to be repeated 1728 times every day (16 rounds on a 108-bead rosary which the devotee receives during his initiation). The recitation of the holy mantra is intimately linked with ISKCON's theological notions. It is believed that Krishna substantively resides in his name, and therefore that the mantra constitutes the godhead (in various aspects) whenever recited (Prabhupada 1985, 11f.). In order to awaken the slumbering soul and reach for higher realities beyond the realm of maya, one has simply to recite the holy names. Quantity equals quality in this respect. ISKCON further asserts that the mantra-recitation is prescribed as the direct means of attaining Krishna Consciousness in Kali-yuga. No other contemplative or meditative processes or techniques are regarded efficient.

Closely related to the mantra-recitation is the process of *sankirtan*, devotional singing and dancing in honor of Krishna. This activity, which may take ecstatic proportions, is very popular and takes place in the temple in front of the deities or in the streets for the benefit of those who may hear the sacred words (Prabhupada 1987, 42).

The worship of the deities, the *arca*, is led by a specialist, a *pujari*, according to traditional standards. Every temple possesses an image of the god. Depending on the spiritual level of the devotees in the particular temple, the image may be one of great mercy (e.g. the

Caitanya incarnation) or one that requires a constant and faultless cult (e.g. the Krishna-Radha incarnation). In every case it is believed that Krishna, like in the mantra, substantively resides in the image, and many devotees will testify that they have seen statues of marble, wood or metal move or change their shape. The deity worship is central to ISKCON's theistic theology. The fact that the images are treated as real persons (they are washed, fed, clothed, put at rest etc.), for instance, is an outstanding example of theistic ritual. Outsiders' lack of understanding is interpreted as a result of 'impersonalistic influence' which contradicts ISKCON's anthropomorphic theology (Vishnupad s.a., 19).

There are two formal stages of initiation. The first 'the sacred name-initiation' (*Hare Nama Diksa*) usually occurs after a period of six months or a year during which the initiate has studied ISKCON's sacred texts and lived according to the basic religious demands. As it appears, the initiate is given a new name during this initiation which leads to normal, initiated membership. The final transformation of the individual takes place during the 'priest-initiation' ('*Brahminical' Diksha*) which is performed for those deeply committed devotees who choose to live full-time as Krishna's servants. The 'journey back' begins with the first initiation, but the commitment to go back to Krishna is not completed before the second initiation is passed. At that stage the past sinful acts in terms of karma can finally be overcomed, it is believed. In order to receive initiation, the devotee selects a spiritual master among ISKCON's gurus and establishes (although usually at a distance) a guru-disciple relation to him (Shinn 1987, 101f.).

The devotional lifestyle may differ from temple to temple depending on the orientation of the local temple president. However, everybody will follow a daily routine defined by Prabhupada around 1975: A.M. 3:30 Rise and shower. 4:15-4:30 Morning deity worship. 5:00 mantra-recitation, 7:30 Scripture reading and lecture, additional chanting, 8:30 Breakfast, 9:00-12:00 Various work schedules, P.M. 12:00 Noon meal, 1:00-4:00 Various work and rest schedules, 4:15 Afternoon deity worship, 5:30 Shower, dinner, and free time, 7:00 Evening class at temple, 8:30 Retire for sleep (Shinn 1987:106).

The ritualized lifestyle also expresses itself through prohibitions and restrictions. From the beginning of Prabhupada's missionary work in the West, he required four vows from his followers, all principles derived from ancient Indian tradition. The devotees are 1. Not allowed to eat meat, 2. Cannot have illicit sex (illicit = outside marriage), 3. Are not allowed to use any kind of intoxicants, and finally, 4. Are not allowed to gamble. These guiding principles are supplemented by numerous other rules.

**Organization**

Until his death Prabhupada himself headed the organization. Being a 'pure devotee' his authority was never questioned, and obviously ISKCON had a major problem at his death. However Prabhupada had appointed a group of twenty commissioners to take over. Twelve of these successors were authorized to take disciples, meaning that they were in fact declared spiritual masters or gurus. Further their authority was linked to geographical sections. In general — but with some alterations — this structure still exists. The Governing Body Commission (of which the gurus are members) is ISKCON's highest authority. At a local level the president of the temple is in charge and will see to it that the individual members behave according to the standards, and that he or she fulfils his or her obligations. By now ISKCON is very well organized and several good means of communication between different parts of the world exist. The Back to Godhead Magazine and the newspaper ISKCON World News being some of the most important. The Bhaktivedanta Book Trust is constantly publishing ISKCON's literature, including translations of the Vaisnava's sacred texts, in very large impressions and in many languages.

The organization provides every necessity to those living a communal life in a temple. To the dedicated members ISKCON becomes the main reference in every respect, and through mission in the streets and distribution of books the members will try to spread their enthusiasm for Krishna.

CHAPTER 8

# ISKCON and Syncretism

As we have seen, TM intensively claims to have established a synthesis between science and religion, and that Maharishi's current ideas of the belief system more than anything rests upon this structure. It has been shown how the basic Advaita-Vedanta assumptions in TM's interpretation could be smoothly identified within the realm of scientific thinking, and it was suggested that the notion of the impersonal divine was the most important precondition to this kind of religio-scientific syncretism. As a major conclusion it was established that science, in certain circumstances, is interpreted as hierophanies in TM. In the case of ISKCON such a harmonious cooperation is far less obvious. Where TM reaches out, ISKCON usually rejects. Where syncretism is the key concept in the case of TM, avoidance and sometimes even hostility is central to the understanding of ISKCON's perspective. As we shall see, the personalistic and dualistic theology of ISKCON — which directly opposes the monism of TM — seems to be an important reason for this.

According to sociologists of religion, ISKCON is characterized as a 'world-rejecting' religion, thus resenting modern society and all it stands for. Characteristic of the world-rejecting new religions is, according to Wallis, a strong emphasis on a clear conception of a personal god who prescribes a clear and uncompromising set of moral demands (Wallis 1984, 9). This is very true to ISKCON and equally irrelevant to TM. We have already seen that TM, being a 'world-affirming' new religion, places no strong emphasis on ethics or morals, and that the personal conception of god remains unimportant (and less 'real') than that of the omnipresent, impersonal divine. Hence a connection between sociological, theological and ontological aspects is evident, but where does it start? One suggestion could be that the lack of direct moral and ethical demands in TM, among other things, makes external influence, and thus syncretistic developments, more likely. The TM members are taught no moral or ethical lessons of importance. It is rendered that once the meditation has started, the individual will accommodate to universal, divine standards, or as it is usually termed, 'natural laws'. Krishna's devotees, on the contrary, submit to a well defined, narrow set of moral, intellectual and spiritual values which, of course, leave little opportunity for external religious ideas to find a place. Through their initiation into the Krishna consciousness movement the devotees have deliberately turned their back to the ideals of modern society, and therefore the individual's inclination to pay attention to external points of view is by nature limited (Shinn 1987, 97-122). The personal god — Krishna — speaks directly to his followers through the scriptures and through the gurus and appears physically to the believers in his arca form in the temples. The devotees see the god's image many times every day and are encouraged to develop intimate personal relations with him (e.g. to be his 'friend') , which indeed is a part of the so-called *Bhakti*-process' (Vishnupada s.a., 15). Very often Prabhupada explicitly warned against any contemplation on 'the divine', Brahman or 'the Absolute', or even to associate with people who do (see Prabhupada 1987, 4, 44-45). As discussed elsewhere, such statements are elements in the old dispute against the Advaita-Vedanta (Chapter 11). What Prabhupada wanted, and indeed what ISKCON wants us to do, is to concentrate on the personal aspect of the godhead: 'When one understands the Personality of Godhead, the reservoir of pleasure, Krishna, he actually becomes transcendentally blissful', Prabhupada says with reference to *Taittriya Upanishad* 2.7.1. (Prabhupada 1986, 708).

The initiation into TM does not imply a corresponding isolation from the surrounding society and its norms. Even the most dedicated member of TM expresses some interest in the ordinary world, although semi-monastic communes among TM members exist. We may conclude that theological notions, among other things, determine how the religions are inserted into society. Turning our attention to ISKCON, we shall see how a morally and ethically strong religion opposes the notions of the surrounding world and in general avoids syncretistic developments. A single quotation sets the scene:

Since I became a devotee I have not bothered to think of what is true and what is not. I have submitted myself to a genuine *guru* in the *parampara* of

Prabhupada and thus to Sri Krishna himself in the form of Caitanya Mahabrabhu. I have found Truth and feel no need to explore other religions or other ideas of how I should live. People may say whatever they want, but I am following Krishna's words. Truth is where Krishna is, and he himself has said that he is in our books.[1]

## Higher Dimensional Science[2]

It would be incorrect to say that science is of no importance to ISKCON. As a matter of fact science occupies a great deal of ISKCON's attention. Contrary to TM, however, this interest is mainly negative and critical. To ISKCON modern science is fundamentally false and unreliable. As we shall see, Prabhupada even attacked the scientists themselves calling them outrageous names.

According to ISKCON's religious aims, a strategy of investigation 'which transcends the limits of traditional mechanistic and biological science' is needed. To ISKCON itself, such a strategy already exists embodied in the Vaisnava-Bhakti tradition, intimately linked with the godhead. This belief system, however, has to undergo a reformulation whenever confronted with modern modes of orientation such as science. It is impossible for ISKCON to debate the suggestions of science, if the arguments derived from the sacred texts of Hinduism are not interpreted in a way that makes them comparable to the scientific statements. To ISKCON the problem is a matter of communication, or put bluntly: The scientists and the lay person are unable to grasp the significance of the sacred texts and the religious expositions. Taken at face value, the religious texts are of no reasonable meaning in a scientific context.[3] Only when the keepers of the texts are able to interpret the religious ideas in such a way that they become meaningful to outsiders, can a genuine discussion commence. This idea reveals itself in ISKCON's way of approaching scientific matters, but it has also been directly explained by some of ISKCON's gurus.[4]

This, of course, is the same phenomenon we find in TM. As a matter of fact, Maharishi's SCI is primarily the result of such a need for a common language. On the other hand ISKCON's case is very different. It is not ISKCON's intention to develop a synthesis with science, and any scientific or pseudo-scientific formulation by ISKCON must be interpreted as a means in the struggle against the traditionally atheistic and/or materialistic world view which is reflected by science. ISKCON maintains that science has only little to offer, if anything, unless it is directly linked with Vaisnava-Bhakti, and the ideas that are held to originate from the sacred texts are thought of as extremely important corrections to the scientific, misleading theories and speculations.[5]

The idea highlighted is that:

... the conflict between religion and science can be resolved by critically examining a number of the theoretical fields that have developed within the body of modern scientific thought. By pruning away unscientific deadwood in these fields, one can increase the rigor and clarity of science and also save important spiritual concepts from the categories of myth and metaphor. (Ramesvara 1984, 27)

Whenever realized this strategy leaves modern science with the theories and results that are acceptable to the theology of ISKCON, and nothing else. The wording does not seek conflict, but in fact the analysis is entirely occupied with ISKCON's perspective: True science is in accordance with ISKCON's theology, 'unscientific deadwood' is that which is not. This is true not only regarding the natural sciences, ISKCON also rejects many of the notions of the humanities, including comparative religion, even if scientific analyses of the movement are welcomed as already mentioned.[6] Most strikingly ISKCON's distinction between science, myth and metaphor, relates to the fact that ISKCON understands the Puranic mythology to be actual historical events and accurate descriptions. For instance it is rendered that the cosmography of Bhagavad Purana's Fifth *Canto* is 'literally correct and not mythological', even if it appears to be so to our ordinary senses:

According to [modern scholars], the cosmology of the Puranas represents an earlier, indigenous phase in the development of Hindu thought, which is entirely mythological and unscientific. This, of course, is not the traditional Vaisnava viewpoint. (Thompson 1989, 15)

The argument which ISKCON advances in many ways is that scientists are mistaking things because of their commitment to a godless ideology. They cannot or will not acknowledge that it is they who are wrong, and the sacred texts are right. The scientists believe themselves to be the superior thinkers while in fact ISKCON maintains, 'Krishna is the supreme scientist' (Bhaktiswaroopa s.a., 13).

The fact that Krishna is identified with the perfected scientist and the fact that ISKCON talks about a 'science of self-realization' which refers to the religious process of the devoted disciple, is of great significance to us. In doing so ISKCON (like TM, but in another way) is transforming the traditional comprehension of science into something different: According to a prominent agitator for ISKCON's ideas, Ravindra-svarupa dasa, it is stated that everything normally associated with religion (in this case Vaisnava-Bhakti) such as beliefs, rituals, scripture, mantras and so on are in fact scientific elements in 'an archaic science, but science non the less' (Deadwyler 1987, 371). At this point it is important not to identify ISKCON's notions with those of TM. The words may seem alike, but the meaning is different. TM imposes meaning upon a modern scientific worldview held to correspond with the religious notions of the Advaita-Vedanta tradition. On the contrary ISKCON claims Vaisnava-Bhakti theology to be truly scientific, contrary to modern science which is looked upon as more or less absurd and certainly (although paradoxically) *not* scientific. The difference is considerable. As a matter of fact ISKCON considers the modern scientific notion of an entirely mechanistic universe a 'grotesque and dangerous superstition' (Ramesvara 1984, 64,)[7] contrary to the Vaisnava teachings and rituals which are based on the direct perception of a mechanistic as well as non-mechanistic universe. The non-mechanistic aspect is concerned with the soul, with god and with the cosmic realities hidden to the normal senses and to the intellect, and therefore out of ordinary scientific reach. In order to overcome modern science, ISKCON claims to be truly scientific, but as ISKCON's science is fundamentally different from ordinary science, the content of the word is totally transformed when used by ISKCON to designate Prabhupada's theology.

The worry about modern science is often used by ISKCON when the outside world is approached: ISKCON's Ravindra-svarupa dasa (William Deadwyler) regards Western society as threatened by its own modes of orientation and interpretation and emphasizes that our scientific and technological abilities are unable to control the situation:

... there is not much prospect for real progress in the present culture of the West. On the contrary we are in great danger — mortal danger — of repeating the horrific mistakes of the past. Hope for progress must lie elsewhere. (Deadwyler 1987, 376)

Deadwyler introduces Vaisnava-Bhakti as the solution and claims the problems of Western society to emerge from the fact that we are presently moving away from 'the karmic ethos' towards some kind of 'theologia negativa', an antithetical challenge to the faith in the personal god. God, Deadwhyler says (attacking deistic notions), is 'written out of ontology' and then denied the effective exercise of any controlling power: 'In this, of course' he says, 'we see...the exact process which accompanied the rise of modern science in Europe' (Deadwyler 1987, 371).

As it appears ISKCON also has a showdown with deistic (contrary to theistic) Christian theologians in mainstream denominations who hold that God's role in the universe is limited to creating and maintaining the laws of physics, a notion not unfamiliar to the Christians since the debates between Newton and Leibnitz:[8] Is God a perfect clockmaker who created the universal machine, set it in motion, and then had no need to intervene further in its operation, or did the creator have to interfere at various times? To ISKCON the existence of permanent divine governing of the universe is obvious, and any religious submission to principles of scientific logic reduces, as ISKCON sees it, a sound and true understanding. God did not simply start the universe and then withdraw. He is constantly present and constantly governing it, ISKCON says. Hence ISKCON regards deistic theology and monistic philosophy in much the same way. In both cases the deliberate involvement in the course of the universe and in the life of men from the personal god is ignored, ISKCON says, and no basis for true understanding is left. Whether Christian deism or Advaita-Vedanta, such beliefs are much more in tune with the principles of theoretical science than a strong theistic religion.

One ISKCON source even said that 'the collapse of Christian theology' is caused by too strong an interest in scientific confirmation. That 'Christianity only sees God as the inventor of the universe rather than the controller' is due to the influence of mechanistic science: 'They (Christianity and mechanistic science) will eventually become one', he said.⁹ Words such as these would never appear in a TM context.

The confrontation with science is not considered an ideal situation. If the world had not been physically and spiritually polluted — so it is stated — ISKCON could concentrate on the pure teaching of the Puranas, the Veda and, the Bhagavad-Gita. I shall just give one example of the status of these texts:

... Srimad-Bhagavatam is a completely transcendental, liberated sound vibration coming from the spiritual world. And, being absolute, it is not different from the Absolute Truth Himself, Lord Sri Krishna. By understanding Srimad-Bhagavatam, consisting of twelve cantos, the reader acquires perfect knowledge with which he or she may live peacefully and progressively on earth, attending to all material necessities and achieving simultaneously supreme spiritual liberation.¹⁰

Further, any didactical adjustment of the form in which the message is spread is due to the poor spiritual situation of modern Man. The development of the non-traditional formulations of the religious teachings, even if totally in harmony with the original standards, is considered a Kali-yuga feature. This is important as it explains why ISKCON accepts to engage in discussions with scientists, when at the same time, science in general is proclaimed disastrous. Accordingly ISKCON does not consider these reformulations as alternative interpretations of the religious dogmas. It is only a matter of necessary pedagogy. At this point we are also able to understand ISKCON's terminology: 'Truly scientific' means 'acceptable according to ISKCON's theology'. Accordingly 'science' in general is not 'scientific'. By all means ISKCON has established an alternative interpretation of the concepts 'science' and 'scientific', and the alternative formulation of the belief system that has developed as the consequence of the confrontation with science is the so-called 'Higher Dimensional Science'.

This kind of relation is not syncretistic, and even if the word 'science' forms a part of the modern designation of ISKCON's belief system, this system is not an expression of syncretism. Hence ISKCON's 'Higher Dimensional Science' and TM's 'Science of Creative Intelligence' are far apart. A typical statement of 'Higher Dimensional Science' is:

To perceive the primordial personality lying behind the impersonal play of cosmic forces, we must go beyond the instruments and reductionistic strategies of present-day science. (Rameswara 1984, 57)

One of the most striking examples of the development and use of this higher dimensional science is the work of ISKCON devotee Sadaputa dasa (Richard L. Thompson), the leading figure in ISKCON's work in this respect. Holding a Ph.D. in mathematics, Sadaputa dasa has written extensively on scientific subjects from the perspective of what he terms 'Higher Dimensional Science'.[11] In one of his books the whole project of higher dimensional science is framed by a quotation from one of Prabhupada's letters, written the year before he died:

Now our Ph.D.'s must collaborate and study the Fifth Canto [of the Srimad-Bhagavatam] to make a model for building the Vedic planetarium.[12] [They] must carefully study the details of the Fifth Canto and make a working model of the universe. If we can explain the passing seasons, eclipses, phases of the moon, passing of day and night, etc. then it will be very powerful propaganda. (Thompson 1989, 1)

In Sadaputa dasa's book the higher dimensional level of science is, among other things, exemplified through the quantum theory of physicist Niels Bohr. According to Bohr, the atomic phenomena must be understood from at least two complementary perspectives, not as a single intelligible whole. The two perspectives are of course the 'wave picture' and the 'particle picture' that seem to contradict each other, even though they are both valid descriptions of nature. The author maintains:

They [the two perspectives] are facets of a coherent theory of the atom, but they cannot be combined within the framework of classical physics. To unite them and show their compatibility, one must go to a higher-dimensional level of mathematical abstraction, which is very difficult to comprehend. (Thompson 1989, 4)

This level of abstraction is contained within what he terms the 'Vedic cosmology'. This term primarily refers to the specific cosmographies in the Puranas (especially the Bhagavad Purana as mentioned above), in the Vedas, in the works of ancient Indian astronomy and mathematics (*Jyotisa Sastra*), in the Bhagavad-Gita and so on, but also relates to any other aspect of the general idea of Cosmos. What is attempted is a multifaceted description of reality, a description that disregards the classical European three-dimensional geometry, which forms the basic assumptions of the modern scientific world view. The outset is that the universe, as described in the sacred texts, is of a higher dimension than those accessible to us by our senses and our Western scientific thinking. Modern science poses a lot of questions, but due to ignorance and 'false identification' (maya) it is unable to give qualified answers. The truth about things are found only in the sacred tradition of Vaisnava-Bhakti, ISKCON claims.

From this point a problem arises. How can we possibly understand higher-dimensional relations when restricted to the realm of three dimensions? How can we understand the message of the sacred texts? Our interpretation is (in this understanding) by its nature imperfect, even if the text is perfect and 'true'. In the statements of Prabhupada the answer is frequently given on different occasions. In his commentary on the Bhagavad Purana he said:

The original purpose of the text must be maintained. No obscure meaning should be screwed out of it, yet it should be presented in an interesting manner for the understanding of the audience, this is called realization. (Prabhupada 1972-85, 1.4.1)[13]

Prabhupada also emphasized that the cosmological statements in the Bhagavad Purana should be accepted as authoritative, and that the reader should simply try to appreciate them instead of asking questions (Prabhupada 1972-85, 5.16.10). Contrary to Western science, the higher dimensional science does not aim at describing one single, rational world model. What it claims is insight into many mutually compatible aspects of one complete whole, indescribable in any ordinary language or scientific system of the modern world. In this way the higher dimensional science, or as it is also termed the 'Vedic science', is looked upon as quite superior to any of the so-called reductionistic scientific disciplines of traditional or ordinary science. This conclusion is inevitable: All of the ordinary scientific disciplines claim to be nothing but tentative, whereas the science that includes the higher dimensions is believed to be absolutely and unchangeably true. This notion points to the basic fact regarding the higher dimensional science of ISKCON: It is from first to last religious. Nevertheless the final answers cannot be given within the lifetime of a single person, no matter how much he or she strives to gain knowledge according to the divine principles. In the Bhagavat Purana it is stated that no person of this world is capable of fully describing the material universe 'even in a lifetime as long as that of Brahma' (Prabhupada 1978-85, 5.16.4.). Even so the missionary work conducted through the confrontation with science will, according to my sources, support the devotee in his spiritual endeavours.

## The Combat with Science as a Theological Discourse

ISKCON's struggle with modern science is an expression of what could be termed 'negative syncretism' (Chapter 1.). In deliberately avoiding scientific influence and through intense argumentation against scientific notions, ISKCON makes modern science an inevitable dimension in the religious minds of the devotees. They understand their religious conviction and experiences in antagonism to science, and because they are constantly reminded of the miseries of science, they are at the same time strengthened in their trust in ISKCON and Krishna. The negative relation between ISKCON and science therefore manifests itself as something which is in fact very much present, and very much at work. While we cannot call this relation syncretistic in the ordinary sense of the word (because syncretism normally refers to the actual merging of two or more systems), we may choose to designate it 'negative syncretism' in order to show that something nevertheless is taking place during the confrontation. The religious body that strives to remain pure and untouched does not remain unaffected, simply because its 'purity' and 'originality' are the products of deliberate avoidance of another religion (or several religions). It is perfectly possible that such negative contact often leads to a strengthened focus on traditional modes. In the case of ISKCON it is obvious that the identification with ancient Indian religion, and the ambition of keeping the teaching pure and unpolluted, are directly supported by ISKCON's surroundings in general working counter to the religious ideas of the group. The religious notions are upheld and theologically considered under the general impact of secular society outside ISKCON. Hence the religious ideas and values of ISKCON are being taught in apologetic terms, always with a clear consciousness that they are antagonistic to the surroundings. On this basis ISKCON has embarked on a new line of argumentation which would not be relevant, had the religio-cultural setting been different. The new argumentation, of course, constitutes the science related theological discussion. That ISKCON opposes the surroundings and tries to escape its influence has, paradoxically, lead to a communication between the two which ISKCON, from a theological point of view, basically would like to avoid. This aspect of the confrontation, I believe, must be regarded as a dimension of syncretism.

Sociologists, anthropologists and historians of religion have, of course, discussed the mechanisms of syncretism and syncretistic development on several occasions, and several approaches to the problem have been suggested. In the academic debate scholars have argued that the social sciences as well as the humanities we may add, lack a general theory of 'tradition' (e.g. Boyer 1990), and obviously the discussion of syncretism has to relate to the concept of tradition. While academics may have been too reluctant to combine syncretism and tradition in their studies, ISKCON has not hesitated. By stressing that syncretism is not possible, nor desirable, simply because 'all good forces should join to ensure the purity and unaffectedness of the Gaudiya-Vaisnava religion and do whatever possible to preach truth to those embeded in lies'[14], ISKCON has specifically related its beliefs as well as its self-esteem to the surrounding world. Through its conflict with science ISKCON has entered a new path of articulation, a new way of expressing religious notions. ISKCON has, to put it briefly, been forced to relate to epistemological elements outside its own divinely sanctioned belief system. This process, which unavoidably affects the group, is what I term 'negative syncretism'. In the following we shall consider some examples.

ISKCON's dominating figure in science, Sadaputa dasa, writes about 'Science: The Vedic View' in every issue of ISKCON's bimonthly Back to Godhead Magazine. The articles are more or less intelligible to readers with some scientific background, but may prove difficult to comprehend for those with no education. Accordingly Sadaputa dasa's articles are not directed to every devotee although Back to Godhead Magazine presents itself as one of the uniting medias of all ISKCON members. The articles are, in my opinion, of detailed interest only to ISKCON's intellectual elite.

In discussing ISKCON's relation to science these articles are excellent starting points, and as Sadaputa dasa is the leading person in this field of work in ISKCON, it is necessary to focus the attention on his contributions. Contrary to TM ISKCON has (deliberately or not) chosen to let a single person cover the field of science more or less on his own. It is nothing but a dimension of ISKCON's activities, contrasting sharply to the religious interpretation of science in TM which currently occupies most of the resources, and in principle every inner-group member. In TM a large team of TM scholars write on the subject, including Maharishi himself, but in ISKCON Sadaputa dasa, assisted by a few researchers, is the single dominating writer on science. TM's material is the result of coordinated, institutionalized activity and strategic planning, while ISKCON seems to improvise much more. This, however, does not mean that Sadaputa dasa is the only devotee who works with science. As we shall see below, ISKCON's 'scientific branch', the Bhaktivedanta Institute, occupies many people, but for the purpose of public relations only a few individuals represent ISKCON's points of view. In the following I shall consider samples of Sadaputa dasa's articles in order to demonstrate the range and line of argumentation implied.

Above all Sadaputa dasa mourns the anathema of reductionistic scientists who insist that everything must obey known physical laws, or at least ascribe to popular theories. The subjects he attacks cover the whole range of science and his arguments are based on different theological notions within the Vaisnava-Bhakti system. In one instance it is theories of cognition and perception:

Commenting on the ideas of a scientist studying the mechanisms of the eye and visual perception, whose theory involves 'a little man inside your head to interpret what you see, and someone else inside his head to interpret what he sees etc. ad infinitum', Sadaputa dasa says:

The basic fallacy of the little man in the brain argument is that it assumes implicitly that consciousness can be understood in physical terms. One tries to explain consciousness by describing a machine that creates a certain display of information. Then one recognizes that the mere presence of displayed information fails to account for consciousness of that information. Then one proposes another mechanism to interpret the information and finally generate consciousness. When that attempt also fails, one takes refuge in the overwhelming complexity of the brain and says that a consciousness-producing mechanism must be hidden in there somewhere. All we have to do is find it. (Back To Godhead Magazine Jan./Feb. 1992, 14)

To ISKCON, of course, consciousness cannot be understood apart from the divine presence of the conscious soul in the perceivers body.[15] Whenever consciousness is explained alternatively, for instance as a result of physiological mechanisms in the nervous system, ISKCON sees it as a grotesque expression of ignorance and human self-assertion at the expense of Krishna, and the theory is ridiculed or otherwise exorcised (a good example is Rameswara 1984, 17-27).

Somewhat outside the frames of ISKCON's traditional dispute with the natural sciences Sadaputa dasa also presents alternative anthropological and archaeological theories suggesting a common core to all ,or at least many religious and spiritual traditions of the world.[16] As it appears to Sadaputa dasa, highly specific Vedic thoughts are identifiable at many places. For instance, focusing on eschatological aspects, he writes:

The traditional date in India for the beginning of Kali-yuga is February 18, 3102 BC. This very date is cited as the time of the Flood in Various Persian, Islamic, and European writings from the sixth to the fourteenth century AD. ... The Norse Ragnarok involves the destruction of the Earth and the abodes of the Norse demigods (called Asgard), and thus it corresponds in Vedic chronology to the annihilation of the three worlds that follow 1000 *yuga* cycles, or one day of Brahma. It is said that during Ragnarok the world is destroyed with flames by a being named Surt, who lives beneath the lower world (appropriately called Hell) and was involved in the world's creation. By comparison the *Srimad-Bhagavatam* (3.11.30) states that at the end of Brahma's day, 'the devastation takes place due to the fire emanating from the mouth of *Sankarsana.*' *Sankarsana* is a plenary expansion of Krishna who is 'seated at the bottom of the universe' (*Srimad-Bhagavatam* 3.8.3), beneath the lower planetary systems. (Back To Godhead Magazine May/June 1991, 11-12)[17]

In the same article (p.10-11) it is suggested that the longevity of Biblical characters (Adam 930 years, Seth 912, Noah 950 etc.) supports 'Vedic chronology' which claims that the time span of a human life, during the yugas, decreases from 100,000 in the *Satya*-yuga to less than 100 years in *Kali*-yuga: The Biblical events are held to have taken place during *Dvapara*-yuga which would allow a life to span 1000 years.

No historical or philological criticism of these arguments shall be discussed here. It is ISKCON's notions we are facing, not scholarly judgements on the same subject. However, we may note that Sadaputa dasa apparently is unaware of important scientific theories such as Georges Dumezil's, while (in my judgement) no theory from the natural sciences escapes his attention.[18] Sadaputa dasa agrees that no final evidence is available, but he suggests that the hypothesis of an ancient global Vedic civilization is supported by the empirical indications found all over the world. This example shows how ISKCON is challenging historical, anthropological and chronological notions of modern science, and likewise the empirical foundation of modern medicine and physiology.

While the above example is mainly occupied with time, a corres ponding example focuses on space, or rather 'meta-space' as it concerns astronomy. Here Sadaputa dasa shows how classical religious cosmographic places recently have been identified as certain stars by modern astronomers. Certain constellations known as *naksatras* are mentioned in the sacred texts and some of them apparently match parts of the southern constellation Scorpio and Sagittarius. Many more details are given and the result is that from the description in (in this case) the Vishnu Purana, we can locate a certain celestial abode — *Pitriloka* (the abodes of the mythological ancestors and the sons of the gods) — in terms of familiar (astro-nomical) celestial landmarks (Back To Godhead Magazine July/ August 1991, 12-15).

Here, of course, we see a positive use of modern science, and indeed a kind of use similar to that of TM. Concerning TM I have used the term scholasticism in order to describe the way science functions, and it seems to be as useful in this connection. ISKCON does not obtain anything new from science. Certainly modern astronomy does not provide with anything that was otherwise missing in the belief system. The astronomical cartography simply confirms what was already known to the religion, just like the theory of the Unified Field in the case of TM. However, ISKCON places no emphasis on this, and by all means ISKCON does not regard astronomy as anything valuable in itself. In this case it proves its worth by affirming the everlasting truth expressed in the Vishnu Purana, but no religious meaning is imposed upon astronomy for that reason. In this respect ISKCON is far from TM.

In his book 'Vedic Cosmography and Astronomy' (1989), Sadaputa dasa outlines the religious critique of modern astronomy. Above all the book seeks to determine that the content of the Fifth Canto of the Bhagavat Purana, contrary to what most people would expect, is not 'mythological' but (together with the *Jyotisa-sastras* which are astrological texts) represent 'distinct yet mutually consistent ways of comprehending a universe with important features beyond the range of ordinary sense perception' (back cover of the book). Obviously the book is written from the perspective of 'higher dimensional science', and a concrete example is useful: Discussing the relations between Brahma in his many expansions and Krishna, Sadaputa dasa writes:

It is interesting to note that the Brahmas visiting Krishna had varying numbers of heads, ranging from four to hundreds of millions. It is rather difficult to understand how millions of heads could be arranged on one body in three-dimensional space, and it is also difficult to see how millions of Brahmas could all be seen simultaneously within one room. We suggest that these things are made possible by the fact that the underlying space is not three-dimensional.

Similar observations could be made about the incident in which Banasura used 1000 arms to work 500 bows and shoot 2000 arrows at a time at Krishna. In this case we are dealing with a materially embodied being living on earth. One might wonder how 500 material arms could be mounted on one shoulder without interfering with one another. And if this is possible, how could they aim 500 bows in the same direction at once? (Did the bows pass through each other?). We suggest that stories of this kind implicitly require higher-dimensional conceptions of space. (Thompson 1989, 39)[19]

A cosmographic example shows the same pattern. In the same book Sadaputa dasa discusses the structure of the universe as described in Bhagavad Purana's Fifth Canto. The text is very complex and therefore cannot be referred to in great detail here. I shall try to cover the essential aspects. The author writes:

The Vedic literature describes the material cosmos as an unlimited ocean situated within a small part of the unlimited spiritual world. Within this ocean there are innumerable universes, or brahamandas, which can be compared to spherical bubbles of foam grouped in clusters. Each of these universal globes consists of a series of spherical coverings and an inner, inhabited portion.

Within the inner region of the brahmanda, the most striking feature is Bhu-mandala, or the earthly planetary system. Bhu-mandala is described... as a flat disc with a diameter of 500 million yojanas, or 4 billion miles (using 8 miles per yojana). The surface of this disc is marked with a series of ring-shaped oceans and islands surrounding a central island called Jambudvipa. (Thompson 1989, 47-48)

According to Sadaputa dasa, the Fifth Canto gives specific figures for the size, shape and position of the geographical or cosmographic structures of the *Bhu-mandala*. These structures involve features otherwise located on an earthly, not a cosmographic, level: Trees, mountains, oceans and islands, but — according to Sadaputa dasa — these objects are all on the same cosmic scale as Bhu-mandala, said to be 12.6 billion billion square miles. The smallest mountain mentioned in this connection is 16,000 miles high and many reaches 80,000 miles or even 672,000 miles according to Bhagavad Puranas Fifth Canto.[20] Among other things Sadaputa dasa presents a computer-model of the plane Bhu-mandala scaled so that the reader, viewing the model from a distance of two feet, is 600 million miles from the centre. While carefully approaching the model step by step in new computer-drawings, more and more details emerge, and the ring shaped oceans and the island of *Jambudvipa* (see the above quotation) is seen. At a distance of 15 million miles, Jambudvipa and the surrounding salt water ocean are clearly visible. Afterwards, as we approach the centre, mountains and canyons are revealed. Some of the models display the view from above, some from east or west. In the text Jambudvipa is described as a disc shaped island 100,000 *yojanas*, or 800,000 miles, in diameter (the sun, Sadaputa dasa informs us for comparison, is currently assumed to be 865 miles in diameter). In the centre of Jambudvipa, Mount Meru raises 84,000 yojanas high, although not shaped like ordinary mountains, rather it is a cylinder on top of which the city of Brahma is situated (Thompson 1989, 47-56).

The judgement of ordinary scientists is well known to Sadaputa dasa:

Modern scholars tend to reject dimensions such as these as ludicrous exaggerations made by poets who were completely devoid of scientific knowledge. However, even common men in primitive societies can tell that the earthly mountains of our experience have heights of thousands of feet rather than thousands of miles. The highly rational philosophical discussion in the Bhagavatam indicates that it was not written by some kind of mad fanatic who was devoid of common sense. We suggest, therefore that the description in the Bhagavatam of gigantic sizes refer to an actual existing world that is built on the scale of the solar system and that contains features built on a similar scale. (Thompson 1989, 48-49)

The notion of Bhu-mandala implies that the Earth can only be considered as a globe in certain circumstances. ISKCON and Sadaputa dasa accept that our everyday perception experiences the Earth as a globe, and it is accepted that this manifestation is the right one to most people:

Yet, even though the earth can be regarded as a globe from the viewpoint of our ordinary sensory experience, we have already argued that there is a sense in which the earth is definitely not a globe. The very idea of a sphere is based on three-dimensional Euclidian geometry. Thus, if the three-dimensional continuum of our ordinary experience is simply a limited aspect of a higher-dimensional reality, it follows that the globe of the earth is also simply an aspect of that higher reality. To properly describe what that reality is, in and of itself, we must go beyond three-dimensional constructs as a sphere or a plane. A yogi who can reach directly to another continent by means of the prapti-siddhi is not experiencing the earth as a sphere. Similarly, a person who is able to realize that Vrndavana in India is nondifferent from the unlimited spiritual realm of Goloka cannot be thinking of the earth simply as a small globe. The earth globe may be one aspect of the reality he is experiencing, but he may choose to describe that reality by emphasizing other aspects that for him are more important. (Thompson 1989, 55-56)

As it appears, Sadaputa dasa's description of the cosmos is seen from the perspective of the rishis and demigods, and he makes no fool out of the scientists who are captured by maya, and therefore see nothing clearly. Their theories are ridiculous, but they themselves are, as most people, confused and disturbed by maya.

In talking of higher dimensional science ISKCON wants to pave the way for a modern, yet literal, understanding of the Puranic cosmography as well as myths. Sadaputa dasa does not want us to believe in multi-headed gods in a simple, earthly way or accept that the earth is flat. He wants to convince us that the scriptures — talking of impossible shapes of gods and worlds — are literally true, but that the level of understanding transcends normal conceptions and ordinary senses.[21] The argumentation involves the notion of higher dimensions. This kind of argumentation cannot be advanced unless modern science is questioned at the same time. Linking his religiously based higher-dimensional science to the ordinary science, Sadaputa dasa says:[22]

Modern cosmology may seem superior to its Vedic counterpart if we stick to the assumption that reality is limited to what ordinary human beings can perceive, using either their unaided senses or mechanical instruments. However, if the Vedic idea of higher realms of existence is even approximately correct, then it becomes clear that the modern scientific approach has caused us to focus our attention uselessly on relatively unimportant aspects of the universe. From this point of view, the technical sophistication of modern astrophysics appears more as an impediment to the attainment of knowledge than as an example of great scientific progress. (Thompson 1989, 121)

The arguments are emphasized again further in the reading:

The point can be made that modern cosmology not only contradicts the Vedic literature but also has its own internal contradictions. These contradictions are quite severe.[23] They indicate that some radical change will have to be made in modern theories to bring them into line with astronomical observations. It is perhaps reasonable to suggest that such a revision should also take into account the empirical evidence for higher-dimensional aspects of reality.[24] Such a new theoretical system might well agree more closely with Vedic cosmology than the present system does. (Thompson 1989, 121)

Finally the relation between science and 'Vedic cosmology' is seen in perspective with the development or evolution of science:

Radical extensions of our theoretical perspective have taken place repeatedly in the history of science. A striking example of this is provided by the revolution in the science of physics that occurred in the twenties and thirties of this century. At the end of the nineteenth century, physicists were almost universally convinced that classical physics provided a final and complete theory of nature. However, a few years later, classical physics was replaced by a new theory, called quantum mechanics, which is based on fundamentally different principles.

The most interesting feature of this development is that classical physics turns out to be compatible with quantum mechanics in the domain of observation in which it was originally applied. The difference between the two theories become significant only in the new atomic domain opened up by the quantum theory. Likewise, our proposed new cosmology would agree with existing theories in its prediction of gross sensory observations, but it would open an entirely new world of higher-dimensional travel. (Thompson 1989, 121-22)

ISKCON maintains that science as yet has not reached a genuine or true understanding of the universe, not even a correct description. Compared to TM's idea of science and scientific achievements the difference is very clear. As it appears to TM science has in fact reached, or is just about to reach, final truths and genuine cosmological descriptions. TM claims to prove what the physicists are assuming by offering the experience from transcendental consciousness as a means of empirical verification.[25] ISKCON still awaits substantial scientific results and will undauntedly present the Vaisnava-Bhakti theology as the only fulfilling and comprehensive description and analysis of the universe. Only if science is willing to broaden its view and engage in close cooporation with higher dimensional perspectives, may it develop into something useful, ISKCON asserts. Under the prevailing circumstances, as indicated by the last sentence in the quotation above, the ordinary, 'profane' science has only something to offer on the level of 'gross sensory observation'. In the words of Sadaputa dasa:

We propose that although the total reality of the world is very difficult, or even impossible to fully describe in words, different aspects correspond to different perspectives, which depend on the different situations and sensory capacities for different observers. Simple geometric imagery may be quite fitting for the description of the universe from many of these different individual perspectives, even though it is completely inadequate to describe the material world as a whole. (Thompson 1989, 56)

### The Bhaktivedanta Institute and the First World Congress on the Synthesis of Science and Religion, 1986

It has been determined that ISKCON claims superiority over science. However, ISKCON maintains a special branch dedicated to scientific research, namely the Bhaktivedanta Institute based in San Francisco and Bombay (with minor departments in Paris and Tirupati). This organization is described as 'an international association of scholars dedicated to coordinating science and religion, especially through consciousness-based paradigms that are meaningful to both' (Singh 1987, xviii). According to what we have already said about ISKCON's relation to science this may come as a surprise. How are we to interpret the aims of the Bhaktivedanta Institute, and indeed how are we to interpret ISKCON's extensive project termed the 'First World Congress on the Synthesis of Science and Religion'? As in the case of TM, I think, one should not be satisfied with the apparent intentions and ideas that are expressed. Obviously TM is not as secularized as it wishes us to believe, and in the following we shall see that ISKCON's engagement with science is not an alliance of equals as the expression 'synthesis of science and religion' might indicate.

The Bhaktivedanta Institute was founded in 1976, the year before Prabhupada died. ISKCON asserts that the set up of the institution was inspired by Prabhupada, and indeed he paid attention to the challenge from science even before then.[26] The aim of the Bhaktivedanta Institute is deepened as follows:

The primary thrust of the Institute is to promote the investigation of alternative paradigms, needed both in science and in religion, to systematically study and understand non-quantitative aspects of the world around us — particularly the nature of life and consciousness. (The Bhaktivedanta Institute 1986, 91)

The phrase 'higher-dimensional science' is not used, but obviously this is what the text refers to.

The most concrete expression of the Bhaktivedanta Institute's work was the 'First World Congress on the Synthesis of Science and Religion' held in Bombay, India during January 9-12, 1986 on the occasion of the 500th anniversary of Caitanya Mahaprabhu's birth. For this conference a group of internationally acclaimed scholars from various disciplines were invited to talk about 'the present status of science and religion, the history of discord between them, and the potential benefits in their reconciliation' (Singh 1987, cover). As a matter of fact ISKCON had been able to gather several high-ranking scientists including five Nobel laureates, the Dalai Lama and other prominent guests. The materials presenting the debate and the issues at stake read:

Science gives us the means and methods to improve material life and to explore the tangible world in which we live, but there is widespread confusion about how to avoid the dangers caused by its misuse. Until recently, religions which concern themselves with values and the purpose of life, were often seen as irrelevant to science. Today, increasing numbers of scholars believe that science and religion can satisfy humanity's needs much more effectively by working together than by remaining apart.[27]

Notice where the emphasis is laid: It is scientists who are turning to religion for answers, not the religions who seek help through science. We also notice that ethical themes are central: Questions of values and conditions and purpose of life. No questions of cosmology are directly mentioned.[28] The official statement of purpose of the congress outlines all the ethical and spiritual problems that have developed 'because modern man has not kept pace with his explosive progress in material technology'. Towards the end the text reads:

The enormity and the seriousness of the global situation demand urgent attention from all thinking men: scientists, philosophers, educationists, and social leaders. The root causes of this malaise have to be identified, and corrective processes initiated.

The World Congress for the Synthesis of Science and Religion is a sincere attempt to focus the attention of leading intellectuals and religious leaders on the urgent need to investigate these multifaceted problems and propound penetrative and durable solutions.[29]

In this respect, as we have seen before, ISKCON also differs from TM. TM's involvement with science aims at a coherent cosmography and cosmology, but only indirectly — somewhat isolated from TM's direct involvement with science — ethical aspects appear. According to sociologist of religion Eileen Barker's personal comments on the congress, the question of world peace was central to the discussions, and apparently the problem was related directly to the relationship between science and religion.[30]

ISKCON is well aware of the differences between Vaisnava-Bhakti and modern science, and the willingness to cooperate is not necessarily the same as suggesting a synthesis. As a matter of fact, according to Eileen Barker, the idea of a synthesis was not popular among all the participants:

So far as the title of the congress was concerned, several of the delegates felt uneasy with the concept of synthesis; many wanted to preserve an analytical distinction between science and religion and were happier with words like 'relationship' or Robert Nelson's suggestion that we should be concerned with a dialectical interaction between the two disciplines. (Barker 1986, 142)

This observation does not correspond to the title of ISKCON's congress, but in my opinion it corresponds perfectly to ISKCON's spirit in this respect. Science, when met positively, is considered a working partner, but not an allied one. When met critically it is looked upon as a manifestation of maya.

The papers read at the conference and a part of the following debate are published in a rather large volume (451 pages) entitled 'Synthesis of Science and Religion. Critical Essays and Dialogues' (edited by T.D. Singh 1987). In an important Editor's Note (placed beside the table of contents) an interesting remark is made:

Though ideas and attitudes expressed in the various articles sometimes conflict not only with those of other articles but also with specific ideas and attitudes of the publishers, this book is intended to be an open forum. We hope that all readers will appreciate the need for freedom of expression in a work of this type.

Obviously the idea of the congress was to present points of view and discussions rather than fixed truths. In this way science becomes a mirror, something for ISKCON to understand itself against. Even if some of the scientists in their contributions acclaim some of the same concepts and notions as ISKCON does itself, the book cannot be regarded as a manifestation of scholarly appraisal of Vaisnava-Bhakti or ISKCON, and certainly not as a religious recognition of science. What it embodies is ISKCON's interest in meeting one of the dominating segments of society, namely science, and confront it with its own (religious) notions and values. Further it is relevant to remember that the scientists present at the Bhaktivedanta Institute's congress were all more or less open-minded and willing to discuss sensitive themes. Even if many of them disagreed with ISKCON on fundamental problems, they all acknowledged ISKCON's interest in bringing the different points of view together for debate. One may well suppose that the majority of scholars in the traditional scientific communities would disregard ISKCON's project — and indeed any project of a similar kind.[31] What ISKCON comprises in the book is a selection of contributions from scholars, philosophers and religious leaders with some kind of interest in ecumenical or inter-disciplinary discourse, either for the purpose of academic analysis or for existential reasons. For that reason we cannot take each and every utterance from the book as an expression of ISKCON's official religious aims. As a whole, of course, the publication is meant to partially fulfill the need for discussion, but *en detail* it does not exclusively support ISKCON's notions. TM, for comparison, exclusively presents scholars from within TM's own body. I know of no current external discussion of TM's perspectives presented within a TM context unless the analysis corresponds perfectly with TM's notions.[32] Not even references to critical articles or books are made. As we have seen academic understandings and religious notions are intermingled in everything TM produces. Consequently any approach in TM's case must be regarded as a carefully chosen direct element in the above all important religious project of the organization. Therefore, at this point, we may consider whether Wallis' notion of TM as 'world-affirming' and ISKCON as 'world-rejecting' is true in every respect (Wallis 1984). Concerning external scientific and philosophical notions, it seems as if ISKCON is more willing to engage in discussions with the surroundings than TM is.

TM and ISKCON individually have developed specialized branches in terms of formulating their teachings. In both cases the foundation is the sacred literature, and basically the traditional structure between the guru and his followers. In scholarly terms the two institutions, the MIU of TM and the Bhaktivedanta Institute of ISKCON, are modern ways of presenting religious beliefs. To TM, however, MIU presents a world-model which is coherent with notions of modern science, while ISKCON's institute presents an alternative to the scientific, non-spiritual understanding of the world. In both cases the institutions are intellectual elements in the total system of organizations and departments constituting the two religions. While TM has developed an institution with formalized public recognition (a university), ISKCON's institute remains outside the formalized systems of education. TM offers actual officially registered educations, grades and so forth, but at the Bhaktivedanta Institute this does not exist. Research on a doctoral and post-doctoral level is explicitly mentioned in the Bhaktivedanta Institute's publications, and it is mentioned that research fellowships will be offered. However, this research remains internal ISKCON business. In terms of how TM and ISKCON in general are inserted into society, this difference is not surprising. Neither is it surprising that an ethical dimension is much more apparent in ISKCON's relation with science. TM's interrelation with science is almost exclusively a matter of cosmology. Referring to the benefits of transcendental meditation and the TM-Sidhi program, TM of course points to ethical aspects as well, and the World Plan of Maharishi contains strong ethical aspects within its millennial notions (p. 31), but focusing on the argumentations with regard to science, the clinical description prevails. At the outset of ISKCON's interrelation with science, ethical considerations are often presented as those which in fact are of greatest concern:

Why do we need to discuss with scientists? It is because their theories are completely out of line with reality. There is no doubt that science can be a great blessing to mankind, but only if we conduct our scientific thinking according to a superior plan, according to spiritual reality. I hope — and I also believe — that our scientists are able to impose that perspective upon their colleagues outside ISKCON. We have to face it: The problems of the Earth today will not be solved unless science changes its focus and accepts that matter is not all. As Prabhupada once said: 'The material diseases and the moral and ethical corruption of the world cannot be cured by artificial medicine'. Ordinary science is artificial. The only solution comes from Krishna himself. He is the real cure. When Vedic science gets its chance, all the troubles will vanish. We are simply obliged to offer Krishna's mercy to our fellow men, be it through *kirtana* or science.[33]

A very clear expression by Sadaputa dasa concludes this description of ISKCON's relation to science: 'If one is at all interested in knowledge of God, one should recognize that such knowledge is not compatible with mainstream science' (Back to Godhead Magazine Nov./Dec. 1992, 20). 'Knowledge of God' is always ISKCON's primary aim, which is not necessarily the case among scientists.

In order to describe TM's attitude towards science I have dealt with the development of the belief system and the notion of sacred as it reveals itself in TM. For the purpose of comparison it would be appropriate to give a corresponding account for ISKCON, but this is only partly relevant. ISKCON has not undergone a development such as TM. Even if ISKCON has changed and adjusted itself to the conditions of modern society, these adjustments or innovations are of a totally different kind than those of TM. In an article on ISKCON's self-perception devotee Ravindra-svarupa dasa (William H. Deadwyler III) reflects on ISKCON's position in today's world by quoting Prabhupada's comment on Bhagavt Purana 1.9.9. Here Prabhupada declared that all the great religious preachers or re-

## 140  ISKCON and Syncretism

formers of the world executed their mission by adjustment of religious principles in terms of time and place:

There are different climates and situations in different parts of the world, and if one has to discharge his duties to preach the message of the Lord, he must be expert in adjusting things in terms of time and place. (Prabhupada's comment on *Bhagavad Purana*. Prabhupada 1972-1985, 1.9.9)

Ravindra-svarupa dasa, who naturally counts Prabhupada among the great religious teachers and reformers, explains how Prabhupada himself did:

In bringing Caitanya's movement to the West, Prabhupada made such adjustments. Most notably, he set the prescribed number of daily rounds of japa [the rosary beads] at sixteen (instead of Bhaktisiddhanta's sixty-four); he simplified ritual, especially with regard to puja; he created an asrama for unmarried women, coining the word brahmacarini; and he gave women disciples brahminical initiation with the gayatri mantra, hence enabling them to assume all priestly functions, including puja, traditionally performed by men alone. (Deadwyler 1989, 73)

Ravindra-svarupa dasa also uses this commentary to describe how ISKCON understands its own position in the modern world:

ISKCON devotees are highly conscious of the innovative nature of ISKCON, and, especially because many devotees have been able to spend time in India, we know very well how much we differ from traditional forms of 'Hinduism'. At the same time, we feel we have not left anything behind that the full tradition has been transmitted to us, and that, by Prabhupada's grace, we have inherited everything that India's ancient spiritual heritage has to offer. We feel very old, and we feel very new. (Deadwyler 1986, 73-74)

The innovations in ISKCON can be grouped in two categories. Some innovative aspects appear as reductions of traditional demands, while others are extensions of traditional possibilities. The *mantra* is recited in the traditional way, but not as intensively as in the original setting, the puja is still carried out, but often in a moderate form. Women are allowed to participate in traditional male activities, but no new rituals or institutions have developed. Hence ISKCON's renewal is confined to structures and modes that are part of Vaisnava tradition. On the contrary TM's innovations are established by introducing elements from outside the original Advaita-Vedanta. While in both cases a development has taken place, the changes are of different kinds.

As a natural consequence of this, it is of only little value to go into details regarding ISKCON's notion of the sacred here, as no innovation takes place in this respect. The only thing to be mentioned is perhaps ISKCON's use of computer based religious texts which makes the sacred writings appear on electronic screens, a phenomenon which I have dealt with elsewhere (Rothstein 1992). It is correct, of course, that this example reveals some interest in modern ways and a slight acknowledgement of the usefulness of scientific knowledge in ISKCON. However, according to ISKCON, it is primarily a question of using modern technology for the benefit of Krishna. One source said:

*Bhagavad Gita* is still *Bhagavad Gita* when it appears on a screen. It does not matter whether it is recited, read in a book or read through a computer. What matters is that we are able to distribute the essence of the *Gita* much more efficiently by using the computer systems.[34]

In ISKCON the sacred is constantly experienced through the traditional channels namely the sacred texts, the gurus, the deities and the rituals (Chapter 7). Through these traditional means of communicating with Krishna, the believers have a coherent platform that does not as yet allow any innovative mechanism or phenomenon as a path to the divine. It is established in the Vaisnava religion that Krishna has defined the ways by which he can be approached, and no alternative methods or ways are recognized. Hence the god only reveals himself to the believers according to the already established standards. It is believed that Prabhupada in his writings (especially his commentary on Bhagavat Purana) has provided the blueprints for an ideal spiritual civilization. As indicated by Ravindra-svarupa dasa, ISKCON is simultaneously innovative and conservative, but regarding the possibility of new ways of approaching Krishna, conservatism reigns. On the contrary, as we have seen in TM's case, the impersonal divine is likely to be discovered in other ways than those prescribed in the traditional Advaita-Vedanta.

ISKCON's offence against modern science also focuses on conservatism, or in ISKCON's own words; 'reductionism'. ISKCON very directly claims its right to be taken seriously, even if its recommendations lead away from established scientific principles:

Given the serious implications of the reductionist approach of modern science, we should hesitate to accept it as completely valid unless forced to do so by truly compelling evidence. Many scientists and philosophers maintain that such evidence has already been found in great abundance. Yet a close examination of current scientific theories reveals that this is simply not so...
Reductionistic thinkers do not have a monopoly on knowledge of life and the universe. Reasonable alternative views deserve as much serious consideration as the reductionistic approach. Otherwise, scientists claim that they are unbiased and objective certainly ring hollow, and people are denied true freedom of choice. (Ramesvara 1984, preface)

'Higher Dimensional Science' in ISKCON means religion, and higher dimensional analysis is what ISKCON needs in order to prove the existence of Krishna, his eternal abodes or any other spiritual, religious or metaphysical notion. Therefore ISKCON's kind of science is an inherent phenomenon which only exists as a part of ISKCON's ontology. TM's science, including for example the Unified Field theory, superstring theory, big bang theory, neurophysiology and so forth,[35] does not differ from the science of ordinary scholars. The interpretations are different, but methods and theories are the same. Of course TM does not stop there. At the bottom line TM — like ISKCON — aims at a transcendental realm outside the reach of ordinary science. The path, however, to that transcendental realm, follows the logic of modern science. It is on the level of interpretation that TM leaves the secular scientific notions. ISKCON's science of the higher dimensions, on the contrary, is precisely — and from the very beginning — of another dimension than that of original science. Therefore no qualified interpretation of the higher dimensional science can be given without a general recognition of ISKCON's ontology, and therefore ISKCON cannot use ordinary science for fundamental purposes. TM confines its argumentation to ordinary scientific theories — not those of higher dimensions, which means that TM's deviances from ordinary science are at the level of interpretation. In this it is seen why TM and ISKCON disagree, and why it is only TM that is engaged in syncretistic intercourse with science.

Discussing ISKCON's relation to science we now turn to a description of how this religion reacts towards a specific scientific theory, namely the theory of biological evolution: TM's darling is the GUTs but ISKCON loves to hate Darwinism.

CHAPTER 9

# ISKCON and Evolutionary Theory

Contrary to TM, ISKCON is very occupied with living nature. As we have seen TM's interest in science is primarily cosmological, but ISKCON's focus is not only on descriptions of the universe's foundation and functioning, it also concentrates on the animal and plant kingdoms. The reason why, I believe, is quite simple. The religious foundation of TM is far less explicit with regard to animals and plants than that of ISKCON. The Puranic mythology is rich in detail concerning animal life, and the iconographic tradition of the Vaisnava religion is always occupied with Krishna's creatures. Indeed Krishna himself is the patron of the animals (e.g. as *Krishna Gopala*), some of his important insignia are related to animals (especially the Peacock) and the sacred texts (e.g. Bhagavad Gita 5,18) again and again declare that the living soul within the human beings is the same as the living soul of the animals (Prabhupada 1986, 293).[1]

It is the intention in the following chapter to discuss ISKCON's attitude towards the theory of biological evolution which is the secularized idea of how life came into being and how it evolves. As we shall see, this aspect of ISKCON's reactions against science, and contemporary ideas of life also point to the 'negative syncretism' discussed in the previous chapter.

## ISKCON and the Theory of Biological Evolution

One of the most popular targets of ISKCON is the biological theory of evolution. The debate, of course, goes back to the discussion that followed immediately after the publication of Charles Darwin's famous work 'The Origin of Species' in 1859, and ISKCON is by no means left alone in the fight. Many modern religious movements — most remarkably Christian groups — maintain (or even rediscover) 'creationistic' points of view. ISKCON, however, confines the argumentation to the Vaisnava theology. The conflict between ISKCON and modern biology, therefore, is an important element in

ISKCON's attitude towards science in general. To TM, biology (apart from human neurology and microbiology which are used to document the effect of the meditation), seems to be of little or no interest. But ISKCON represents a vast, traditional mythological system including detailed cosmogonies dealing with the origin of life. Consequently ISKCON has to relate to the modern ideas opposing ISKCON's own notions. The origin of life is not directly on TM's agenda, and the question of how to comprehend biological life becomes of little significance.

In Europe and the United States the basic aspects of the debate were immediately recognizable once the theory of biological evolution became known. More than anything Darwin's theory was seen as a challenge to the authority of the cosmogony of Genesis, but more precisely 'the dignity of Man' was considered threatened. From the position of being created in the image of God, Man, in the theory of evolution, was (roughly speaking) degraded to a descendent from ape-like creatures, according to Christian interpretations. Nevertheless, the theory of evolution found its place within the Christian culture. Today only Biblical fundamentalists strongly reject the theory.[2] Most Christians seem to accept evolution as a fact, superimposing God as the originator and sustainer of a naturalistic process (evolution): As God created the universe in such a way that life (including human beings) would arise and evolve, Man is still God's creation, they say.[3]

This kind of syncretising of the naturalistic account with God's creativity has not found its place within ISKCON. No modified interpretation of the religious dogmas is allowed, and only criticism is shown. In ISKCON the mere existence of the evolutionary theory can be explained and dealt with within the limits of the Vaisnava-Bhakti religion: It is a Kali-yuga feature, an idea arisen in the minds of people isolated from any true knowledge of the divine and thus any true knowledge at all. Indeed evolutionary theory is identified as a dominating and horrific aspect of the cultural and spiritual collapse awaited in the present Age of Death. In the words of devotee Sadaputa dasa:

Religious beliefs are compatible with Darwinism only if they hold that God is simply a human idea having something to do with moral imperatives.

But if this is what you believe, then instead of having religious beliefs, you have 'scientific' beliefs about religion.[4]

There are several good reasons to compare this attitude of ISKCON to that of Christianity in the last part of the 19th Century. What people reacted against in Europe at that time is very much the same as ISKCON is up against now. The philosopher Ernan McMullin describes Darwin's immense impact upon Christian religious thought during the 1860s as follows:

First of all, he undermined the design argument which had become a motive for religious belief among Christians. He undermined the notion that we can discover God by looking at the living world and seeing in that world a testimony to God's direct interventive action. The more familiar consequence of Darwin's ideas was that the human organism itself came to be seen as a simple product of selection over many millenia. One of the central notions in the Jewish and Christian traditions had always been the uniqueness of the human, the thought that somehow the universe focuses on man, that the reason of the universe somehow lies in man. If one accepts an evolutionary theory which claims that man was simply and, as it were, accidentally brought about, man's uniqueness appears to be compromised. In that case, man seems to become just one possible outcome on this small and insignificant planet. He might never have been. And on other planets, there may be forms of life quite different. (McMullin 1987, 79)

ISKCON of course should not be compared to the Judean-Christian tradition in general. In this respect, however, there are patterns of considerable likeness. In the following I shall give an account of this, based on material from the earlier days of ISKCON as well as more recent material.

### A Note on Style and Argumentation

Before I turn to a description one thing should be mentioned: ISKCON's way of arguing has been strongly developed since the days of Prabhupada. Today the arguments are primarily put forward by ISKCON devotees with an academic, scholarly upbringing within the traditional scientific community. They know what they are talking about, and they are very well aware of how to discuss these matters in a way that gives most trouble to scientists. As a matter of fact ISKCON's specific religious alternative in this debate is frequently left out when the criticism is forwarded, even in ISKCON's own publications. Instead the devotees will argue from opposing platforms within the scientific tradition itself. A good example is Rameswara 1984, 29-35 where theories of biochemistry are questioned or elegantly torn apart without introducing religious arguments, or the mathematical and statistical calculations concerning the possibility of life arising by chance, in the same volume (p. 34-35). Another example of high intellectual quality is devotee Ravi Gomatam's discussion of real and artificial intelligence which contains only one reference to the Bhagavad Gita (Gomatam 1986). In these and other cases the problems with scientific theories on evolution (and other matters) are dealt with intellectually and in a great many details, including numerous references.

Of course this line of argumentation is a matter of strategy. The sayings of Prabhupada, dating from the last three or four years of his life on the other hand, seem quite insufficient as arguments. An example:

Darwin is a scoundrel. What is his theory? We kick out Darwin's philosophy. The more we kick out Darwin's philosophy, the more we shall develop in spiritual consciousness.[5]

Another example:

[If] a scientist does not know the supreme authority what kind of man is he? He is simply a third class man, a rascal. A civilized man knows about God. Your science is not civilized.[6]

And equally:

Though today's scientist has devised a lofty technology, essentially he knows about as much as his dog: How to eat well, how to sleep peacefully, how to have an enjoyable sex life, and how to defend against enemies. (Burr 1984, 179)[7]

His rejection of any interpretation of Life apart from his own is carried on by his successors, but where the leading contemporary devotees express themselves according to scientific terminology and attempt — apart from the religious arguments — a traditional line of scientific argumentation in their criticism, Prabhupada restricted his discussions to a harsh challenge in a rather condescending form as the example above indicates. Indeed social anthropologist Angela Burr points to the fact that the devotees are highly impressed by Prabhupada's intellectualism, although from an academic point of view he is not intellectually sophisticated (1984, 17). In this connection it is interesting to observe that ISKCON, although very eloquent scientists exist within the group, again and again promote the sayings of Prabhupada himself. Sadaputa dasa quotes Prabhupada for saying that the inhabitants of the moon would be 'almost invisible' with subtle material bodies, which he takes to mean that 'the world of the demigods, including their dwellings, food, conveyances, and so on, would also be invisible to us'. The topic leads Sadaputa dasa to questions of whether or not astronauts actually traveled in three-dimensional space to the moon 'we directly perceive in the sky' (Thompson (i.e. Sadaputa dasa) 1989, 131 f.). From Prabhupada's rather simple statements, Sadaputa dasa unfolds a vast theory on the subject based on Vaisnava theology. In this case it is Sadaputa dasa, not Praphubada, who develops the exegesis. In the book 'Life Comes From Life' published simultaneously in many countries in many languages during 1989-90,[8] tape recordings of Prabhupada's conversations with his disciples and others dating from 1973, are presented in print. His line of argumentation is straightforward and condemning in a much more radical manner than that of his intellectual followers of today. Obviously the use of Prabhupada, even if unsuitable and out of line with the current strategies of ISKCON, is explained through his position as an infallible Master. Being a 'pure devotee' he cannot be mistaken, and every utterance from his mouth is of immense importance. The position of Maharishi is very much the same in TM, but what he has to say about scientists is very much different.

Apart from this use of the spiritual master, the style of argumentation in ISKCON has undergone changes. The debate on biological evolution is a good example of this development, though the same process is recognizable when other scientific disciplines are discussed. It should be added that devotees with no scholarly background also use modern science as an indication of the wrongs of the modern, secularized world. Their arguments, however, are not as elegantly presented as those of the former professional scientists among the devotees. On the contrary — as will be shown — they often tend to be rather primitive.

## The Theory of Evolution as a Spiritual Problem

Apparently Prabhupada considered the evolutionistic understanding of people in the West to be one of the primary obstacles to further spiritual development, as the theory disregards the role or even the existence of a personal divinity. When the role of science is given a status superior to that of God (Krishna), it is stated, we are left with an empty shell instead of a guiding, ontologically valid religion. The problem is, ISKCON maintains, that modern Man has faith in 'simple, mathematical explanations of highly complex phenomena such as life, the origin of species, the origin and structure of the universe etc.' (Ramesvara 1984, 57). The result is a world view where:

...values and ethical norms can no longer be understood as fundamental principles, originating from a transcendental creator who defines the ultimate purpose and meaning of human life. Rather they become mere strategies for survival that originated by chance, were perpetuated because of their effectiveness under certain circumstances, and will be swept aside by inexorable physical transformation as those circumstances change. (Ramesvara 1984, 1)

According to ISKCON humanity has to acknowledge its origin in terms of divine creation in order to develop spiritually. The notion of biological evolution counteracts the desired spiritual attitude. As ISKCON sees it, it reduces the human being to a load of chemicals with no other goal than physical survival. In Danish ISKCON's radio broadcast ('Radio Krishna') this theme is dealt with again and again (October 1992. Repeated during January 1993). During a six hour broadcast it was repeated over and over again that 'the way we understand life will determine the way we live': If a person believes that life evolved by coincidence, that he developed from another species, and that he shall never live again, he cannot understand the purpose of his life and will blindly seek 'sense gratification'. The consequence of evolutionary ideas, therefore, is a materialistic attitude towards life. The only basis of a sound and meaningful life, ISKCON maintains, is the awareness of life as something spiritual and everlasting. To accept that the species have developed according to physical laws, and that no creation has taken place, contradicts the religious explanation and the important conceptions of karma and samsara, and is totally unacceptable to ISKCON.

All the movement's endeavors must be understood in accordance with this alarming problem. Any attempt to persuade people of the superiority of ISKCON's religious notions focuses on what is looked upon as the erroneous basis of scientific thought. It may be that ISKCON does not always refer to scientific points of view, but every major problem that is discussed in the movement's propaganda has been considered by science (questions of life, death, creation, time and space). This is why scientific answers or suggestions are very often introduced as victims in ISKCON's rethoric.

This makes the dispute against the modern theory of biological evolution a part of ISKCON's general strategy. The discussion is carried out as a means of religious argumentation in order to awaken the slumbering people of the modern Western world. The salvation of humankind, ISKCON says, depends on people's orientation. Therefore it is of the utmost importance to argue against the false teachings of the scientists. The world finds itself in a tremendously fortunate position right now thanks to Caitanya's and Prabhupada's grace, and the liberation of many, many souls is expected even in the present Kali-yuga. In this way ISKCON's propaganda against science is linked with the movement's general soteriological notions.

**Theory and Speculation versus Knowledge**

Of course ISKCON has discovered that the traditional Darwinian perspective has undergone a remarkable development since the time of Darwin himself. The basic ideas of evolution may be the same, but through the recent insight gained from genetics and the science of molecular biology (of which Darwin knew nothing), the theory has undergone some very important developments. The focus of ISKCON's criticism, however, is still the traditional material, as is Charles Darwin himself. As an example Darwin's own confusion regarding his theory is brought forth as something typical — what it is not. From 'On the Origin of Species' Darwin is quoted:

To suppose that the eye with all its inimitable contrivances for adjusting the focus to different distances, for admitting amounts of light...could have been formed by natural selection, seems, I freely confess, absurd in the highest degree. (Rameswara 1984, 47)

In a book entitled 'The Scientific Basis of Krishna Consciousness', Bhaktiswaroopa Damodar Swami writes about Darwin and his contemporary colleague biologist A.R. Wallace, referring to an often cited correspondence between the two. Darwin is quoted: '...I am a firm believer that without speculation there is no good and original observation', and the ISKCON devotee's comment runs as follows:

Thus, one does not need to make an extensive study in order to understand this theory. His theory was completely based on his own speculation and mental manipulation, based on some data collected during his 'Voyage of the Beagle' (1831-36). Every sensible person knows that speculative knowledge is quite fallible. (Bhaktiswaroopa, s.a., 33)

The rhethorical appeal to 'every sensible person' is typical of ISKCON's texts. In this connection it serves to underline the idea that the theory of evolution is absurd. The negative criticism is primarily based on the ISKCON dogma of 'true knowledge' as identical with what is found in the sacred texts and what is established by the *gurus*. The cosmogonies of the Puranas and the cosmogonic fragments of the Bhagavad-Gita (e.g.10.8) clearly contradict the modern idea of evolution, ISKCON says.

The tentativeness of scientific thought appears to ISKCON as the weak point indeed. There is no final authority to judge the validity of scientific theories, and one must always be prepared to change the scientific conclusions. On the contrary, a firm authority does exist within ISKCON's religious tradition. Apart from the body of sacred literature, this authority is primarily Prabhupada, who, being 'a pure devotee of Sri Krishna', upheld the position of the ultimately developed guru. According to the dogmas of ISKCON, such a person is infallible as he is fundamentally linked with Krishna himself. After his death, Prabhupada's writings and the numerous audio and videotapes/films with his speeches and conversations are consulted as authoritative sources. In this way Prabhupada and his work rank more or less equally with the original religious texts, all in all forming a divinely sanctioned body of teachings (Rothstein 1992). Compared to the solely manmade construction of modern science this is far superior, ISKCON claims. The philosophical or methodological arguments presented by ISKCON against the scientific community stress this difference: The Vaisnavas are talking on behalf of the divine being, whereas the conventional scientists retail manmade fiction. The difference, of course, is immense:

[Darwin] could not provide any logical answer expect his speculative argumentation...He did not know that all species of life have been existing since the dawn of creation (Bhaktiswaroopa s.a., 34).

Relating to the Bhagavad Gita, such claims are typically supported by Prabhupada's commentaries to the passages dealing with creation. A good example is his comment on the Bhagavad Gita 9.8. which partly reads:

The different species of life are created immediately along with the universe. Men, animals, beasts, birds — everything is simultaneously created, because whatever desires the living entities had at the last annihilation are again manifested. (Prabhupada 1986, 463)[9]

The notion of karma and reincarnation is of course of primary interest to ISKCON in this respect. Darwin, as far as I am informed, had no awareness of such alien religious ideas. To ISKCON this fact is an absolute proof to his insufficiency. He knew nothing of the spirit soul and its transmigration from one body or species to another, and the evolution described by Darwin is, therefore, far away from the *actual* evolution of the spirit soul through different bodies, ISKCON claims. But today, ISKCON says, the idea of karma and reincarnation is (more or less) commonly known among scientists, partly because ISKCON has very strongly tried to inform biologists, paleontologists and zoologists on the subject.[10] In this way Darwin's successors carry an even bigger responsibility, although they may not recognize it themselves. As a matter of fact the 'evolutionist's propaganda' is considered a threat to ISKCON's spiritual life, and especially to the devotee's children. A column from Back to Godhead Magazine, entitled 'Schooling Krishna's Children' by Urmila Devi dasi, includes an article with the heading 'Kick Out Darwin' (a reference to Prabhupada's statement quoted above), beginning:

The doctrine of evolution is difficult to hide from. It is so pervasive in textbooks of science, geography, history, and literature that the reader, numbed by repetition, hardly notices the constant drone.
Our children need help to remain awake to spiritual life amidst this sleepy cloud of propaganda. We need to teach them, clearly and specifically, how evolutionists are lying.[11]

Apparently the criticism of the Darwinian perspective is not only based on a philosophical concern. It is a matter of spiritual welfare, and therefore — as already mentioned — it also forms a part of the ideological basis for ISKCON's extensive and ever expanding contribution to ecological preservation. Since 1986, when the WWF-International launched a cooperation between the organization itself and the world's religions (the so-called 'New Alliance'), ISKCON has been the leading representative of Hinduism, promoting Hindu points of view on ecology and nature conservation (references in note 1). T.D. Singh, one prominent representative of ISKCON's 'Center for Advanced Study in Science and Applied Theology' at the Bhaktivedanta Institute, writes:

In the Darwinian definition of life, geologic life consists only of chemicals; God is not involved, and thus there is no question of any share being allotted by Him. With this understanding, man often misuses his intellect and disrupts the balance of nature by unnecessarily killing certain groups of trees, animals, birds, fish, and so on. Thus he causes ecological disasters and various problems for himself. (Singh 1987, 94)

Such attacks on the theory of evolution are only rarely expressed straightforwardly in connection with nature preservation. More often notorious Hindu religious ideas are presented as arguments in ISKCON's work for ecological responsibility including among other things *ahimsa*: the notion of God as the owner of the earth (as expressed in the *Isa Upanishad* v. 1), the sacredness of cows and other natural objects, and pantheistic ideas of the divine as being present in nature. These aspects are derived from the sacred texts, thus forming the Hindu perspective. By introducing the criticism against Darwinism, ISKCON marks the gap between their own understanding and that of the secularized West. In fact the antagonism between the two perspectives serves to legitimate the religious understanding as ISKCON sees it.

Here we shall briefly return to TM where no programatic care for animals is seen. As a matter of fact TM has been criticized for mistreatment of animals in relation to TM's Ayurveda program. The international edition of Hinduism Today (May 1992) ran an article under the heading: 'Animal Testing in Ayurveda. Ethics Collide With Old and New Science'. Here it was established that TM scientists (and scientists with affiliation to TM) systematically have given animals lung and breast cancer in order to observe the animals' reactions to certain Ayurvedic remedies. One of the scientists is quoted:

Dr. Hari Sharma, a long-time Transcendental Meditation initiate and head of anatomic pathology at Ohio State University, is a chief researcher for the Maharishi ayurveda line. He explained to Hinduism Today that 'it is necessary to sacrifice a few for the benefit of the greater public' when asked about the ethics of animal experimentation. (p. 13)

According to the newspaper the case has damaged TM's reputation among mainstream Hindus and among religious Hindu groups in particular. TM, however, pointed to the fact that the scientists who had been criticicized had been working on their own and not under the authority of the TM movement, but this statement did not improve TM's image considerably. Above all many Hindu commentators interviewed by Hinduism Today assert that the violation of *ahimsa* is unforgivable. ISKCON agrees to that. When a leading member of ISKCON in Denmark read the article (on my suggestion) he declared that TM's activities were unforgivable and distasteful; 'Some of them even eat animals!' he proclaimed.[12]

This example seems to indicate that TM's ambition of being modern and scientific may well lead to a declining awareness of traditional Hindu notions. On the contrary ISKCON, struggling against the ways of modern society, strongly conforms to the traditional ethics of Hinduism, in this case the notion of *ahimsa*. While people with relation to TM apparently use vivisection because it is very often a requirement in Western science, ISKCON does without for exactly the same reason.

We now return to the discussion of evolutionary theory: ISKCON's position is, of course, reasonable within the framework of the religious tradition, and when exclusively scientific arguments are promoted they are usually well researched and well documented. On the other hand, the devotees have not always payed justice to the theory of evolution, and not always followed the line of scientific argumentation they claim. As an example, it is a severe misinterpretation of the theory of evolution always to expect a process of radical change to take place within a few thousand years. Nor can the biological theory of evolution, from a scientific or intellectual point of view, be criticized by mythological arguments, that is by beliefs alone. Both faults are at work in this example which argues against the evolutionary perspective:

As an example, the species portrayed in the ancient Egyptian pyramids were the same as those we meet at the present day. Similarly, since time immemorial the peacock, whose colorful feathers so nicely decorate the transcendental head of the Supreme Personality of Godhead Sri Krishna, has been the same as the species we find today. With his poor fund of knowledge, Darwin concluded that some species became extinct in the process of evolution. This is completely wrong. (Bhaktiswaroopa s.a., 35)

In order to support such claims, arguments with no scientific value whatsoever are occasionally put forward. A devotee, associated with the ISKCON scholars at the Bhaktivedanta Institute, introduced the possibility of living dinosaurs in remote places somewhere in central Africa, as an argument against the otherwise unquestionable fact of the total distinction of dinosaurs 65 million years ago. His concern was not the question of dinosaurs themselves, but rather the principal errors of modern zoology and paleontology. There is, he said, every reason to believe that species unknown to humankind are represented on Earth, because an unknown multitude of forms of life are required to fulfil the needs of the uncountable souls that have to take birth again and again on their way towards liberation.[13]

Relating to ISKCON's work for nature preservation this notion offers a paradox: It is a well established fact among conventional scientists that around 20,000 species of life become extinct every year, primarily due to deforestation. More than two species an hour. In ISKCON's projects this is mentioned as one of the environmental problems. But according to the idea of karma and samsara, these species are all needed for the incarnation of the billions of souls transmigrating through the multitude of bodily forms. How can ISKCON accept the fact that species become extinct when it is simultaneously claimed that all living entities are needed for the process of samsara which is governed by Krishna himself? How can the cycle of birth, death and rebirth continue if certain bodily forms disappear? And why bother at all: The Bhagavad Gita 2.11. says: 'Those who are wise lament neither for the living nor for the dead' (Prabhupada 1986, 87).

This question was answered by one of the leaders of ISKCON in Sweden during an interview. He was asked how the process of samsara could go on when species became extinct, but rejected the logic of the question. It is true, he said that species become extinct in various parts of the world, and perhaps even totally extinct from Earth, but this does not mean that the species are 'out of existence'. They may live on other planets, in other realms or in other forms.[14] This notion obviously is derived from passages in the Bhagavad Gita such as 14.4 and 14.5, although my source did not refer to them. In 14.5 Prabhupada's comment reads:

Living entities are seen not only on this planet but on every planet, even on the highest, where Brahma is situated. Everywhere there are living entities; within the earth there are living entities, even within water and within fire. All these appearances are due to the mother, material nature, and to Krishna's seed-giving process. (Prabhupada 1986, 685)

One has to suppose that the same ideas lie behind Prabhupada's comment on Darwin's theory: During a talk on biological evolution, someone referred to Darwin's theory and said that some species would become extinct, while others would survive. Prabhupada's reply was a straightforward rejection: 'Nothing becomes extinct. The monkey has not been extinct. Darwin's closest ancestor, the monkey, still exists' (Prabhupada 1990, 15). Several monkey species have been extinct from Earth. Prabhupada's words only make sense if related to ISKCON's general cosmology which leaves room for extraterrestrial life and life at other (spiritual) levels of existence. Further, the extinction of an earthly species may be interpreted as a response to 'karmic' needs. This became obvious when another source answered a similar question:

The living souls are not to be judged by their appearance during incarnation. The bodily form is a tool. Nothing but a tool. I can well understand if Krishna lets a certain form disappear if there is no need for it any longer.[15]

When asked how the sad story of the Passenger Pigeon could be explained within the frames of this understanding, the devotee answered that it was beyond his knowledge to explain. The Passenger Pigeon, once the most numerous of all bird species in the world, became extinct within a few years due to human interference in 1914.[16]

Devotees with less connection to the leading individuals of ISKCON's scientific branch have taken the assumptions of 'non-typical' survival of species even further, thereby approaching the field of 'crypto-zoology', a discipline avoided by conventional science. Without suggesting any actual proofs, devotees have said that creatures such as the Loch Ness Monster, the Yeti of the Himalayas, 'Bigfoot' and so on are likely to exist.[17]

The ordinary 'crypto-zoologists' hardly consider their interest in unknown or even nonexisting animals an existential or religious project. The interest is driven by an understandable curiosity and a simple fascination of the unknown or grotesque. As an element in ISKCON's more or less officially expressed arguments against modern science, the same ideas of odd creatures must be interpreted within the realms of the religious teaching. Obviously the dinosaurs, the Sea Serpent and the Yeti are placed in the belief system, focusing on the process of reincarnation, and it has been shown how such examples are used as arguments against the Darwinian model of biological evolution.

At this point it is interesting to ask why ISKCON takes interest in confronting the surrounding community with such provoking statements. The same points could be pursued in other ways as well. For instance no dinosaurs or monsters are needed to support ISKCON's notion of the existence of unknown species. Modern biologists and zoologists find new species every year and everybody knows that many existing forms of life are yet to be discovered in the tropical forests and in the deep seas. As a matter of fact many zoologists point to the fact that unknown species become extinct every day due to the deforestation in South America (mainly, but certainly not solely, insects).

There are reasons for believing that the mythology of ISKCON carries some of the responsibility in this respect. The vast mythological tradition poses entities of any thinkable and unthinkable kind. The avataras of Vishnu let alone include among other things the giant fish, the giant boar and the horrifying Man-Lion creature. The myths are understood literally, and the wonders of Krishna are without limitation. With this outset ISKCON often claims that 'reality is far more unbelievable than any fairy tale or fiction'. With our limited senses we may not be aware, but the world in which we live is in every respect incredible and fantastic. It is not hard to understand a Central African dinosaur to be more exciting than a newly discovered black beetle of 2.5 mm found in the soil of the South American rain forest. A huge and strange animal, a survivor from the late mesozoic era more than 65 million years ago, corresponds much better to the mythological creatures of the religious tradition than does an inferior beetle.[18] In this way ISKCON devotees contribute to the construction of a new mythological structure. The 'crypto-zoological' elements form a part of the coherent anti-evolutionary perspective, thus presenting the religiously based alternative to the scientific ideas.

It is important to stress that this does not necessarily mean any further coordination between the genuine myths and the semi-mythologies we see. The dinosaur does not belong to the Puranic stories, but the latter — as the devotees see it — surely supports the idea of a prehistoric leftover somewhere in Africa. What we find is a line of argumentation based on the religious dogmas, but with ingredients taken from the spectacular semi-scientific subjects which always hit the headlines and always provoke during the silly seasons. Anyhow, the fact that such ideas occur is far more interesting than the ideas themselves, if we want to understand the mechanisms at work in a situation where ISKCON critically faces the notions of modern science.

## Principles for Classification

The 'complete and perfect knowledge of evolution' ('evolution' referring to the process of samsara) is, according to ISKCON, in minute detail available in the sacred texts. These details include among other things, a register of the earthly forms of life, their kind and the number of them. From the *Padma Purana* the following passage is cited:

There are 9,000,000 species of aquatic life; 2,000,000 species of plants and trees; 1,100,000 species of insects; 1,000,000 species of bird life; 3,000,000 species of beasts, and 400,000 species of human life. (Bhaktiswaroopa s.a., 36)

Of course these figures should by no means be judged against the statistics or principles of modern botany and zoology. As a matter of fact something quite different than the normal use of the concept is meant by the term 'species' in this connection. Nevertheless such a comparison is what ISKCON aims at. Apparently the idea is to show that the system of classification used by modern scientists is inapplicable. It only applies to the physical appearance of the creatures whereas the taxonomy of ISKCON goes beyond the morphological features and focuses on the level of consciousness. In this way the scientific taxonomy based on morphological discrepancies vary fundamentally from ISKCON's spiritually based classification of the living entities. Still, as ISKCON claims the Puranic account to be 'perfect' and persistently measures its own system of classification to that of modern science, we may briefly compare the statements of the sacred text to that of contemporary biology. If so we shall find some severe discrepancies. Of course there is no possible harmony between the two systems of classification. Two examples: Firstly, modern science assumes that about 250,000[19] types of trees and plants exist, ISKCON says 2,000,000 and secondly, modern ornithologists reckon with less than 8,600 species of birds, ISKCON claims 1,000,000.

To ISKCON these discrepancies act as evidence of the failure of modern science, simply because the figures are so very different.

As far as systems of classification are central elements to every religion, ISKCON's taxonomy of the living entities reveals to us something very important. It points to the fact that every level of existence is understood within an epistemological framework totally isolated from that of the surrounding society. Nature is not nature in the ordinary sense. Animals are not animals in the ordinary sense and plants are not plants as we usually understand the term. Each natural element, ISKCON claims, represents something for which the Western world has no qualified expression. As far as ISKCON is concerned modern science is totally unable to describe that which exists. The scientific system of classification is unable to grasp what it is actually designed for. This understanding, of course, is nothing new as every culture expresses different systems of classification and different interpretations of the single elements within the taxonomies. In the case of ISKCON, though, we find ethnic Westerners to whom a totally foreign system of classification has become essentially meaningful. They even try to overtake the established system of classification in favour of their new conceptions of reality. What we are witnessing therefore is an alternative system of classification which sociologically exists within another, but different system of classification. Of course this is true in the most general sense, but focusing on the devotee's conception of nature, some interesting details are revealed. For instance, according to one informant, birds are regarded poor creatures born into a horrible form of life which gives them no rest (Rothstein 1990, 83). The bird is not looked upon as an animal with specific features. Rather the bird is understood as a current incarnation of a struggling soul, working its way through the 8,400,000 earthly species on its way towards liberation. Likewise fish are considered lower species than plants in terms of incarnation. Beholding a picture of a fish, a devotee said that its unintelligent appearance was due to the fact that it embodied a very low incarnated soul, and that the creature was unintelligent indeed. The beauty of flowers, to the same source, was an indication of plants' spiritual superiority to fish. Hence, the fish is not primarily an aquatic vertebrate which breathes by gills, as we would say. It is primarily looked upon as an incarnation of a soul of low status. One the contrary the plant, being put at our disposal for food by Krishna, is venerated for positive reasons. A plant is also relatively lowly incarnated, but its purpose as human food (and the fact that it will be offered to Krishna before it is eaten by humans) will lift it to higher levels and bestow much blessing upon it. In contradistinction to ordinary Western taxonomy, ISKCON frequently characterizes people as 'non-humans'. A good example is Prabhupada's comprehension of secular scientists, especially those who reject any divine precondition to life. The scientists themselves, but also those who listen to them or even acknowledge their teachings, are termed dogs, pigs, camels and donkeys. Prabhupada said: 'We do not recognize them as being human. An animal is praised by another animal' (Prabhupada 1990, 18).[20] Likewise any political or sociological idea of how human society works or ought to work is disdained in favour of the so-called *Vedic Varnasrama* system which is thought to be divinely instituted (Vishnupada 1981[21]). In this way the sciences of sociology, social psychology, ethnography and so on are discredited.

At this point TM also differs from ISKCON. As we have seen, sociological and social psychological methods are employed in order to prove the effects of transcendental meditation and the Maharishi Effect and thus promote TM. Aron and Aron, both engaged in TM, emphasize that they are in fact educated scientists and researchers in their account for the Maharishi Effect (Aron and Aron 1986). At the same time we note that TM never mentions the Varnasrama system but rather depicts a future society very much according to Western ideals.

At this point we may conclude that ISKCON's conception of animals, plants and human beings is fundamentally different from the surrounding society's. The criticism of Darwinism, therefore, is primarily a criticism of a system of classification which disregards the essence of ISKCON's own religiously based taxonomy. Once again it is the foundation of a secular scientific theory that makes it invalid to ISKCON. This mechanism is often demonstrated and I shall quote one devotee to whom the problem with modern science was obvious. When he was asked by a guest during a lecture whether science had anything to offer the devotee answered:

ISKCON will not surrender to science before the very foundation of scientific thought has changed. Today science rests upon lies and bewilderments. Krishna is not taken into consideration but it is he who creates, upholds and destroys the universe and everything in it. Unless this is accepted, the scientific notions will per definition always be wrong. Unless Krishna is installed in the center of scientific thinking, science will take us nowhere but to death and destruction, but modern scientists will not accept that a supreme person reigns over them. The bhakti-process is truly scientific. It is by far superior to the ordinary scientists.[22]

**Common Ground between ISKCON's Notion and Evolutionary Theory**

No matter how different the religious anthropology of ISKCON is from the naturalistic account based on the theory of evolution, there are some interesting structural similarities worth mentioning:

Firstly, biological science claims all forms of life to be interlinked in some way, as every living entity has developed from a common source. So does ISKCON, but in another way: 'Every soul or self is part-and-parcel of Krishna', ISKCON says. Secondly, the theory of evolution claims that the forms of life develop from lower (less complex) forms to higher (more complex). A corresponding evolutionary perspective is also fundamental to ISKCON in terms of the process of samsara, eventually leading the soul to perfection, with the incarnation in a human body as an utmost important phase. Further science maintains a distinction between humankind and animals, even if humankind is understood to be an integrated element in the total of biological evolution: Science will usually claim humankind's ability to reason and to think rationally distinguishing it from the animals whose activities are restricted to what is governed by instinct. To ISKCON this, and other observations, lead to a similar conclusion, although the living soul in all living organisms are considered of the same kind. Humankind, however, is something special because the souls incarnated in humans have progressed far more.

It is interesting, then, to observe that ISKCON has by no means tried to make use of these structural resemblances between science and religion, as has TM whenever possible. Why, we may ask again, has ISKCON not sought some kind of understanding with the scientific community in this connection? The answer, as I have already suggested, is found in the basic assessments of ISKCON. The premises of science, in this connection zoology and related fields, are considered wrong and the scientific notions can therefore be nothing but false. Even if some conclusions would turn out to be in harmony with ISKCON's notions, their foundation (and therefore the conclusions themselves) would be unacceptable to ISKCON. One source said:

If scientists tell us that a bird can fly because it has wings it is a correct statement, but it does not explain everything. Why does the bird have wings? How did the wings get there? These are the interesting questions, and science cannot answer them because the answers are with Krishna, and science does not care about Krishna. So we may agree that the bird is flying because it has wings, but what really lies behind this phenomenon the scientists are not interested in. To them a bird is just a bird. To us it is one of Krishna's creations. Nothing is just what it appears to be. Everything is linked with Krishna.[23]

ISKCON's outset is considered perfect in every respect, being determined by Krishna. The only reason why ISKCON members have engaged in argumentation is the challenge from the modern world. The believers are forced to make up their minds. In order to confirm their religious beliefs they are willing to combat any idea, phenomenon, theory or fact that may contradict their notion. Obviously the argumentation serves internal purposes as much as missionary obligations. Through the rejection of modern ideas of biological evolution, internal ideas are highlighted in a way that supports the group's internal bounds. Through the rejection of biological evolution, a theory intimately linked with secularized society, devotees also reject one of the most important cornerstones of modern culture in favour of their own sub-cultural group and its world view. Therefore the antagonisms between science and the Vaisnava-Bhakti are of great importance to the self-esteem of the devotees, and of a considerable relevance to the way in which the religious doctrines are formulated and promoted. In other words what I have termed 'negative syncretism' is at work.

ISKCON has rightly pointed to the fact that Darwin's theory of biological evolution is nothing but a theory. The final proofs of its validity are yet to be seen although some definite progress has been made during the last decades. On the other hand other scholars have questioned basic evolutionary assumptions, and to the critical mind such arguments may well appear as evidence against the theory. ISKCON relates to the latter. One of ISKCON's strongest arguments is the rather meagre support of fossils to document the ascent of humankind. Very often paleoanthropology is used to exemplify the faults of evolutionary theory, and ISKCON is very much aware of the internal ruptures and occasional dishonesty in this particular field of research. While this is being written, ISKCON-devotees are preparing a bulky (more than 1000 pages) volume on archaeology and paleoanthropology entitled 'Forbidden Archaeology'. This book will sum up everything on the subject already presented by ISKCON and add new findings and interpretations (some of these data are already presented in Ramesvara 1984, 48-55). Presently ISKCON offers a 30 minute videotape on the subject entitled: 'Human Evolution: A Confrontation of Fact and Theory'. In the video it is claimed that the fossil and archaeological evidence of human evolution are nothing but a small, anomalous fraction of what is gathered, and it is argued that substantial evidence going against the theory of evolution has been systematically ignored and discredited. Aiming at a general audience, this video has been widely distributed. Another video on a similar subject entitled, 'Models of Natural Selection' is aimed at a more scientifically oriented audience. It discusses the Darwinian theory of evolution which 'assumes all existing organisms to be connected to one another by viable intermediate forms' and claims to prove that the neo-Darwinian theory of evolution is unclear, illogical and — most importantly — that the intermediate forms fail to exist for some of the key models imposed by the evolutionists themselves in order to describe the process.[24] The forthcoming book will, according to one of the authors, eliminate the very foundation of modern evolutionary theory because it brings into focus the major shortcomings of not only paleoanthropology but modern science in general: Science is ruling out in advance any nonmaterial, nonmechanistic explanation, and therefore will never discover the truth.

Relating to what has been said about the similarities between the way ISKCON reacts today and the way Christians reacted during the 1860s a further comment may be relevant: Contrary to the Christians at the time of Charles Darwin, ISKCON is not confronted with new ideas. As a matter of fact it is the Vaisnava theology which is new to the devotees and the naturalistic account of how life originated that is supported by their original culture. While the Church had to defend itself against the scientific notions, ISKCON holds the part of the aggressor today. ISKCON feels an obligation to conquer the world through Krishna Consciousness while the Church during the late 18th Century had to defend itself against the offensive Darwinism. I conclude this chapter with a quotation from one devotee who is particularly hostile to the theory of biological evolution:

What the Bible says about creation is not correct, but it is more correct than what the Darwinists say. It is Sri Krishna who governs the universe and it is his servant, Brahma, who is in charge of the creation of the material universe. Everything, every species is created by him. It is madness to suppose that some natural force, some 'cosmic principle' is responsible. Darwinism is totally destructive because it is purely materialistic. Brahma is a person, and the species are here according to his will and they look the way he wants them to. ... You cannot understand life unless you accept the transcendental reality of Sri Krishna.[25]

We have seen how TM's monistic beliefs make identification with scientific notions possible, and we have seen how ISKCON's theism works the other way around. In order to determine more precisely how the preconditions for syncretistic developments with science vary between ISKCON and TM, the following chapter discusses, among other things, some of these basic theological differences, especially the notion of the divine.

CHAPTER 10

# TM and ISKCON: Basic Differences

**Monistic Theology (TM)**

It is difficult indeed to overlook the many Vedanta traditions. Each Vedanta philosophy corresponds to different interpretations of the sacred texts, and even if similarity in terminology is apparent, the systems vary considerably and the traditions often engage in theological rivalry. TM, relating to Sankara, therefore does not cover the whole spectrum of the Vedanta philosophies, and by no means is the organization generally recognized among the Vedanta traditions. It is, however, not surprising that TM claims to represent what is termed 'the perennial philosophy' of ancient India, a claim indicating that TM's heritage is the true one while other systems are more or less erroneous. While acknowledging all the chief branches of Vedanta as relevant at certain levels of understanding, the Advaita-Vedanta is always favoured. To some extend aspects of the so called 'qualified nondualism' (*Vishistadvaita-Vedanta*) represented by Ramanuja is accepted, while the pure dualistic teaching of the *Dvaita-Vedanta* of Madhva is rejected. These teachings only represent a partial insight into the true Self, TM says. TM claims every religion to be relevant, and no direct attempt is ever made to persuade people to change their religious affiliation. On the contrary it is claimed that every religion will benefit from the practice of transcendental meditation (Hollings 1982, 7, Goldhaber 1976, 182-83, Smith 1983). Consequently the theistic traditions within Hinduism are recognized only as relevant to those who do not comprehend the significance of the Advaita-Vedanta as it manifests itself in TM. In TM's motto (which we have already seen) this idea is directly expressed: 'Knowledge is structured in consciousness' Maharishi says, which means that any perception is interpreted according to the spiritual level of the perceiver's consciousness. The phrase, derived from Rig Veda, tends to show that the spiritual insight into Being increases as the level of consciousness rises (Russell 1978, 169-70). At certain levels only fragmentary understandings of the ultimate truth are possible. To TM the theistic notions belong to a relatively low level, although Maharishi explicitly states that the personal god is an intellectual necessity, and that any rejection of his existence would indicate 'poor understanding'. To Maharishi the personal god is the head of Creation, and he describes him in quite theistic terms:

The personal aspect of God necessarily has form, qualities, and features, likes and dislikes, and the ability to command the entire existence of the cosmos, the process of evolution, and all that there are in creation ....
Ultimately on the top level of evolution, is He whose power is unlimited, whose joyfulness is unlimited, whose intelligence and energy are unlimited. All knowing is He, all powerful is He, all blissful is He, almighty is He who dwells on top level of evolution. (Maharishi 1968, 269-70)

However, the personal god manifests himself within the realm of relative existence. He is not transcendental:

Anything in the relative field cannot be omnipresent; relative means bound by time, space and causation, whereas the plane of the omnipresent is unbounded by time, space and causation.
The realization of the personal God, then, by necessity, will be on the level of human perception, on the level of the sensory experience. Realization of the personal God means that the eyes should be able to see that supreme Person and the heart should be able to feel the qualities of that supreme Person. The realization of personal God has to be in the relative field of life. Thus, the realization of the impersonal God is in transcendental consciousness, and the realization of the personal God is on the level of consciousness of the waking state. (Maharishi 1968, 272-73)

To obtain the highest state of consciousness (i.e. unity with the impersonal divine) human consciousness has to transcend the limits of the relative realm and enter 'the transcendental field":

It is necessary for the conscious mind to be brought from the present level of experience to the subtler levels of experience and eventually transcend the subtlest level of relative experience to consciously arrive at the transcendental field of existence. (Maharishi 1968, 273)

To Maharishi and TM, theistic religion is constantly captured by maya, as the personal manifestation of the impersonal divine is erroneously considered the ultimate manifestation. Maharishi's understanding is very clear:

> From a cosmic standpoint, Vedanta explains the relationship of the unmanifested absolute Reality (Brahman) with the manifested relative aspect of life by introducing the principle of maya. The word maya means literally that which is not that which does not exist. This brings to light the character of maya: it is not anything substantial. Its presence is inferred from the effects that it produces. The influence of maya may be understood by the example of sap appearing as a tree. Every fibre of the tree is nothing but sap. Sap, while remaining sap, appears as the tree. Likewise, through the influence of maya, Brahman, remaining Brahman, appears as the manifested world...
> Under the influence of maya, Brahman appears as Ishvara, the personal God, who exists on the celestial level of life in the subtlest field of creation.(Maharishi 1979, 491-92)

Commenting on a complicated question 'What did Sankara [Samkara] really mean?', historian of religions Frederick Copleston writes:

> The reader who is aware of Samkara's theory of non-dualism may feel inclined to protest that I have been trying to represent the Indian philosopher as a theist, so far as this is possible in the case of someone who described the supreme Lord as the material as well as the efficient cause of the world. Did not Samkara believe that the ultimate reality, Brahman, was supra-personal and that the human spirit was identical with Brahman?
> The reply is that, for Samkara, the concept of Isvara or a personal creator is the form in which the Absolute appears to discursive thought, operating with the subject/object distinction .... To the mind operating within the framework of the subject/object distinction the highest reality is the supreme Lord, Isvara. (Copleston 1980, 74)

Obviously the notions of Maharishi and those of Sankara as referred by Copleston are the same: The personal god — whether he is called Ishvara, Vishnu or Siva — is Brahman; Brahman 'appearing to or conceived by discursive thought', as Copleston puts it.

On this basis one could expect some kind of outward interest for the personal divine. Such a personal divinity, however, is not something that TM by now officially cares about. The idea is only expressed directly through Maharishi's earlier writings. But indirectly there are signs of such an interest. During the initiation ritual (which is called by the standard term; *puja*), where several Hindu deities are mentioned, pictures or even figures of Hindu gods are placed on the alter. Apparently the person performing the initiation is free to choose, although the pictures of Brahmananda Saraswati and Maharishi himself are prescribed. According to two sources, both former TM teachers, Krishna and Vishnu are preferred, but other gods may be used as well.[1] The intention, so the former TM teachers say, is to provide those participating in the ritual with an object for identification: 'It is harder to talk to an impersonal, unmanifested Reality, while much more easy to address a god or a guru', one source said. The only important personification of the divine is Brahmananda Saraswati. Praising him, Maharishi called him the living expression of *'Purnam adah, purnam idam'*, meaning 'That Unmanifested (Brahman) is perfect and This manifested (Brahman) is (also) perfect'. In a rather direct expression Maharishi presents him as a manifestation of the Absolute:

[When he died] the Manifested merged with its original, the Unmanifested, and *'Brahma Leena Brahmanandam'* is now appearing in the hearts of His devotees as waves of Brahmanandam (Bliss). (Maharishi 1965, 11)

As mentioned elsewhere Brahmananda Saraswati, the Shankaracharya of Joythir Math, was sometimes addressed as 'Vedanta Incarnate' (Truth Embodiment), a fact indicating his position in Hinduism in general and TM in particular. Maharishi claims his example to be ideal in every respect, and he urges his followers to regard him as their personal guardian and guru. In sum, Brahmananda Saraswati is the closest to a genuine divinity appearing in TM's official image. Of course his status is primarily that of the guru, but thinking of him as the embodiment of the Absolute, he obviously means more to Maharishi's followers.[2]

Maharishi, contrary to Prabhupada, concluded his Bhagavad Gita commentary after the sixth chapter, thus avoiding the part of the text where the idea of bhakti is presented and developed. According to TM representatives, Maharishi has planned a commentary of the remaining chapters, but to this point nothing has appeared. His commentary on the first six chapters was originally published in 1967 (the manuscript was completed in early 1965). This is not surprising at all. Maharishi's teaching recognizes the personal godhead, but not as the supreme manifestation of the ultimate truth (Maharishi 1968, 269 f.). In order to communicate his message as clearly as possible, Maharishi may wisely have chosen to ignore the parts of the Bhagavad Gita that seemingly contradicts his fundamental idea. To Maharishi himself of course, and to the inner-group of TM, the whole of the Bhagavad Gita is important, as the theistic parts of the text, in Maharishi's interpretation, are in harmony with the monistic beliefs. Maharishi, commenting on Vedanta as one of the six systems of Indian philosophy, clearly defines the personal manifestation of the divine as the highest relative manifestation. I quote once more: 'Under the influence of maya, Brahman appears as Ishvara, the personal God, who exists on the celestial level in the subtlest field of creation' (Maharishi 1979, 492). But there are more references of importance.

In 'The Science of Being and Art of Living' Maharishi touches upon 'the emotional path to God Realization' which he also terms 'Path of Devotion'. He never uses the word 'bhakti'. The reading shows a deep concern for the devotional process as an element in the spiritual regeneration, and the formulations appear to be as 'bhakti' as those of Prabhupada:

The feeling of love is the vehicle which enables man to advance on [the path of devotion]. The increasing capacity of love, emotion, happiness, kindness, devotion, and surrender are the qualities of the heart which sustain the path of devotion. Love increases, and, as it advances, it leaves behind fields of lesser happiness and gains ground on more stable, more important, more valuable fields of happiness. (Maharishi 1968, 281).

It is, however, significant that Maharishi's kind of devotion towards the divine avoids any pronouns and any names. The text talks of 'capacities', 'paths', 'fields' and 'emotions' which are all abstract concepts. There is no clear object for the devotion. The devotion leads to 'happiness', not to a personal divinity. Contrary to Prabhupada, Maharishi also maintains that the practice of transcendental meditation is the precondition to any bhakti advancement towards the divine:

## Monistic Theology 171

This [transcendental meditation] is what rows the boat of love and brings fulfillment to the path of love. The path of devotion without the practice of this transcendental deep meditation, without greater experience of great happiness, is not practical. (Maharishi 1968, 284)

Above all, Maharishi's explanation in his commentary on the Bhagavad Gita reveals his attitude towards bhakti. Referring to the inevitable loss of knowledge due to Man's poorly developed consciousness he writes:

When Shankara's high ideal of transcendental devotion disappeared from sight, Ramanuja, Madhva and other teachers upheld the path of devotion, even though without its proper basis in Being. People followed them, and thus there arose many devotional sects all on the level of emotion and every one founded on the comfortable basis of hope that 'some day our prayer will be heard, some day He will come to us and call us to Him'. Indeed a comfort to the heart but, alas, such devotion is on the imaginary plane of feeling! It is far, far away from the reality of actual contact between the devotee and his God. Awareness in the state of Being alone makes the whole field of devotion real. (Maharishi 1979, 13-14)

Thus Maharishi resents the core of Vaisnava theology and thereby the essence of ISKCON's teachings. He explicitly rejects the ultimate importance of the personal god. As a matter of fact one of the clearest statements concerning TM and science I know of was given with reference to this notion during an introducing lecture prior to actual initiation. One of the guests (apparently a Christian investigating a strange and obscure religion) asked how the foundation of the universe (which was explained in terms of the Unified Field by the speaker) could be interpreted as anything but God? The answer was covering two important aspects of TM's ontology. Firstly it was stated that the notion of a personal god was erroneous:

The foundation of the universe are forces, natural laws. This has been established by science long ago. It is the force behind it all that now has been identified as the Unified Field. 'God' is a rather rigid way of dealing with these things. The forces of nature is no entity, no person. They are forces. Principles in nature. You do not have to name them. They are understood either through scientific calculations or through meditation.[3]

Secondly it was emphasized that the ancient Veda already knew all the answers, and the speaker concluded:

During the last years the physicists have developed theories that are similar to what the Vedas describe. Modern science is not based on the assumption that a personal god is ruling the universe. Scientists know that natural forces are behind it all, and that everything eventually will come out on formulas. Science has managed to reach the same conclusions as the Vedas, and through transcendental meditation and the TM-Sidhi program human beings have free access to enjoy the benefit of this knowledge.[4]

Had TM's interest in theistic ideas been any stronger, such categorical statements would be impossible.

## Theistic Theology (ISKCON)

ISKCON occupies the opposite position. Being an entirely theistic religion Madhva's, Ramanuja's and of course Caitanya's dualistic teachings are favoured, while Sankara's religious system is considered false. Indeed there are close connections between the theology of Ramanuja and Madhva and that of Chaitanya, and ISKCON very deliberately makes Ramanuja and Madhva, some of Hinduism's most prominent theistic theologians, their allies against the Advaita-Vedanta school (Gelberg 1983, 179-80). ISKCON also points to the fact that there are similarities between Advaita-Vedanta, Jainism and Buddhism. Emphasizing the principle atheism of Buddhism, this is not meant to be a compliment. One thing in particular is promoted as an intellectual argument against non-theistic Advaita-Vedanta: The fact that Shankara did not comment on texts which emphasizes theistic ideas is taken as a proof of his poor understanding (Gelberg 1983, 178). There is, however, an important theological detail of considerable interest in this connection. According to ISKCON, Shankara was sent to 'confuse' humankind in order to enliven the religious sentiment of those hearing him. The Advaita-Vedanta, ISKCON claims, is a Kali-yuga feature imposed upon humans in order to bring them doubt and frustration so that they, through close consideration, may be able to reject it and thus find the devotional path towards Krishna, the supreme Lord. With references to Padma Purana and Siva Purana it is explained that Sankara accepted the role of the impersonalist, but that his so-called *Mayavada* philosophy was in fact a divine intervention meant to work against the purely atheistic Buddhism (Satsvarupa s.a., 86-88, Deadwyler 1989, 71-73). In this way Sankara's monism is explicable within the framework of the Vaisnava theology, and in this way devotees of ISKCON occasionally cope with TM and similar groups[5]:

Well, as a matter of fact they don't understand Sankaracharya. They only know him as he appears superficially. Not in essence. You know, you can't reach Krishna if you reject him from the beginning. This is what they do. Well, I guess they are attached to the material world to a degree that prevents them from going in the right direction. It's so very easy to say that everything is one, and that no distinctions exist, far easier than understanding the existence of the supreme Lord which is Krishna. But Krishna is so merciful. If they want to know his lower energies, his lower aspects, they are invited to do so, but this will lead them nowhere near Krishna himself.[6]

Maharishi's notion of the relationship between the impersonal god, the personal god and humanity reflects that of Shankara himself. Because of the popularity gained by the Bhagavad Gita in his days, Shankara made room for the personal deity, Krishna, and made him a valid image of worship for the 'unliberated', even though he constantly relegated Krishna to a lesser realm of reality than Brahman, the qualityless divine. The result was a theological system with opportunities for devotional service to personal gods such as Vishnu or Krishna, along with the mystic submission to the impersonal divine. This development, according to historian of religions J. Stillson Judah, was the result of public demand rather than obligingness from the religious Brahman establishment (Judah 1974, 47). Today TM asserts that the Bhakti/Vaisnava tradition is fully acceptable at a certain level, and that the practice of transcendental meditation will prove beneficial even to those who choose to contemplate on the personal aspect of the divine. But ISKCON sees Krishna as the supreme manifestation of the divine. The Brahman of the Upanishads, the attributeless, differenceless Absolute, in the teaching of Chaitnaya is only one aspect of reality, and not the ultimate manifestation. The ultimate reality is 'Brahman with qualities', highly personalized as the anthropomorphic Krishna. To Prabhupada Brahman is primarily the effulgence or halo of Krishna, the *Brahmajyoti*, which includes everything in cosmos. Brahmajyoti is identified as 'material nature' when the halo is influenced by maya. But Brahman is also the spirit in which living entities form a part without loosing their identity (Prabhupada 1986, 231 f.).

The conflict between the two poles become even more clear in Prabhupada's commentary on the Bhagavad Gita. One verse (7.24) in Prabhupada's translation reads:

Unintelligent men, who do not know Me perfectly, think that I, the Supreme Personality of Godhead, Krishna, was impersonal before and have now assumed this personality. Due to their small knowledge, they do not know My higher nature, which is imperishable and supreme. (Prabhupada 1986, 400)

In his commentary Prabhupada says:

Those who are worshippers of demigods have been described as less intelligent persons, and here the impersonalists are similarly described...

Persons who are under the impression that the Absolute Truth is impersonal are described as *abuddhayah*, which means those who do not know the ultimate feature of the Absolute Truth. In the Srimad-Bhagavatam it is stated that supreme realization begins from the impersonal Brahman and then rises to the localized Supersoul — but the ultimate word in the Absolute Truth is the Personality of Godhead. Modern impersonalists are still less intelligent, for they do not even follow their great predecessor Sankaracarya, who has specifically stated that Krishna is the Supreme Personality of Godhead.[7] Impersonalists, therefore, not knowing the Supreme Truth, think Krishna to be only the son of Devaki and Vasudeva, or a prince, or a powerful living entity. (Prabhupada 1986, 400-2)

The idea of Krishna's avataras (numbering around 30 depending on criteria) takes the personalistic image of the divine even further, culminating in the anthropomorphical manifestation of the god in the shape of Caitanya (the so-called 'Golden Avatar') especially present in the prevailing Kali-yuga (contrary to most Kali-yugas) as an expression of Krishna's compassionate love and care. As a matter of fact Chaitanya is taken to be an embodiment of both Krishna and

Radha (Krishna's feminine aspect) a divine form with no equals (Prabhupada 1984, 154-61).

## Sankhya in Different Interpretations

ISKCON also attacks Sankhya philosophy, which, being in principle atheistic, is identified as some kind of ideological foundation of modern scientific thinking. I am aware of no comment or analysis which in scholarly terms links TM to Sankhya, and apparently ISKCON maintains an unambiguous focus on TM's Advaita-Vedanta aspect. However, TM seems to be inspired by Sankhya notions. ISKCON's theological criticism of Sankhya philosophy therefore indirectly forms a criticism of TM and science, and, of course, it reveals important elements of ISKCON's self-understanding.

According to Prabhupada there are two aspects of Sankhya-philosophy: The ancient Sankhya derived from *Kapiladeva* (in fact an incarnation of Krishna) which explains 'how to loose the grip on matter and find Vishnu in ones heart'. 'Modern' Sankhya on the contrary, was designed by 'the atheist' Kapila and, according to Prabhupada, is only occupied with the understanding of the material universe. Hence he makes an important distinction between the two: While the original Sankhya, derived from a divine person, in fact is a form of bhakti-worship, the atheistic Sankhya of human origin is comparable to modern science (Prabhupada 1990, 30-31). According to the Bhagavad Gita 7.5., ISKCON maintains, there is another divine energy apart from that which constitutes the material universe, namely Krishna's energy 'which comprises the living entities who are exploiting the resources of this material nature' (Prabhupada 1986, 371). It is this higher, spiritual energy which is ignored by the modern Sankhya-philosophy as well as modern science, Prabhupada claims. Scientific analysis is restricted to material elements, just as is 'modern' Sankhya. Neither science, nor Sankhya have knowledge of the spirit soul. This, to Prabhupada, explains why Sankhya philosophy will always fail. Facing the same pitfalls as science, it does not take the controlling, sustaining and creating divinity into account, and will never be able to explain how and why the material elements in creation are arranged and how and why they interact. Consequently the resentment towards Sankhya as well as science is evident. What interests us most in this connection is the fact that the criticism, in both cases, rests on the same kind of arguments and the same kind of reasoning. Indeed ISKCON's current attempt to disprove science is the latest phase in a continuum which starts with theological rivalry against monistic Hinduism several hundred years ago.

Contrary to Prabhupada's devastating judgement, Maharishi claims the practice of transcendental meditation to verify the teaching of Kapila (whom in Maharishi's writings refers to one single individual). Maharishi's positive interest in Sankhya, however, is not as developed as Prabhupada's rejection. For instance he never bothers to discuss the nature of Kapila. In Maharishi's words Sankhya philosophy asserts that knowledge of an object will not be complete without the knowledge of its components (Maharishi 1979, 480). Through transcendental meditation, which brings the mind through all the gross and subtle levels of creation to the state of pure consciousness, the teaching about these various elements of creation (according to Sankhya counting 25), can be verified.

None of the six *darshanas*, the classical schools of Hinduism, is inferior to Maharishi: 'Knowledge is true only when it is acceptable in the light of each of the six systems of Indian philosophy', he says (Maharishi 1979, 472). Even if some of the philosophical schools may seem contradictory to Maharishi's main line of argumentation, his interpretation leaves space for all of them, including Sankhya.

Maharishi's use of Sankhya, and the way in which Sankhya has apparently laid some of the foundation of TM's scientific strategy, may be understood through his commentary on the Bhagavad Gita.[8] In their commentaries on the Bhagavad Gita, Maharishi and Prabhupada more / or less directly relate certain passages to intellectual interpretation and understanding of the universe, each with his attitude. Commenting on the Bhagavad Gita 2.39 Maharishi says:

Intellectual understanding of Reality convinces man of the existence of a nobler and more permanent field of life that lies beyond and underlies the ordinary level of phenomenal existence. That has been the purpose of the discourse up to this point. Now Lord Krishna wishes to introduce Arjuna to the practice whereby his intellect will become established in Reality. (Maharishi 1979, 116)

Here Maharishi is referring to Sankhya philosophy, which, according to his interpretation, has been the core subject of Krishna's teachings up to this point in the text. This interpretation is of great importance in Maharishi's teaching, and it reveals some of the basic ideas. Most relevant to our subject is the clarification of the relation between Yoga and Sankhya. Maharishi writes:

The Sankhya of the Bhagavad-Gita presents the principles of all the six systems of Indian philosophy, while the Yoga of the Bhagavad-Gita presents their practical aspects. (Maharishi 1979, 116)

Thus Maharishi claims Sankhya to be an intellectual discourse while Yoga remains the active, practical and transformative discipline. It is deepened further in the reading:

By using the word 'Intellect'[9], the Lord makes it clear that the mind, purified or settled by the wisdom of Sankhya, becomes established in the Self through the practice of Yoga. (Maharishi 1979, 117)

This characterization corresponds with TM's idea of the meditation technique as the practical aspect of SCI, which in itself is considered the ideological or scientific — that is 'intellectual' — exposition of Life and Being (Forem 1984, 100). The SCI occupies the position of the traditional Sankhya philosophy, and the meditation ritual is identical with 'the practice of Yoga'. In Maharishi's comments on the Bhagavad Gita 2.12-2.15. the theme has already been touched upon. Here it is shown that no practice is involved in gaining the understanding of life through Sankhya. The practical aspect is Yoga. In this respect (the connection between Sankhya and Yoga) Maharishi is in line with the traditional understanding.

So far it is obvious that the belief system of TM rests upon a two dimensional structure: The intellectual and the practical, or in the vocabulary of Maharishi's commentary on the Bhagavad Gita; Sankhya and Yoga. It is also obvious that this structure underlies the notion of the meditation ritual as the practical aspect of the SCI. As modern science forms a substantial part of the SCI, Maharishi's idea of Sankhya apparently is the philosophical or ideological platform from which the *use* of science gets its legitimacy. Thinking of Sankhya philosophy in general this it not surprising. The system is fundamentally non-theistic, and usually more concerned with speculation and theoretical investigation than beliefs which makes it a suitable parallel to science. Maharishi has as already mentioned declared that 'knowledge is true only when it is acceptable in the light of each of the six systems of Indian philosophy' (Maharishi 1979, 472). Sankhya, which is considered the third system, 'enumerates the different components of the object' (Maharishi 1979, 472). Discussing the twenty-five categories which, according to Sankhya, are lying at the basis of creation and the process of cosmic evolution, Maharishi (among all the others) mentions *Prakriti* (which he terms 'nature') : 'Prakriti is the primal substance of which the entire creation arises. Its constituents are the three gunas, *sattva, rajas,* and *tamas*. They are responsible for all change and form the basis of evolution' (Maharishi 1979, 481). In the same chapter of his Bhagavad Gita commentary Maharishi also gives a description of the five elements (*Mahabuthas*) of which creation is constituted (space [*akasha*], air [*vayu*], fire [*tejas*], water [*apas*] and earth [*prithivi*]) (Maharishi 1979, 483). Although no direct linkage between such conceptualizations of nature and the descriptions of modern science is seen in TM's publications, it seems as if the principles of Sankhya are recognized in the modern materials. In both cases we find systematic classifications and systems of exploration. While the concrete notions of modern science seem to be in harmony with the structures of Advaita-Vedanta, which remain the main aspect of TM's religious heritage, there are reasons for believing that the Sankhya part of TM's heritage supports the rendering of the belief system into scientific language.

Not surprisingly Prabhupada's commentary on the Bhagavad Gita verses discussed above shows an entirely different picture, as the basic understanding of the Bhagavad Gita is another. Following the arguments related above, the intellectual approach is ignored as meaningful along with the author's theistic/devotional (bhakti) assumptions. Referring to the two Kapila's, the 'True Lord Kapila' and 'the impostor Kapila', Prabhupada describes various Sankhya philosophies depending on different interpretations. He rejects any connection with 'impostor Kapila' and maintains, by quoting Krishna, that only the less intelligent class of people make a distinction between Sankhya and bhakti (Prabhupada 1986, 125). The Sankhya followed by Maharishi and TM, therefore, in the eyes of Prabhupada and ISKCON is that of 'impostor Kapila', while Prabhupada himself and ISKCON only relate to the true Sankhya of the divine sage *Kapila*, an incarnation of Krishna himself.

## Sacred Time

In ISKCON's salvation history, science is an obstacle, but in the salvation history of TM it has become a valuable tool.

Mircea Eliade sees the linear view of history as a novel development which arose in Israel when the prophets began to interpret catastrophic events as what he terms 'negative theophanies', the wrath of Jahwe (Eliade 1974, 104). The linear view of time, which describes an irreversible course pointing in a definite direction, serving a definite purpose, is contrasted with the 'archaic' notion of time as possessing a cyclical structure (Eliade 1974, 117). As we have seen, both TM and ISKCON rest upon cyclical time structures. Both religions believe themselves to appear under certain, predictable cosmic conditions and both define what role each of them is meant to play. In both cases the changing yugas of Hinduism are at stake, and in both cases succession and continuance of ancient traditions are believed to be governing the process. There is, however, one major difference. While TM believes in inaugurating the Age of Enlightenment (Maharishi 1986), ISKCON maintains that the world has entered the Age of *Kali*, the Age of Death and Destruction (Prabhupada 1981). According to ISKCON, nothing good can be expected during *Kali yuga*. The existence of ISKCON itself is seen as a very special event which is due to the appearance of Krishna's avatar Caitanya Mahabrabhu approximately 500 years ago, something that usually never happens in Kali yuga. ISKCON therefore, as something quite natural, regards the dominating system of understanding in the West — science — to be fundamentally influenced by the dark forces of Kali yuga. TM on the contrary sees this age as benevolent and prosperous. Under such happy circumstances human beings have developed all sorts of benefits for themselves, including science, which, if used properly, is considered a blessing. Accordingly TM does not disregard science, nor its possibilities.

As it appears TM and ISKCON stand on two different cosmological platforms, and we cannot assume corresponding

# 180 TM and ISKCON

attitudes towards modern ways of life and modern notions of the cosmos. However, as we will understand from Eliade's idea, they have one thing in common: Both are opposing the time structure of the Western world which is determined by the Judeo-Christian notion of time. Due to TM's and ISKCON's idea of time they can both argue that certain circumstances or conditions prevail, and that their specific points of view must be understood accordingly. None of the two religions can claim any authority through Christianity, but through a combination of alternative conceptions of time and alternative use or disapproval of science, both religions are able to find a place in modern society. However, it is correct that TM at the same time has assumed the Western, European belief in future scientific accomplishments, thereby accepting linear conceptions of time. Considering that TM's ambition is to bring science back to 'the Veda', it seems as if cyclical as well as linear conceptions of time are also present.

## Sacred Space and Places

SCI, I have argued, initiates science into the sphere of the sacred, making it a hierophany. Accordingly MIU (and to a lesser extent similar TM institutions), which is where the religio-scientific system primarily is being developed and from where it is primarily articulated, can be seen as a sacred place.[10] Again we may quote Eliade who says:

... every sacred space implies a hierophany, an irruption of the sacred that results in detaching a territory from the surrounding cosmic milieu and making it qualitatively different. (Eliade 1987, 26)

It is at MIU Maharishi very often dwells, it is here the crowds of *Sidhas* gather to perform their ritual that will eventually lead to paradise on Earth, it is here that videotape recordings with Maharishi are stored and it is here many of the agents of the Age of Enlightenment are educated. Sometimes the cite of MIU is depicted as the radiating centre of the world on posters, showing the global influence of TM, quite resembling Jewish or Christian religious geography which places Jerusalem in the centre of the world, or

Muslim examples with Mecca in the centre. From MIU a radiation of peace and spirituality — literally drawn on the poster maps — spread throughout the world. There is no doubt that MIU, being officially a university with public recognition, is at the same time a sacred place at the heart of a religious movement. What we see is an elegant harmony between the syncretistic belief system which involves religious and scientific elements, and the main institution of the movement which is also a conglomerate of religious and secular structures and phenomena.[11]

If we compare this situation to that of ISKCON yet another difference is seen. ISKCON has no new sacred places in the same way as TM. The religious geography focuses on *Vrindavan* where Krishna according to Vaisnava mythology was engaged in his 'transcendental pastimes' (*Krishna liila*) while on Earth in his original bodily form. In this area a multitude of shrines are celebrated and physically maintained by the devotees including the *Govardhana Hill*, the trees that are supposed to have witnessed Krishna's activities 5000 years ago, numerous temples, saints' graves and so on. The only new shrines established by ISKCON are those with relation to Prabhupada; the apartment where he first gave lectures in the U.S., the place in Vrindavan where he lived shortly before his death, and of course his *'Samadhi'*: His tomb. These sacred places, however, are in tune with Vaisnava standards. Any departed guru may be the object of cultic devotion which focuses on places of importance in his life. In the same way ISKCON carries on a well established tradition by opening new temples. Nothing actually new is happening.

## Cosmology and Ethics

Contrary to most traditional mythologies, TM's SCI does not imply well developed ethics. It is true that inner members of TM live according to specific standards recommended by Maharishi, standards derived from traditional Hindu monastic (or semi-monastic) systems. It is also true that the outward appearance of TM members clearly point to strong group mechanisms,[12] and it is clear that the organization (although at a low scale) directs new initiates in ethical matters. However, these aspects cannot be linked with the belief system such as it is presented at courses, in papers and so forth. The ethics of TM are primarily derived from Maharishi's early writings where he often concentrates on interpersonal relations and questions of human fulfilment. SCI as a conglomerate of Hinduism and science avoids such things. The ethic of TM is clearly separated from the present philosophical or theoretical outlining of the belief system. In other words no social (moral, ethical) etiology is found in SCI. No descriptions of how people should live, no divine standards regarding the structure of society, no moral, no demands, and indeed no entities, no divine actors, are promoted in this modern myth. SCI is more than anything a cosmology. A description of the universe, and actually a rather technical account of how it works. Very often the term cosmography may be more suitable. Secondly it is a cosmogony, although its primary ambition remains to describe the universe as it is, not to explain how it came into existence.[13]

Accordingly TM's mythology does not relate directly to human society and culture in any detail. The millennial promise contained within the notion of the 'Maharishi-effect' (Rothstein 1991d) embodies everything of relevance to human society and human ethics since everything, so it is believed, will function perfectly once the right foundation is laid through a highly developed consciousness within the individual and within society, but the question of how, more precisely, this perfect society will manifest itself seems to be outside the scope of TM's outward propaganda. I quote a typical example of how TM is promoting the vision of 'Heaven on Earth':

We are now in possession of that supreme knowledge of Natural Law — the scientific knowledge of the source of nature's perfect order and how to access it — that can bestow perfection on any individual and on any government, and can raise life everywhere to the level of Heaven on Earth.

Now should be the time for all those custodians of this knowledge in the country to offer their services to the national government to create an ideal administration. This will automatically bring the Support of Nature to the whole population and raise the ability of he government to satisfy everyone and create a problem-free nation.

In this way the government will do justice to its sovereign authority and the whole nation will enjoy perpetual peace, happiness, and prosperity — Heaven on Earth. (Advertisement text by Maharishi in The Independent, March 16. 1992)

In this respect it is right to say that the scientific aspect of SCI has taken over. TM's mythology is above all descriptive just like science.[14] But this does not interfere with the fact that the religious dimension ensures an internal meaning which places the system outside the realm of traditional science. SCI is without ethical and moral meaning, but as it describes and expounds divine realities, it also embodies spiritual meaning. Once meditators relate to this inherent meaning (the meditation being 'the technical aspect of SCI') , they will enliven the human (social, moral and ethical) ideals that lie implicitly in the inherent meaning and fulfil all human potential. The point is that the ethical dimension only reveals itself through meditation, as a high state of consciousness is necessary in order to experience the full consequences of SCI's cosmology. Only through meditation the spiritual (and thereby full) understanding of SCI is possible, and consequently the belief system presents itself in rather formalized ways whenever it is approached intellectually.

The ethics of ISKCON, and how it influences the religion, have been touched upon elsewhere.

Most important, in this chapter, it has been established that the personalistic views of ISKCON prevent any close identification with modern science and that the impersonalistic notions of TM, on the other hand, make such identification more likely. We have also seen how traditions remain viable in new contexts by either assuming new forms or faithfully sticking to the classical ways. In the next chapter we shall consider some concrete examples of disputes between ISKCON and TM in order to demonstrate the different positions from another perspective.

CHAPTER 11

# Disputes between TM and ISKCON

I have mentioned that TM and ISKCON only rarely engage in discussions with one another. In the following, however, two examples of deliberate dispute against TM from ISKCON reveal important aspects of how the opposing theologies react towards science (and towards each other), and what kind of reasoning they are advancing. Although no historical account of the dispute between Advaita-Vedanta and Vaisnava-Bhakti has been attempted, this chapter gives an impression of the most recent development in the old theological discussion.

ISKCON's theistic theology explains why no attempt to merge with science has occured. The notion of the personal god, Krishna, is of paramount importance to ISKCON and no single element in Prabhupada's teaching can be understood apart from this concept. Whenever scientists talk of forces or principles, ISKCON will find the personal god, the conscious creator and sustainer of the universe, behind it. A common ground which makes a syncretistic development possible cannot be seen, as in the case of TM where according to one source: 'the divine is a metaphor for the Unified Field and vice versa'.[1] This difference between ISKCON and TM is of great importance for the present analysis, and as a matter of fact this problem is very clearly presented in a discussion against TM's points of view, conducted by ISKCON's leading commentator regarding science, Sadaputa dasa. This discussion is presented in the following, but first we shall look into another example of how ISKCON regards TM/Advaita-Vedanta and science.

There are only a few sources revealing Prabhupada's understanding of Maharishi, but to my knowledge none cast light upon Maharishi's understanding of Prabhupada. The little we know, however, is relevant if we want to understand TM and ISKCON's positions today. Although the fundamental theological discrepancies originated a long time ago, the more recent debate will clearly support our understanding of the present state of affairs.² As we would expect, ISKCON, being far more aggressive than TM, has published material which (indirectly) criticizes TM. TM on the contrary keeps a low profile and never engages in debate with other religions.

The only place where Maharishi — according to my knowledge — is discussed directly in an ISKCON context, is in a transcript of a conversation between Prabhupada, a Sanskrit professor, other guests, and some of Prabhupada's disciples. The text, published in the series 'Conversations With Srila Prabhupada' is dated February 12, 1975, and involves primarily one new disciple who apparently had been a close associate of Maharishi's until shortly before the conversation (and the disciple's conversion) took place.

The theme discussed is why some people are attracted to 'bogus' gurus, while others — such as Prabhupada's disciples themselves — are blessed with a 'bona fide' guru, and Maharishi Mahesh Yogi is mentioned by one of the guests. Prabhupada, commenting on Maharishi, answers: 'I think he doesn't speak anything about God'. Guest: 'No. He's teaching the transcendental meditation'. Prabhupada: 'He speaks something of material prosperity. So he has nothing to do with God'. During the conversation a young man is introduced to Prabhupada as a former secretary of Maharishi's. Answering Prabhupada's questions about Maharishi (whom Prabhupada apparently knew almost nothing about) the young man reveals that Maharishi in fact considers 'Krishna consciousness' the highest truth. According to the young man, Maharishi came to this conclusion during his study and transcription of the *Brahma-sutra*, and that the insight left him in a very solemn mood (Conversations 1989, 227-31).³

It is impossible to verify this information, but what we learn is of course of great moral and religious relevance to ISKCON. A 'Mayavada-philosopher'⁴ (Maharishi), succeeding from a former Shankaracharya, who acknowledges Krishna to be 'the highest truth', truly is a victory. Discussing the passage with a leading representative from Danish ISKCON, it was explained to me that Maharishi — as far as my source could understand — was in a position quite similar to that of Sankara. His job is to 'confuse in order to clear peoples minds'(p. 173). Regarding Maharishi and TM's positive interest in science he said:

## 186  Disputes between TM and ISKCON

There is no doubt in my mind that his [Maharishi's] idea of science and spiritual life as the same thing is meant to confuse us. According to this conversation [the one cited above] he really knows better, just like Shankaracharya did. You know, Shankaracharya was in fact a devotee of Krishna, but he had a mission. So, therefore he could not reveal himself as a devotee of Krishna. I think Maharishi has a similar role to play today. Now we know that he knows better, and I suppose that his followers will learn it too some day.[5]

To my source it was clear that the TM movement will in the future accept the personalistic theology as superior to Advaita-Vedanta, and that those practicing transcendental meditation by that time will have matured into genuine worshippers of Krishna. This prediction, which is not officially promoted by ISKCON, has not been fulfilled yet. On the contrary TM shows no sign of a development in that direction.[6]

Maharishi's former pupil, according to the text, also told Prabhupada that Maharishi in fact had completed a translation and commentary on the Bhagavad Gita in its full length, but that people in the West were not ready to receive the last chapters. Chapters 1-6 were originally published in 1967 (Maharishi 1979), but the later — and preferably theistic chapters — (as mentioned elsewhere) still await publication.[7] According to the internal ISKCON conversation, Maharishi's commentary on the theistic part is very similar to that of Prabhupada himself (Conversations 1989, 230). If so, an internal contradiction (to say the least), exists within TM.

What interests us in this connection is that the first part of the Bhagavad Gita is used in TM's present strategies, while the theistic part only with great difficulties is adaptable to TM's official image. To ISKCON this is a dear opportunity to reveal the faultiness of the Mayavada philosophers and their organizations and consequently TM's compassionate merging with science. It may be that TM maintains good arguments against ISKCON's view, but as far as I am informed no response to ISKCON's criticism has ever been articulated. Accordingly I have nothing formal for quotation, only the remarks from unofficial members of TM: The prevailing idea is that the personalists of the ISKCON type are restricted to a lower realm of cognition and spiritual understanding. Returning to the TM belief system and the Advaita-Vedanta of Sankara this means, in philosophical terms, that devotees of a personal god are unable to understand that even their god is a product of maya. This is what Maharishi means when he says that 'ignorance' (either as avidya or maya) prevents the individual from perceiving Brahman, which instead appears as Ishwara (Maharishi 1979, 492).

In sum the discussion in ISKCON's cherished book(s) about Prabhupada and his conversations with various people confirms that the relation to science depends on the theological foundation. As long as TM sticks to the impersonalistic philosophy, ISKCON identifies the organization with maya, which is also the main characteristic given to science. If, however, Maharishi turns the attention towards devotional service to the supreme, personal god, then clearly TM changes into something else in the eyes of ISKCON. According to my source quoted above, TM's 'scientific identity' only prevails as long as the monistic perspective dominates. 'Science' he said, 'is only relevant if you are unable to ask the right questions'. During the interview he linked TM's project to Zen in saying that the Zen master will often refuse to answer an improper question, but contrary to Zen masters, he said, Maharishi is willing to answer any question, even if it is illogical: 'The answers he gives', he said, 'are derived from atheistic science'.

On the contrary we have already seen (in the previous chapter) how TM argues that the notion of the personal god will prevent any true understanding of the forces governing the universe. It is interesting to observe that the conversation between Prabhupada and Maharishi's former pupil took place in 1975 when TM's scientific image was well established, the same period when Prabhupada himself irreconcilably argued against science and scientists. ISKCON is combining the classical Vaisnava criticism of the Advaita-Vedanta tradition with an attack on modern science.[8] During this process ISKCON argues that the faultiness of science is meaningful to TM only because Advaita-Vedanta is based on erroneous assumptions. How, more precisely, this argumentation is articulated is exemplified in the following.

This example of a more or less explicit criticism of TM is officially issued by ISKCON, but as it appears, TM and Maharishi are only mentioned indirectly. The discussion was published in Back to Godhead Magazine and is highly informative for our purpose. In an article entitled 'Collapsing the Cosmic Hierarchy', Sadaputa dasa, argues directly against one of TM's most prominent physicist and leaders of the organization, physicist Dr. John Hagelin of MIU. Sadaputa dasa is very well aware of Hagelin's position, but he elegantly avoids mentioning TM or Maharishi by name:

Hagelin follows the teachings of a yogi who claims allegiance to Shankaracharya, the founder of the Indian school of philosophy known as Advaita Vedanta. (*Back to Godhead* November/December 1991, 16)

The disparaging tone shines through. Sadaputa dasa comments on a paper delivered by Hagelin at a conference, and as Hagelin — as we would expect — concentrates on the Unified Field (p. 42f.), Sadaputa dasa's reaction is a concrete example of how ISKCON looks upon TM's darling.

Sadaputa dasa refers to an article by Hagelin in a MIU publication and explains how the author claims the Unified Field of the physicists to be identical with the unbounded consciousness of Vedic science.[9] Exactly as TM would have put it, Sadaputa dasa sums up Hagelin's idea:

In the latest theories of physics, all the matter and energy in the universe are thought to be generated by a single, unified entity called a quantum field. In Vedic science, both material phenomena and our consciousness of these phenomena are said to flow from a unified source of absolute, unbounded consciousness. (*Back to Godhead* November/December 1991, 16).

And he continues, not quite as TM would have done:

By equating the unified quantum field with this unbounded consciousness, Hagelin reconciles modern science with ancient Vedic wisdom. Thus he provides an ultimate, unified explanation for both subjective and objective aspects of reality.

It sounds good — but unfortunately it's bogus.
Even though there are many schools of thought in ancient Indian tradition, certain features are common to all of them. Hagelin's theory requires the wholesale elimination of many of these important features. (*Back to Godhead* November/December 1991, 16)

To Sadaputa dasa it is clear that Hagelin ignores theistic conceptions, and as we have already seen, he immediately links Hagelin's conclusions with the notions of Advaita-Vedanta. In doing so Sadaputa dasa claims that 'the only truth Shankaracharya taught, is the field of absolute, undifferentiated consciousness known as Brahman', and he rightly identifies Hagelin's 'unbounded consciousness' as Brahman. One main criticism of Hagelin's theory, and thus of TM's cosmology, rests upon the fact that Sankara also spoke about a personal divinity as the creator and sustainer of the universe (a fact almost completely overlooked by monistic religious groups in the West), but that this personal god remains unimportant to Hagelin and his analysis.[10]

According to Vaisnava theology Krishna is the cause of all causes and Brahman is his impersonal effulgence, and according to Sadaputa dasa, Shankara accepted Krishna to be 'at least as real as everything else in the manifest universe'. He confirms that Shankara placed Krishna within the realm of maya, but at the same time regarded him (Krishna) to be the controller of the universe, which he also regarded as illusory. There is no easy solution. The discussion has lasted for centuries, and we shall not judge in the matter. What interests us is the positions of the opponents, not who is right.

In the eyes of Sadaputa dasa and ISKCON Hagelin's and TM's grievous offence is that they place the personal divinity within the realm of maya. Referring to 'the great teachers of Vaisnava philosophy', Sadaputa dasa claims that such notions will block one's advancement in spiritual life, and that Shankara in fact 'inwardly accepted Krishna's transcendental status'. If so only little logic remains in Maharishi's explanations regarding the personal god and maya. To Maharishi the experience of the personal god (and hence the level of 'God-consciousness') remains a partial understanding below that of the experience of Brahman (and hence 'Unity-consciousness') (p. 22). To Maharishi the personal divinity (termed Ishwara) only appears under the influence of maya, and therefore this manifestation ranks below Brahman in the cosmic hierarchy. To ISKCON this collapse of the cosmic hierarchy is disastrous. While TM feels supported by Shankara in this respect, ISKCON claims that the notion of Brahman's superiority also discharges Shankara's true teaching. Thereby ISKCON also finds the modern theory of the

Unified Field totally incompatible with the views of Vaisnava theology. TM is wrong because the personal god is ignored, and accordingly modern science is erroneous. This, ISKCON explains, is also why monistic systems such as TM's go so well along with the scientific speculations. It is a negative coalition. As ISKCON interprets the theory of the Unified Field (and science in general), personality does not lie behind the universe but generates when evolution produces suitable elements so that brains and nervous systems can emerge (Back to Godhead Magazine November/December 1991, 17).

Further, as far as I can judge, TM pays no (or at least no official) attention to other Hindu divinities such as Brahma, Varuna, Agni and so on, all of whom are considered demi-gods with administrative functions under the auspices of the supreme creator of the universe. To ISKCON, on the contrary, such entities (comprising millions according to Vaisnava theology) are considered to be actual persons in the cosmic system.[11] For instance, ISKCON may ask, what happens to important demi-gods such as Yama who punishes the dead and sees to their transmigration to other planets for future incarnation. Is there room for such an entity in the Unified Field cosmology? It appears not. In general ISKCON feels deprived of the mythological space of the Vaisnava-Bhakti tradition whenever the scientific realm is considered. The spiritual planets, the demons, the gods in all their incarnations, the space in which the soul moves during the process of reincarnation and so forth is not accounted for in Unified Field theories, nor in any other scientific cosmology.[12] The structure which makes close identification possible in the case of TM is missing. ISKCON is witnessing a cosmological burst whenever scientific notions are considered. In the eyes of one TM source this is what makes ISKCON 'dogmatic' contrary to 'Vedanta [TM] which is the opposite'.[13]

The cosmological breakdown which modern science represents to ISKCON is at the same time an ontological provocation. Science describes something which is not, or at least something which is more than it appears to be in the scientific description. Reality as perceived by science is meaningless to ISKCON. ISKCON's theology and modern science do not suit one another and consequently no syncretistic development emerges.

The theological differences are basically the same as 500 years ago when Chaitanya opposed the monistic philosophers of his days, but because ISKCON and TM find themselves placed in a world where science is an unavoidable dimension, they naturally integrate it — not only into their internal considerations or public statements — but also into their mutual confrontations. Science does not only affect the belief systems of the religions. It also determines the way theological disputes are conducted.

CHAPTER 12

# Conclusion

**Introduction**

After ISKCON's big conference in 1986 Eileen Barker (see Chapter 8 note 30) wrote:

> The relationships that are assumed to exist between science and religion are complicated and frequently contradictory. Sometimes science is invoked to prove, justify, support, or merely give permission for the truth claims of a particular ideology; sometimes it is used to disprove or to question the ideological presuppositions of others; frequently science is vilified as the demon that is responsible for secularism, materialism, and the horror of modern military technology; but it is almost invariably a demon that is respected, and it is commonly assumed that 'proper use' of science would bring about a better (more enlightened or more spiritual) world of peace. (Barker 1986, 143)

Each in its own way, and in certain ways unanimously, the religions discussed here correspond to Barker's description. We find all kinds of strategic use of science, and although we have to agree that the relationship between science and religion is complicated and often contradictory, the material presented here, rather precisely suggests how science is looked upon and how it works in two particular religions. Above all it is established that none of the religions were able to ignore the challenge from science.

This necessity for new religions to find solutions to the questions posed as a result of the confrontation with the surrounding culture — in this case represented by science — makes the question of adaptability central to our survey. What are the preconditions for adaptability? Does anything encourage adjustment? Does anything work the other way round? In the introduction I emphasized that the present analysis is dealing with new religions of Hindu origin, rather than Hinduism in a foreign setting. Nonetheless, as historian of religions, Frank Whaling, points out, there are connections between

## Introduction 193

the new and the traditional Hindu religions, also with regard to their present situation and inclination to find a place in the modern world:

... Hinduism in Europe, America, Africa and further Asia have to cope with different environments and face different questions from those posed to Hindus in India. The many Hindu movements working outside as well as inside India...: the Hare Krishnas, The Sathya Sai Babas, the Raja-Yogas and Transcendental Meditation, have had to take cognizance of the wider perspective, as have Hindu ecumenical movements which have tried to unite Hindus on a global basis. (Whaling 1987, 173)

The variety, adaptability and assimilative power of the Hindu tradition are often praised (p. 79f.), and indeed TM and ISKCON each in its own way reflect this ability to accommodate to new demands.

In the Introduction (Chapter 1) it was suggested that what we need in order to study syncretistic processes is a strategy that will allow us to determine how the dynamic process of religious and cultural coalescence takes place. Why, it was asked, are syncretistic developments with science allowed in TM's case and rejected in ISKCON's? Why are religious notions sometimes brought into harmony with science, and why is religion at other times looked upon as completely antagonistic to science? What are the preconditions that allow Advaita-Vedanta and TM to embrace modern science, and what are the preconditions that prevent Vaisnava-Bhakti and ISKCON to do the same?

In order to explore these and other questions I have primarily looked into the analogies and homologies of or conflicts between religion and science. I have also discussed how new languages, new symbols and new modes of expression emerge during a syncretistic process such as the one known to TM, and I have tried to show that a corresponding development was irrelevant to ISKCON. Finally I have considered how, more precisely, science and scientific notions are placed in TM and ISKCON respectively. In this connection, as a major conclusion, I pointed to the fact that science or rather certain scientific notions and expositions manifest themselves as hierophanies to TM which is not the case in ISKCON.

As it appears this strategy for investigation has been useful. On the previous pages we have seen how syncretistic processes can be understood through analysis of the preconditions and structural resemblances or differences between the religions (and in this case science) involved. The following pages conclude the analysis.

No doubt TM's heritage from Sankhya philosophy has nourished the intellectual dimension of the SCI as Sankhya relies on distinct and recognizable patterns of enumeration and methods of enquiry. With its emphasis on the the equilibrium of the three gunas, the idea that matter is one, and that the evolution of a number of things out of that matter is understood as causation, it forms a structural parallel to modern scientific thinking. TM apparently sees a structural resemblance between Sankhya and modern science which makes science a part of a tradition which has Sankhya at its basis. Together with the Advaita-Vedanta notion of the unpersonal omnipresent Brahman, which in a great many ways resembles modern scientific ideas of the forces governing nature, Sankhya therefore leaves TM with good opportunities for a syncretistic development with science.

On the contrary ISKCON, with its unconditional focus on an anthropomorphic, personal god, has placed itself outside the realm of scientific theory and positions. The aspects of ISKCON's theology that structurally correspond to physics and other natural sciences — for instance the notion of the *Brahmajyoti*, the halo or effulgence of Krishna which includes all that exist — are of secondary importance to the devotees because it belongs to the realm of maya, which, of course, also is where science belongs. Consequently no syncretistic development will be able to take place unless science puts the personal god on the agenda. Furthermore ISKCON regards modern science to be reductionistic in the sense that it does not take the 'higher dimensional levels' into consideration, and above all, ISKCON claims the right to be taken seriously.

Focusing on the structures of the scientific dimension of the SCI, it is clear that the development from monistic Hinduism (Advaita-Vedanta) and Sankhya philosophy to science was potentially contained within TM from its birth. Structures of considerable likeness to those of science were already present in the traditional religious material. The example from TM's newspaper advertisement, and the model which equates quantum physics with transcendental meditation are excellent expressions of how TM identifies traditional religious notions in scientific theory and scientific models. The secular demands did not provoke the development of a fundamentally new belief system. Rather it made the already existing belief system develop in a specific direction.

The demand for scientific verification in the modern Western world is strong. In TM's case Maharishi's teaching contained the structural preconditions to a merging, and, as time went by, ever stronger identification with science. Thereby we have ascertained that the scientific image of TM, in fact owes more to traditional Hindu thought, than we would perhaps be inclined to expect.

ISKCON's perspective on Hinduism, however, points in the other direction. The lack of a common ground with science was clear to Prabhupada from the very beginning. He had some scientific training himself, and in the earliest records regarding his preaching, as we have seen, hard attacks against 'materialism' in terms of science were made. Prabhupada disregards the intellectual or philosophical Sankhya, but refers to the 'true Sankhya' which unambiguously supports theistic notions. Hence every dimension of his theology contradicts current scientific notions.

Further more the difference between TM and ISKCON may be considered through the outer appearance of the believers.

In her study of ISKCON, social anthropologist Angela Burr is occupied with body symbolism. Among other things, she shows how the appearance of the devotees (shaven heads, deviant clothing etc.) signals distaste and rejection towards the surroundings: 'Body symbolism...is employed to criticize and symbolize what the devotees consider to be the main problems and ills of the outside 'karmi' world' (Burr 1984, 178). While this aspect of 'world rejection' (to use Wallis' term) is physical and bodily, the strong antipathy to science is ideological and intellectual. Both aspects, however, form a unity in the religious community where specific religious points of view are articulated at all levels. We might even say that modern theoretical science gets a physical alternative in ISKCON as the rituals (which are bodily exercises) are promoted as 'truly scientific' contrary to ordinary science.

The situation in TM is quite different. Here we find no body symbolism which opposes traditional Western standards. On the contrary Maharishi has, as we have already touched upon, encouraged, or even demanded, people to dress and wear their hair according to the norms of ordinary society (McCutchan 1977, 148). Accordingly TM accepts modern science and does whatever to align with it.

A syncretistic process is not necessarily harmonious, nor 'fair' to the traditions implied. As a culturally determined pattern the new belief systems may be the results of challenge and combat. Most scientists will probably feel TM's use of physics to be rather far-fetched, but when it comes to a point the scientists' points of view are of no interest. The standards and the procedure of the process are set by TM alone. Even though many meditators, including the most prominent of the movement's theorists, are scientists, and even though the Maharishi International University (MIU) is officially credited, the general acknowledgement of TM and the SCI is limited. It is true that various analyses of the effect of the meditation technique have been published in many prominent scholarly periodicals (especially those focusing on medical science, neurology and psychology), but the publications do not reflect a corresponding, lasting interest in the TM perspectives outside TM itself.[1] For that reason there is no basis for understanding the syncretistic process as something going on between groups, what we see is rather a meeting of ideas: TM uses science, though some would say that TM violates it. This is, I believe, important to note. The premises are solely TM's.

It is also important to note that TM does not claim SCI to be a 'new paradigm'. The notion of a new paradigm permeates the New Age movement and even parts of the scientific community, but to TM nothing new is at stake. It is believed that no new knowledge has been obtained, as the Veda has always embodied all knowledge and wisdom. What is fostered is merely a new language, a new way of expressing this knowledge. In this way TM to some degree avoids a problem otherwise pointed to by scholars. Historian of religions Ingvild Gilhus, as an example, claims that the attempt to merge science with religion, does not lead to an actual new paradigm (Gilhus 1989, 157). She points to the fact that the New Age notions rest upon monistic assumptions while science is based on dualistic patterns. Commenting on a book on the 'new paradigm' by New Age writer Erik Dammann (Dammann 1987), Gilhus shows how the author places the monistic notion as superior to the dualistic pattern. On this basis, so she says, the attempt to conciliate two different paradigms is doomed. The premises will automatically favour the religious, monistic understanding. The result is not a new paradigm, but some kind of coordination of two separately existing patterns of understanding. Contrary to the natural scientist Henri Atlan, who follows a similar line of argumentation (Atlan 1986), Gilhus does not neglect the fact that the incoherent alliance between science and religion is coherent indeed to the believer.

TM never left its religious origin, but a thorough transformation of language has resulted in what apparently is a secularized belief system. The idiomatic language of SCI is one of TM's strongest characteristics. The merging with science has resulted in a mixture of formulations, and above all a reevaluation of what can be said in scientific terms. The transformation of Advaita-Vedanta into the syncretistic SCI required a new language where the sentiments of monistic Hinduism or mysticism was aligned with the abstract language of natural science (primarily physics). Hence we see a corresponding development in beliefs and language. In addition, as indicated by the pictures in the previous chapters) a new iconography has been developed in order to demonstrate the synthesis of Advaita-Vedanta and science.

Turning to ISKCON the picture shows more signs of ambiguity. As we have seen, ISKCON strongly has rejected any deliberate syncretism, and undoubtedly a traditional religious language dominates ISKCON's texts. To demonstrate this we may choose randomly among ISKCON's literally several hundreds of publications. Whenever strict religious business is dealt with, the language is religious in the traditional sense of the word. However, resulting indirectly from ISKCON's fight against science, some kind of scientific influence on the language *is* seen. Most profoundly this development is observable in the formulations of the 'Higher Dimensional Science'. Even if ISKCON's notion of 'science' and 'scientific' is special, the language used in order to describe the science of higher dimensions frequently goes into traditional scientific conceptions in order to discuss them. Sadaputa dasa's writings are examples of this strategy. The change in language is a fact even if ISKCON seems quite unsusceptible to influence on the level of beliefs. Contrary to the case of TM, we therefore find a change in language but no corresponding change in ideology or beliefs.

It seems correct that new religious orientations in terms of syncretistic developments lead to a deliberate change in language, but ISKCON's example also suggests that a negative confrontation with another religion or another system of understanding, may lead to a change in language. This phenomenon, I believe, is a part of the 'negative syncretism' which I have suggested as relevant to the understanding of ISKCON. ISKCON has, to a certain degree, accepted a new language, which primarily serves as a device in the missionary work.

The main consequence of ISKCON's meeting with the scientific Western ideologies, so it appears, has been a strengthened identification with 'the Vedic knowledge'. ISKCON is firmly consolidated in its Gaudia-Vaisnava identity, and in its 'world-rejection' (i.e. ISKCON's hostility towards modern society). This identification with India and a specific Indian religion is partly a consequence of the believers' dissatisfaction with Western society, and partly a positive interest in the exotic. Focusing on the first aspect, we may conclude that the self-perception of ISKCON primarily is derived from its opposition to Western society (and ideals), which — once again — makes the paradoxical notion of 'negative syncretism' relevant. In the introduction I proposed to discuss the new languages, new symbols and new modes of expression that emerge as a result of the encounter between science and religion, whether positive or negative. As far as ISKCON is concerned, it seems that this religion currently is intensifying its identification with its religious origin in every respect thus consolidating a traditional articulation of its beliefs. On the contrary TM, being 'world-affirming', is intensifying its identification with modern ways of saying things, although the movement firmly holds on to the religious message contained within its modern 'mythology'.

Eliade's notion of hierophanies was introduced as a method for detecting the nature of TM's naturalistic accounts of spiritual matters. With references to TM's publications of different kinds and through quotations from conversations with the members of TM, I have suggested that science in TM forms some kind of hierophany. I have not gone into a discussion of the nature of those experiences, although I am convinced that such an undertaking would prove most useful for our future understanding of TM and SCI. What I have tried is merely to show that the syncretistic belief system, SCI, leaves room for rather traditional, religious interpretations although the religious language is an innovation. In designating SCI as some kind of myth, I have focused on the functional aspects of the belief system, and by relating it to TM's ritual aspect I have, hopefully, demonstrated that it is intimately linked with religious behaviour.

SCI is an expression of syncretism, but it does not add anything morphologically new to the concept of religion. What may appear to be a scientific domination over religion in TM is, in fact, the opposite. What TM has done is to transform secular science into something which expresses religious meaning. TM has imposed the ontology of Advaita-Vedanta upon science, and thus (within its own mental and physical boundaries) made science 'religious'. This has happened, essentially because TM claims that science by now is able to reach beyond the limits of the relative realm into which the physical universe is otherwise confined.

With a focus on their relationships to science we have seen how TM aligns itself with scientific notions while ISKCON rejects them as being meaningful. The same observation has been made from a sociological perspective. The social dispositions of these religions may correctly be interpreted as strategic, and this analysis — from the perspective of history of religions — has demonstrated how the basic traditions of TM and ISKCON are determining their strategies, in this case their relationships to science. Indeed the examples here show that tradition is not only a matter of reference to the past, but just as much a question of contemporary production of beliefs, modes and practices. In both cases we may correctly describe the mythological transformations as a continuation of tradition or simply tomorrow's beliefs in the making. In this sense the study of new religion's bindings to 'tradition' adds to the general picture of these groups which is primarily determined by sociological analysis. No religion appears out of nothing, and no religious phenomenon can be understood detached from its history. It has been demonstrated that traditional and religious determinants are affecting the development of new religions, and that recognition and recruitment strategies as well as sociological characteristics in terms of 'world-affirmation' and 'world-rejection' only form a part of the total picture.

Further, due to the fact that the syncretistic new religions are observable at close range in every respect, it is obvious that the study of syncretism in general would benefit tremendously from a closer study of these groups.

What TM has done is to reformulate a classic belief system with just the right emphasis. With science in focus TM tries to overcome modern society's present reservation towards religious interpretations of life, but traditional religious structures are maintained in the new articulation. TM has made the secular myth of science religiously meaningful, and tries to conform to the normative order of the surrounding community.

ISKCON is against the normative order of the society in which it exists. The opposition to science is one particular dimension of this antagonism. ISKCON's understanding of the potentials of modern science, which concludes this survey, is framed by Prabhupada's clear statement: 'There will not and cannot be any arrival at truth through this [scientific] process'.[2]

# Notes

**Notes to Preface**
1. All books and otherwise identifiable publications are placed in the bibliography and will be referred to as such. Other kinds of written material that require a specific reference are outlined in the notes.
2. It is sufficient to refer to sociologist of religion James A. Beckford's well known description of internal social differentiation in new religious movements (Beckford 1985).

**Notes to Chapter 1**
1. Quoted in Bang 1989, 210.
2. Having completed the present analysis I have become aware of the existence of a new book by Mary Midgley entitled 'Science as Salvation. A Modern Myth and its Meaning' (Routledge. London 1992).
3. 'When the concept of syncretism is used in describing phenomena, the application of the term is still not the result of an analysis; rather, it serves as a disparaging judgement on certain manifestations, a judgement assumed to be obvious' (Cople 1987, 219).
4. The similarities between the mystery religions and gnosticism of the ancient world and the new religion of today are not ignored, but much more work along these lines wait ahead. It is obvious that new perspectives of importance will emerge from that comparative perspective.
5. At this point it should be stressed that any generalization from this material to the problems of syncretism by and large need close consideration. The attention to the historical and cultural situation and the time in which this religious phenomenon appears, is needed as much as ever. It seems likely that some general features of the syncretic process are common indeed, and there is no reason why we should not compare TM's merging with modern physics with the mixture of e.g. the Israelite and Canaanite elements forming the religion of The Old Testament. But in each case a thorough understanding of the general cultural and historical context is needed. What seems to be common, however, is the need for structural precondition of the merging of two (or more) religious traditions.
6. As it will appear, I do not believe, as do some sociologists, that the emergence of today's new religions should be primarily understood as

an expression of social protest. Certainly this is often the case, but as pointed out by scholars such as Wallis (1984), Beckford (1985) and Nelson (1987), it is necessary to introduce light and shade into the matter. Some new religions (of which TM, Scientology, many UFO-cults and others are examples) apparently exist by virtue of — not in spite of — dominant traditions of the modern world, such as science. In some cases a straightforward 'scientism' even seems to be a dominant feature.

**Notes to Chapter 2**
1. Short accounts are given in Melton 1986, 187-92, Barker 1989, 213-14, Bancroft 1989, 167-79 and Needleman 1972, 128-41, but most information is integrated in the various other titles. For further references see bibliography.
2. 'Maharishi' has become the usual designation, although it is not a name but a title meaning 'Great Seer'. In this book, for the sake of convenience, I shall stick to this practice. 'Yogi' refers to someone who masters *yoga* while Mahesh remains his actual name.
3. Maharishi 1965, 11 states: 'He [Brahmananda Saraswati] cast off His mortal coil, but left behind a few others in mortal coils to keep up the light of His grace and pass on the torch of His teachings from hand to hand for all the millenium to come.' Apparently Maharishi was one of those left behind but to my knowledge, no information exists concerning the others.
4. Some meditators believe that Maharishi and Brahmananda Saraswati deliberately planned a modified meditation program for lay persons prior to Maharishi's mission, but this is contradicted by Maharishi's own explanations. He maintains that no alterations have been made (Maharishi 1965, 11).
5. In this study I shall focus on the cosmological level. It is important though, to note that the bodily advantages that, according to TM, are the results of the meditation, are understood to be microcosmic manifestations of the overall influence of the meditators upon cosmos in general.
6. There is a good chart showing the seven states of consciousness on p. 109 in Campbell's book.
7. I have discussed the TM-Sidhi technique in Rothstein 1991c and 1991d. See also Richards 1985, 12-16 etc.
8. In Denmark about 36,000 persons have learned to meditate since 1962 when TM arrived in this country. However, less than 2500 are members of TM's supporters organization in Denmark (the only parameter for

determining the number of persons with an active involvement). From my observations I suggest that the inner-group of Danish TM numbers less than 300 individuals.
9. TM in Denmark reacted strongly against a chapter in a recent book (Jensen, Rothstein and Podemann Sørensen 1994), where the organisation was presented as a religious movement. It was not the analysis itself that provoked TM. Rather it was the fact that TM was designated 'a religion'. Intense discussions with the publisher and the scholars behind the book, lead to one thing: TM's arguments were integrated as references in the scholarly argumentation.
10. Woodrum (1977) points to the same dichotomy, but never relates the sociological difference to the grade of initiation. Focusing on the religious aspects of the internal differentiation a linkage to the initiations, however, seems natural.

## Notes to Chapter 3

1. At MIU, TM and SCI are systematically related to virtually every major science (MIU 1991).
2. TM very often emphasizes that Maharishi is 'a scientist'. It is, however, as indicated already, impossible to determine his actual scientific competence. It may very well be that his close associates carry out most of the work. But it may also be himself. Officially TM leaves us with the impression that there are no limits to Maharishi's abilities.
3. Interview, August 1991.
4. It should be observed that TM's explanations also assert that 'The Veda' in fact is the most well established system at all times. This notion, however, is not articulated to the surrounding world with the same intensity as the scientific verification of Maharishi´s claims. The reason, of course, is that the Veda is deprived of any authority to the ordinary public in the West.
5. One important exception is Deepak Chopra M.D., an Indian endocrinologist in charge of Maharishi's international efforts to establish Ayurvedic principles for treatment.
6. Members of TM's elite with regard to the articulation of the SCI are behind every book, article or paper distributed by MIU on that subject. They are promoted as highly qualified lecturers and interpreters of Maharishi's wisdom. Their lectures are available on videotape and their writings are published in books and periodicals such as 'Modern Science and Vedic Science' (MIU World, MIU Press 1991).
7. Translation of my Danish notes. Copenhagen. March 1990.
8. Interview, Copenhagen, May 1990.

9. Smith 1983 is a good example. It is a book published by Christians to whom TM is a tool for 'Christian growth'.
10. Editor's Notes in MIU publications explain that it has been decided to adopt the convention of 'Ved' (pronounced Vade), which is used by Maharishi himself because it 'produces the most accurate pronunciation of the original Sanskrit form'.
11. Contemporary physics is very often highly speculative, and — contrary to the traditional physics of Newton — it is occupied with theories of the most subtle and far-reaching kind. In fact scientists have to consider questions that are totally different from what was previously discussed (Davis 1986). In this sense it is correct, as TM claims, that modern science only recently has achieved a level that can be compared to Advaita-Vedanta which has, since long, been occupied with questions (and answers) of that nature.
12. In this case a scientific process is compared to a spiritual notion in order to explain the latter. Usually TM's use of science is for the purpose of identification.
13. Interview, Copenhagen. 1.10.1990.
14. Actually from 1983 but with special emphasis since 1988.
15. A widely distributed booklet entitled 'Scientific Research on The Maharishi Technology of the Unified Field: The Transcendental Meditation and TM-Sidhi Program' (1988) is one of the most accessible publications in this respect (MIU Press 1988).
16. The organizational predecessor of TM.

**Notes to Chapter 4**
1. Brahmananda Saraswati (guru Dev), the incarnation of the Divine, passed down the eternal wisdom to his student Maharishi. This is why Maharishi could speak with the same authority as his own teacher from the beginning. (Notes from lecture given by a TM teacher in Copenhagen September 5. 1991).
2. The Danish materials from this period are of little interest to the subject discussed here. TM's internal letters, invitations to lectures etc. were held in a neutral language with emphasis on words such as 'peace', 'fulfilment' and 'happiness' (A sample of mailouts etc. dating from 1966-68 was lent to me by a member of TM in Denmark).
3. The numbers of initiations have changed dramatically over the years culminating during late 1975, followed by a development in the opposite direction the year after (Bainbridge and Jackson 1981, 145) These are the only solid statistics on TM demography known to me. The figures are American, but nothing indicates that things were different in Europe.

4. According to the late sociologist of religion Roy Wallis, Robert McCutchan was once Maharishi's secretary (Private conversation 1988).
5. Rothstein 1989, 48 gives other examples.
6. Interview, March 1990.
7. A new volume entitled 'The Maharishi Effect' which contains 'results of scientific research 1974-1990' has been published by MIU Press just recently (1991). I have not seen the book but apparently it is even more detailed than Aron and Aron 1986, and up to date.
8. This is very often given as an example in lectures etc.
9. Interview, March 1990.
10. Interview, August 1989.
11. Here it is important to note that the Vedas, according to TM, already contained the same truth as Maharishi spoke of. Maharishi's task was to bring the 'knowledge' or 'truth' to human beings, and thus bless them with every conceivable benefit, not to invent something new. At first he walked the same paths as his predecessors in the Advaita-Vedanta tradition, but soon he found another way of expounding his message.

**Notes to Chapter 5**
1. It should be remembered that TM is not the only agent of a 'theology of science' today. Among the agitators of the New Age movement, for example, there are several ideologists with similar notions. Initially physicist Fritjof Capra argued that an intimate connection between physics and mysticism exists (Capra 1975, 1982). During the years many people have come forward with the same message. There is, however, no official contact between TM and other organisations or teachers. Nevertheless many meditators will take part in various New Age activities outside TM.
2. According to one of Eliade's pupils, professor Bruce Lincoln, Eliade never discussed 'modern modalities of the sacred', either because he did not find them attractive, or even more likely, because they did not exist to him (private conversation, November 1992).
3. According to Eliade's plan for the concluding volume of his 'Historie des croyances et des idées religieuse' (Vol. 4) he intended to analyse how the sacred has become 'totally camouflaged' in the final phase of secularization, i.e. how 'the sacred has merged with the profane' (Eliade 1983-1991, Vol. 1, 15). Eliade's death prevented him from writing Vol. 4, but Richard Schaeffler has summarized Eliade's basic notions, although with no reference to modern science. It is likely that Eliade's thoughts in this respect would add something to his theories, and it is true that he expected the difference between sacred and profane to

eventually obliterate in every religion. However, I shall not discuss what Eliade might have said (Eliade 1983-1991, Vol 4., 366-400).
4. The quotation below is from the 1968 edition. According to the publishers no alterations have been made.
5. According to physicists, the theories of the Unified Field have not been further developed since they were presented in 1986 (private conversation with physicist Jens M. Bang of The Niels Bohr Institute, University of Copenhagen). This may explain why TM has been able to hold on to this subject. Very often scientific theories are quickly altered, but the GUTs are still there.
6. It is interesting to observe that Sheldrake occasionally refers to religious notions in order to establish his theories as something known — although unconsciously — throughout history.
7. Danish science writer Tor Nørretranders elegantly makes a critical point out of TM's overwhelming mathematical argumentation which he finds incomprehensible but 'magnificently done from a lithographic point of view'. TM approached him in 1984, and he critically includes the incident in his biography on physicist Niels Bohr. Nørretranders' observation is that TM rejects the fact that the new physics takes us to unknown land. According to Nørretranders TM has 'domesticated' theoretical physics because it is unbearable to realize that the scientific description of reality makes everything uncertain. TM, he says, has made the theories become something which they are not. (Nørretranders 1988, 274-82)
8. Meditators are told that actual mystic experiences will come whenever the individual's consciousness is prepared (although the phrase 'mysticism' may not be used). Usually it will take a while before anything of that sort happens, but occasionally new initiates react strongly during their very first meditation. In such cases (which are considered more than welcome by the TM teachers), it is explained that the individual's level of consciousness was higher than most people's. It is certainly not everybody who learns to meditate who has mystical experiences, but among TM's inner-members everybody will testify to some kind of mystical experiences.
9. Interview, April 1990.

**Notes to Chapter 6**
1. Already in 1875 The Theosophical Society was established in New York. Although outside the actual Neo-Hinduistic movements, the hyper-syncretistic theosophical movement was one of the most influential actors in the articulation of Hindu thoughts in the West (Ahlbäck 1990).

It is interesting to observe that TM and the Theosophical Society share basic notions concerning the relation between religion and science. I have looked closer into the matter, but even if the similarities are striking, no connection whatsoever is seen between the two groups.
2. This issue 'A Special Supplement to The India Times; Maharishi Mahesh Yogi and His Movement' (24 pages tabloid!) represent the most direct example of TM's missionary endeavors towards an Indian audience. Contrary to the newspaper 'Hinduism Today' which often carries critical articles on movements like TM, The India Times straightforwardly recommends TM to its readers.
3. During my field-work I have learned of many internal conflicts. However, I have never experienced a criticism of Maharishi nor of TM's official image.
4. No data. Obtained from a source who had used the papers during a course in Holland 1991. Probably 1990-91.
5. TM asserts that the initiation-puja is carried out in Sanskrit in honor of the tradition to which it belongs. A closer examination, however, shows that the initiation only works if the texts are recited in Sanskrit. Focus is not centred on intellectual understanding of the text, but on its magical ability to initiate the individual, or more precisely, to establish the preconditions so that the mantra may work and thus expand the individual's consciousness (Further examined in Rothstein 1989, 160-83). TM's official explanation is given in Johnston 1980, 351 note 4. Related subjects are dealt with in Rothstein 1991c and 1991d.

## Notes to Chapter 7

1. A good example is Gelberg 1983 which is based on an ISKCON initiative. Further, ISKCON has set up the publication 'ISKCON Review. Academic perspectives on the Hare Krishna Movement' in affiliation with The Institute for Vaisnava Studies, Dept. of Philosophy and Religion, The American University, Washington, to promote scholarly interest in ISKCON. Most important in this respect, however, is the ISKCON Communications Journal, which is 'a biannual journal of news and views on Communications training and practice' edited by ISKCON devotee Saunaka Rishi dasa. The Journal is primarily a means for internal communication, but it serves just as much as a forum for dialogue with scholars. Hence the ISKCON Communications Journal signifies ISKCON's principle interest in good relations to the academic world.
2. Like in the case of TM and 'Maharishi', I use 'Prabhupada' when speaking of Bhaktivedanta Prabhupada. This is the form used in all ISKCON's materials.

3. While simultaneously serving as religious guides revealing the example of the guru, these biographies are, from a scholarly point of view, well researched and well written. Apart from those referred to in the text, a six volume book about Prabhupada and his life, modelled after the traditional biography of the sage Caitanya (the 'Caitanya Caritamrita') exist. The author of this 'Srila Prabhupada-lilamrita' is also Satsvarupa Dasa Goswami. A good biographical sketch is finally given in Shinn 1987, 34-42.
4. Revised listings in Back to Godhead Magazine 1991-92.
5. It is difficult to determine the number of adherents, and ISKCON's figures may be too optimistic.
6. Most important: 1) ISKCON allows the sexes to live in the same temple, although in separate sections. The requirements to austerity among celibate monks and nuns would traditionally forbid this. 2) The requirements regarding mantra-recitation and temple worship is less demanding than originally (see further below).
7. Back to Godhead Magazine, January/February 1991, 1.
8. Anthropologist Angela Burr 1984, 172-90 etc. has an excellent analysis of ISKCON's hair and dress code (see also p. 193).

**Notes to Chapter 8**
1. Interview with devotee, March 1990.
2. In order to give an impression of this concept a sample of statements and descriptions from important ISKCON publications will be quoted in the following.
3. Here, of course, we must think in terms of the natural sciences.
4. Interview with two of ISKCON's leading gurus Suhotra Swami and Harikesa Vishnupad during their visits to Copenhagen 1990-91.
5. A parallel of considerable interest is ISKCON's notion of modern technology like computers, telex, telephones, etc. According to my sources all these material things are accepted for use whenever it is done in Krishna's honor, and for 'spiritual purposes'. This means that devotees may use devices otherwise identified with the ignorant materialists of the surrounding world.
6. A thorough criticism of philology, comparative religion and indology from the viewpoint of *Vaisnava-Bhakti* has been published in Satsvarupa 1977, Chapter 2. One of ISKCON's gurus Sohotra Swami declared in a ISKCON radio broadcast that philosophy, and indeed all the fields of the humanities, are a 'play with words', and that the philosophical discourse 'follows no plan' (Jan. 1993)(see also Thompson 1989, 6).

7. This wording is inspired by physicist W. Heiler's book: 'Man and Science'. Basic Books. New York 1963, p. 97.
8. J.C. Polkinghorne 1987 is a good example of 'deistic' scientific theory. Polkinghorne is a theoretical physicist and at the same time serves as a priest. See also Back To Godhead Magazine April/March 1991, 12-16.
9. Interview, August 1991.
10. One of ISKCON's gurus Hridayananda dasa Goswami quoted in Danish ISKCON's news bulletin 'Krishnas Venner' No. 4. 1991, 6. The text is a comment to the Bhagavat Purana's 11th Canto's 2nd part.
11. In order to appraise Sadaputa dasa's scientific competence, I have shown a substantial part of his production to a leading physicist at the Niels Bohr Institute of the University of Copenhagen. The scholarly judgement was in favour of Sadaputa dasa. His work was considered competent, although the physicist emphasized that he himself did not share the conclusions. As a matter of fact scholars from the Niels Bohr Institute were willing to meet with Sadaputa dasa for scholarly purposes. It should be noted, however, that they felt unable to host him at their own institute, but arranged (through this author and ISKCON in Denmark) a meeting at the University of Copenhagen. Unfortunately Sadaputa dasa, due to various circumstances never arrived in Denmark.
12. ISKCON has for a long time wished to establish exhibitions and educational centers all over the world. The planetarium mentioned is one of these initiatives. Now, during the early 90s, show rooms have appeared in the USA, Europe and India.
13. Prabhupada's Bhagavat Purana edition is called *'Srimad Bhagavatam'*. At this instance it comes in 34 volumes. As far as I know more are in preparation. The figures in the reference refer to the number of 'book', 'chapter' and Prabhupada's explanation in the Bhagavat Purana.
14. Lecture given by a Danish devotee in Radio Krishna, March 1991.
15. The soul *Jiva-atma* cannot be seen or measured by any scientific standard being smaller than the smallest, ISKCON says. Nevertheless it is regarded as some kind of entity.
16. See note 6.
17. The author also mentions a line of differences.
18. I merely make this comment in order to point out that the natural sciences at this point are closer to ISKCON's attention than the humanities. This may be due to Sadaputa dasa's educational background, but it may also reflect that the natural sciences (or 'exact' sciences) are more directly connected with current cosmological notions of the industrialized West than the social sciences or the humanities.

However, as mentioned elsewhere, ISKCON has also been focusing on archaeology and paleontology.
19. See also Thompson 1989, 62-71. See also note 17.
20. Sadaputa dasa also gives a line of corresponding examples from other parts of the Puranic literature, as an example Bhagavad Purana 4.6.32, 8.2.42, 8.7.9 and 8.24.44.
21. It is interesting to observe that ISKCON's rich iconographic tradition depicts situations like those described here, but, of course, only in two dimensions. As a matter of fact, it is not in ISKCON's most popular books that suggestions of higher dimensions are promoted, and therefore the ordinary devotee is left with pictures of, for instance, gods with their shoulders strangely burdened with an overload of heads and limbs. Sources have explained to me that 'in the past everything was possible' or 'In the world of Krishna no limits exist', but the iconographic standards still struggle with the problems of the two dimensions.
22. Sadaputa dasa is focusing on astronomy in this connection, but in principle any scientific discipline is criticized in the same way.
23. Sadaputa dasa discusses these internal contradictions in Chapter 7 in his book.
24. These aspects Sadaputa dasa discusses in Chapter 5 in his book.
25. In a way ISKCON also points to religious techniques (yoga) as a means of obtaining correct knowledge (Rameswaram 1984, 27). This knowledge, however, is not that of experimental physics, but the knowledge contained within the sacred texts.
26. See for instance the examples published in Prabhupada 1990, dating from the late 1960s and the early 1970s. I shall return to Prabhupada's person in Chapter 9.
27. Xerox copy summarizing the themes of the debate: 'First World Congress on the Synthesis of Science and Religion. The Bhaktivedanta Institute 1987'. Received from Danish ISKCON.
28. Some of the contributions were indeed focusing on cosmology. What I am commenting on is ISKCON's principle intention with the whole arrangement.
29. 'World Congress for the Synthesis of Science and Religion: Final Announcement'. Leaflet from the Bhaktivedanta Institute. January 1986 pp. 1-2.
30. After the congress ISKCON asked Eileen Barker to give a personal account of her experiences during the congress. Her article appeared in ISKCON Review later the same year (Barker 1986).

31. Apparently some of the delegates had hesitated to accept the invitation due to the nature of the hosts.
32. Maharishi's discussions with newspaper men and Christian clergy took place during the sixties. See as an example Floor 1968, 83-98.
33. Interview with devotee, March 1991.
34. Interview, November 1992.
35. Examples of how TM looks upon scientific theories apart from those discussed in the present study is given in Dam 1985.

**Notes to Chapter 9**
1. A closer examination of ISKCON's relation to nature and the role of animals in the belief system cannot be pursued here, but no doubt ISKCON's growing engagement in nature preservation derives its inspiration from the Vaisnava theology. For references see Jensen and Rothstein 1991, 67-89 (on nature preservation) and Rothstein 1990 (on the conception of nature in ISKCON) and the ISKCON publication Prime 1990 (on nature preservation).
2. One good example is the Jehova Witneses': 'Life — How Did It Get Here? By Evolution or by Creation?', International Bible Students Association. New York 1985. Within mainstream churches the creationist movements are growing as well.
3. This deistic notion is also discussed in Chapter 11.
4. Back To Godhead Magazine November/December 1992, 20.
5. Quotation from Danish ISKCON's internal bulletin: 'Krishnas Venner' no. 6, 1989. Corresponding statements are found in Prabhupada 1990.
6. Quotation from Danish ISKCON's internal bulletin: 'Krishnas Venner' no. 9, 1990. Corresponding statements are found in Sarva Jnana das (ed.) 1991, 10 ('Srila Prabhupada Speaks Out on Science and Belief') .
7. Burr is quoting Prabhupada in Back To Godhead Magazine Vol. 12. No. 5. p. 4. (s.a.).
8. The bibliography refers to the Danish edition; 'Liv kommer fra liv' (1990).
9. ISKCON's notions of creation involve the well known myths of *Maha-Vishnu* from whom the universes emanate and *Brahma* who is in charge of the material realms. A comprehensive collection of these (and other Puranic myths) are found in Dimmitt and van Buitenen 1978.
10. Leading members of ISKCON in Denmark asked me for advice regarding an offensive against biologists and zoologists in Denmark. What the devotees had in mind was to produce a sample of papers about 'spiritual evolution' and donate it to various scientists in order

to provoke their evolutionary notions. How do we approach them most successfully, they asked? (Spring 1992).
11. Back To Godhead Magazine January/February 1992, 15-16.
12. Interview, July 1992. Ten or twelve years ago a group of TM's Danish members left the organization because some of the more advanced meditators were professionally engaged in producing and selling cages for vivisection animals. One of the apostates told me that when such a thing could happen, then clearly Maharishi's technique was not at all as good as promised. It had not made people become more humane.
13. These ideas were presented during a conversation with American devotees visiting the ISKCON temple of Copenhagen in February 1991.
14. Interview in Malmö, Sweden during August 1991.
15. Interview, August 1991.
16. Of course we cannot expect qualified answers from any general member of the group. The reason why I asked about the Passenger Pigeon is the grotesqueness of the event. The example made my point clear to my informant. We may also notice that the rejection of animal extinction seems quite out of tune with ISKCON's work for nature preservation. However, even if animals (souls) will live (incarnate) elsewhere in the many universes, humans are — according to *ahimsa* — obliged to protect them.
17. Interview, August 1991.
18. The tremendous succes of the novel and motion picture Jurassic Park, which tells the story of revived dinosaurs, may serve as an indication of how secular society feels about the creatures of the past. It is perfectly possible that religious groups, or individuals within such groups (in this case ISKCON), have been affected by the public interest in dinosaurs.
19. This figure was obtained through inquiries to botanists.
20. Even if ISKCON and TM may seem far apart in this respect, Maharishi's writings actually contain similar considerations: 'One who has not realized the truth ... does not deserve to be called man' (Maharishi 1979, 279).
21. Not all devotees will agree with the details put forward in this particular publication.
22. Field notes, May 1991.
23. Interview, September 1991
24. The videos (released during 1991) are obtainable from The Bhaktivedanta Institute in San Diego.
25. Interview, February 1992.

## Notes to Chapter 10

1. Practicing TM teachers are usually not inclined to reveal anything about the initiation ritual. Certain xerox copies of the ritual text have circulated during the years, and Anti-Cult Movements and Christian apologetics have frequently been able to present the text or at least drafts from it. My Danish sources were never willing to discuss esoteric matters of initiation with me. They persistently presented the official explanation, which obviously is only true to a certain degree.
2. It should be noted, of course, that Maharishi himself holds a similar position. However, TM, carefully sees to it that Maharishi is presented more as a philosopher, an idealist and a genius, than as a guru.
3. Field notes, September 1991.
4. Field notes, September 1991.
5. Elsewhere I have considered the fact that ISKCON at other times promotes Sankara as being in fact a theist (p. 184, 187).
6. Interview with devotee in Copenhagen, March 1991.
7. See note 5.
8. Indeed passages in the basic texts of TM and ISKCON seem to be advantageous in terms of understanding the more specific statements on modern science in both groups, and obviously it is relevant to show that the divergent religious and ideological arguments concerning modern science are rooted in some of the most renowned and sacred texts. However, direct references to modern science only rarely appear in the commentaries to the classical texts, although more often in Prabhupada's expositions than in those of Maharishi.
9. Maharishi's translation.
10. Some sources disagree that MIU is the heart of the organization. However, from an outsider's position, MIU seems to be very essential, not only to the organisation TM, but also to the development and distribution of the belief system itself.
11. For an internal presentation of MIU and the activities going on there see 'MIU World. Documenting the Rise of Heaven on Earth through Maharishi's Transcendental Meditation' Vol. 1. No. 1. MIU 1991.
12. All inner-group members dress in much the same way. Male members typically wear suit and tie and keep their haircut short. Female members prefer dresses to pants, and very often grow their hair long. Both sexes confirm classical (masculine/feminine) ideals. As no social anthropological analysis is attempted here, I shall merely refer to Robert McCutchan who claims that the outward appearance of the inner-group members is part of a deliberate strategy: They are supposed to confirm to the ideals of mainstream society in order to appear as attractive as

possible (1977, 148). This, of course, is a parallel to the use of science in the belief system (SCI) which (among other things) was introduced in order to appear sympathetic to the surroundings. It should be stressed, though, that the dress code among today's members of TM may be understood much as 'tradition' rather than 'strategy' not to mention 'obedience'.

13. Questions of creation only rarely appear in TM's materials. In my article on mysticism and ritual in TM (Rothstein 1991c. With an English summary), I have tried to show how the meditation re-actualizes the cosmogonic act, namely the original meditation of the Creator, thereby designating the meditation 'an internal ritual drama'. In this sense, if I am correct, the re-creation of the universe through meditation is an integral part of TM's project, but most significantly the mythology of the movement remains a description of the universe. This problem highlights yet another dimension outside the direct scope of the present study, namely the relations between belief system and ritual practice (a problem which McCutchan also touches upon 1977, 153). In a few cases the theory of the Big Bang has been promoted by TM representatives, but only rarely as official TM points of view (Dam 1985).
14. While science by itself does not constitute a value, it is obvious that scientists have to submit (or at least relate) to the ethical and moral standards of their society.

**Notes to Chapter 11**
1. Interview, January 1992. (cf. p. 71).
2. The following description and analysis follows up what has already been said about the theological differences between TM and ISKCON. A good presentation of the theological dispute between Advaita-Vedanta and other schools of thought is found in Copleston 1980.
3. No commentary or translation of the *Brahma-sutra* has yet appeared from TM, but Maharishi 1986, 589 indicates that he worked on such a commentary during 1969. Sankara wrote a commentary on that particular text, and therefore it is not entirely unlikely that TM's inner-group uses the text. However, I have not been able to learn more about this question.
4. 'Mayavada' is the doctrine affirming that the world is an illusion, a notion contained within speculative monistic ideas, and especially applied to the Advaita-Vedanta by ISKCON.
5. Interview, August 1991.
6. It should be noted, however, that at least four of the inner-group members of ISKCON in Denmark were involved with TM prior to their

initiation into ISKCON. Also note how the content of the conversation printed in an official ISKCON publication is accepted without any questions.
7. My inquiries into this matter left my TM sources with surprise. None of them had heard of a complete Bhagavad Gita commentary. This, however, is not to say that it has not been prepared at all, only that the text — if it exists — remains unpublished and unknown to ordinary members of TM.
8. It also appears that this discussion on TM took place just as TM experienced the most remarkable success ever in terms of attracting peoples' interest (See Bainbridge and Jackson 1981).
9. John S. Hagelin: 'Is Consciousness the Unified Field? A Field Theorist's Perspective', MIU, Fairfield, Iowa. S.a.
10. Sadaputa dasa refers to Sankara's poems 'Sri Krishnastaka' in S.D. Kulkarni: 'Adi Sankara', BHISHMA. Bombay 1987, 316 which reads: 'The whole universe with its sky, wind etc. has sprung from Him. The life of this earth is sustained through his blissfulness. He is the destroyer of the demon Madhu. At the time of deluge, the whole universe merges into Him. He is all-pervading. May such Sri Krishna appear before my eyes.

He resides in the universe and controls its activities. But this the universe does not know. This is the way the Vedas describe him. He, the Lord, is pure and is the Controller of the universe. He is fit to be meditated upon. He liberates the seers, the gods and men. May such Sri Krishna appear before my very eyes'. (*Back to Godhead* November/December 1991, 16)
11. To ISKCON nature also manifests personal divinities. A good example is ISKCON's promotion of the goddess Bhumi who is identical with planet Earth. This demi-god is often mentioned in connection with ISKCON's work for nature preservation.
12. This notion is expressed over and over again. The basic reference remains Bhagavad Purana, First Canto, Chapter 3.1-5 and Brahma-samhita, Chapter 5.
13. Interview, January 1992.

**Notes to Chapter 12**
1. Some of the most important articles until 1976 have been collected by TM and published in Orme-Johnson et. al. (eds.) 1977. See also Bloomfield et al. 1977.
2. Broadcasting in Danish ISKCON's radio ('Radio Krishna'), July 1992.

# Bibliography

*A Special Supplement of The India Times; Maharishi Mahesh Yogi and His Movement*. The India Times 23 November 1990.

Acquaviva, S.S. 1979. *The Decline of the Sacred in Industrial Society*. Oxford: Blackwell.

Ahlbäck, Tore 1990. The Theosophical Society. A New Religious Movement Based On A Conglomerate of Traditions. In: Niels G. Holm (ed.), pp. 49-60.

Aron, Elaine and Aron, Arthur 1986. *The Maharishi Effect. A Revolution Through Meditation. Scientific Discovery of the Astounding Power of the Group Mind*. Walpole: Stillpoint Publishing.

Atlan, Henri 1986. *A tort et a raison; intercritique de la science et du mythe*. Paris: Édition du Seuil.

Bainbridge, William Sims 1987. Science and Religion: The Case of Scientology. In: Bromley and Hammond, pp. 59-79.

Bainbridge, William Sims and Jackson, Daniel H. 1981. The Rise and Decline of Transcendental Meditation. In: Wilson, Bryan (ed.): *The Social Impact of New Religious Movements*. New York: The Unification Church Theological Seminary.

Baird, Robert D. 1971. *Category Formation and the History of Religions*. The Hague & Paris: Mouton & Co.

Bancroft, Anne 1989(1976). *Twentieth-Century Mystics and Sages*. London: Arkana.

Bang, Jens M. 1989. Naturvidenskab, tro og overtro. In: Gule og Laugerud, pp. 202-12.

Barker, Eileen 1989. *New Religious Movements. A Practical Introduction*. London: HMSO.

Barker, Eileen 1985. *The Making of a Moonie — Brainwashing or Choice?* Oxford: Blackwell.

Barker, Eileen 1986. World Congress for the Synthesis of Science and Religion: A Personal Account. *ISKCON Review. Academic perspectives on the Hare Krishna Movement*, Vol. 2. Washington, pp. 133-47.

Basham, A.L. 1989. *The Sacred Cow. The Evolution of Classical Hinduism* Zysk, Kenneth G. (edited and annotated) London: Rider/Beacon Press.

Bastide, Roger 1978(1960). *The African Religions of Brazil. Toward a Sociology of the Interpretation of Civilizations*. Baltimore and London: The Johns Hopkins University Press.
Beckford, James A. 1985. *Cult controversies — The Societal Response to the New Religious Movements*. London: Tavistock.
Bellah, Robert N. 1976. New Religious Consciousness and the Crisis in Modernity. In: Glock and Bellah pp. 333-52.
Bhaktiswaroopa Damodar Swami: *The Scientific Basis of Krishna Consciousness*. New York (s.a.): The Bhaktivedanta Book Trust.
The Bhaktivedanta Institute (publ.) 1986. *Interviews With Nobel Laureates and Other Eminent Scholars*. Bombay: The Bhaktivedanta Institute.
Bloomfield, Harold H.; Cain, Michael Peter; Jaffe, Dennis T. and Kory, Robert B. 1979. *TM. En gennemgang af Transcendental Meditations principper, virkning og anvendelsesmuligheder, belyst ud fra de senere års videnskabelige forskning*. Copenhagen: Nyt Nordisk Forlag.
Boyer, Pascal 1990. *Tradition as truth and communication: A cognitive description of traditional discourse*. Cambridge: Cambridge University Press.
Bromley, David G. and Hammond, Phillip E. (eds.) 1987. *The Future of New Religious Movements*. Macon: Mercer University Press.
Bromley, David G. and Shinn, Larry D. (eds.) 1989. *Krishna Consciousness in the West*. Lewisburg: Bucknell University Press.
Burr, Angela 1984. *I Am Not My Body. A Study of the International Hare Krishna Sect*. New Delhi: Vikas.
Campbell, Anthony 1974. *Seven States of Consciousness: A Vision of Possibilities Suggested by the Teachings of Maharishi Mahesh Yogi*. New York: Harper and Row.
Capra, Fritjof 1975. *The Tao of Physics*. USA: Wildwood House.
Capra, Fritjof 1982. *The Turning Point*. USA: Wildwood House.
Chopra, Deepak 1991. *Unconditional Life. Mastering the Forces that Shape Personal Reality*. New York: Bantam.
Chopra, Deepak 1989. *Quantum Healing. Exploring the Frontiers of Mind/Body Medicine*. New York: Bantam.
Copleston, Frederick 1980. *Religion and the One. Philosophies East and West*. New York: Crossroad.
Colpe, Carsten 1987. Syncretism. In: Eliade, Mircea (ed.) pp. 218-27.
Colpe, Carsten, August 1977. Syncretism and Secularisation: Complementary and Antithetical Trends in New Religious Movements? *History of Religions. An International Journal for Comparative Historical Studies*. Vol. 17. No. 1. pp. 158-76.

*Conversations With Srila Prabhupad,* Vol. 2. 1989. Los Angeles: The Bhaktivedanta Book Trust.
*Creative Intelligence no. 2.* London s.a.: SRM (Spiritual Regeneration Movement) Foundation.
Dam, Max ten 1985. *Consciousness and Matter. The Unified Field of Consciousness and the Latest Developments in Physics.* The Hague: SOMA.
Dammann, Erik 1987. *Bag tid og rom.* Oslo: Dreyer.
Dandekar, R.N. 1968. Hindu Intellectuals Under Recent Impacts of Modern Culture. *The Impact of Modern Culture on Traditional Religions Vol. 1.* Proceedings of the XIth International Congress of the International Association for the History of Religions. (California 6-11.9.1965) Leiden: Brill. p. 73-91.
Davies, Paul 1986(1983). *God and the New Physics.* [Book] Harmondsworth: Penguin.
Davies, Paul 1983. God and the New Physics. [Article] *New Scientist* 98, 872-74.
Deadwyler, William, H. III. (Ravindra-svarupa das) 1989. Patterns in ISKCON's Historical Self-Perception. In: Bromley, David G. and Shin, Larry D., pp. 55-78.
Deadwyler, William 1987. The Contribution Of Bhagavat-Dharma Toward A 'Scientific Religion' And A 'Religious Science'. In: Singh. pp. 366-80.
Diehl, Carl Gustav 1969. Replacement or Substitution in the Meeting of Religions. In: Hartmann, Sven S. (ed.), pp. 137-61.
Dillbeck, Michael D. 1989. Experience of the Ved. Realization of the Cosmic Psyche by Direct Perception: Opening Individual Awareness to the Self-Interacting Dynamics of Consciousness. *Modern Science and Vedic Science* Vol. 3. No. 2. pp. 117-54.
Dimmitt, Cornelia and van Buitenen, J.A.B. 1978. *Classical Hindu Mythology. A Reader in the Sanskrit Puranas.* Philadelphia: Temple University Press.
Ebon, M. 1967. *Maharishi, the Guru.* New York: New American Library.
Eliade, Mircea 1983-91. *De religiøse ideers historie, 1-4.* Copenhagen: Gyldendal.
Eliade, Mircea 1960. *Myths, Dreams and Mysteries.* New York: Harper & Row.
Eliade, Mircea 1983(1958). *Patterns in Comparative Religion.* London: Sheed and Ward.
Eliade, Mircea (ed.) 1987. *The Encyclopedia of Religion* [Vol. 14]. New York: Macmillan. London: Collier Macmillan.

Eliade, Mircea 1974. *The Myth of the Eternal Return, Or, Cosmos and History.* Princeton: Routledge and Kegan Paul.
Eliade, Mircea 1976. The Occult in the Modern World. *Occultism, Witchcraft and Cultural Fashions. Essays in Comparative Religions.* Chicago: The University of Chicago Press. pp. 47-68.
Eliade, Mircea 1987(1957). *The Sacred and the Profane — The Nature of Religion.* London: Harcourt Brace Jovanovich.
Ellwood, Robert S. and Partin, Harry B. 1988. *Religious and Spiritual Groups in Modern America.* Second Edition. Englewood Cliffs: Prentice-Hall.
Flor, Margherita 1968. *Maharishi Mahesh Yogi og Transcendental Meditation.* Copenhagen: Thaning & Appels Forlag.
Forem, Jack 1984(1973). *Transcendental Meditation — Maharishi Mahesh Yogi and the Science of Creative Intelligence.* London: Unwin Paperbacks.
Gelberg, Steven J. (ed.) 1983. *Hare Krishna, Hare Krishna. Five Distinguished Scholars on the Krishna Movement in the West.* New York: Grove Press.
Geertz, Armin W. 1992. *The Invention of Prophecy, Continuity and Meaning in Hopi Indian Religion.* Aarhus: Brunbakke Publications.
Gilhus, Ingvild Sælid 1989. *Bak tid og rom i religionshistorisk perspektiv.* In: Gule og Laugerud. p.157-63.
Glock, Charles Y. and Bellah, Robert N.(eds.) 1976.*The New Religious Consciousness.* Berkeley: University of California Press.
Goldhaber, Nat (et al) 1976. *TM — An Alphabetical Guide to the Transcendental Meditation Program.* New York: Ballantine.
Gomatam, Ravi 1986. Real And Artificial Intelligence. Towards a Hierarchical Model of Consciousness, Intelligence, Mind and Body. In: Singh. pp. 302-35.
Gosling, D.L. 1976. *Science and Religion in India. Christian Literature Society.* Madras.
Goswami, Satsvarupa dasa 1983. *He Built a House in Which the Whole World Can Live.* Los Angeles: Bhaktivedanta Book Trust.
Goswami, Satsvarupa dasa 1980. *Planting a Seed — New York City 1965-1966: A Biography.* Los Angeles: Bhaktivedanta Book Trust.
Gule, Lars og Laugerud, Henning (eds.) 1989. *Vitenskap og verdensbilder.* Bergen: Ariadne.
Hartman, Sven S. (ed.) 1969. *Syncretism (Scripta Instituti Donneriani Aboensis III).* Stockholm: Almqvist & Wiksell.
Hinnells, John R. (ed.) 1991. *Who's Who of World Religions.* London: Macmillan.

## 220 Bibliography

Hollings, Robert 1982. *Transcendental Meditation. An Introduction to the practice and aims of TM.* Wellingborough: The Aquarian Press.

Holm, Nils G. (ed.) 1990. *Encounter With India. Studies in Neohinduism.* Religionsvitenskapliga skrifter nr. 20. Åbo: Åbo Akademi.

Holm, Nils G. 1990. Introduction. In: Holm, Nils G. (ed.) pp. 7-24.

IAASCI (International Association for the Advancement of the Science of Creative Intelligence) (publisher) 1978. *Enlightenment To Every Individual Invincibility To Every Nation.* West Germany: MERU Press.

Jensen, Tim og Rothstein, Mikael 1991. *Gud — og grønne skove; Religioner og naturbevarelse.* Copenhagen: Munksgaard.

Jensen Tim, Rothstein Mikael og Podemann Sørensen, Jørgen (red.) 1994. *Gyldendals religionshistorie. Ritualer. Mytologi. Ikonografi.* Copenhagen: Gyldendal.

Jensen, Tim og Rothstein, Mikael 1990. *På sporet af det hellige. Om Mircea Eliades hierologi.* Psyke og Logos nr. 2. Copenhagen: Dansk Psykologisk Forlag.

Johnston, Hank 1980. The Marketed Social Movement. A Case Study of the Rapid Growth of TM. *Pacific Sociological Review,* Vol. 23..

Judah, J. Stillson 1974. *Hare Krishna and the Counterculture.* New York: Wiley.

Kvastad, Nils Bjørn 1980. *Problems of Mysticism.* Oslo: Scintilla.

Maharishi Mahesh Yogi 1965. *Love and God.* Oslo: Spiritual Regeneration Movement (SRM).

Maharishi Mahesh Yogi 1968a. *Meditation of Maharishi Mahesh Yogi.* New York: Bantam.

Maharishi Mahesh Yogi 1979(1967). *On The Bhagavad-Gita. A New Translation And Commentary. Chapters 1-6.* Harmondsworth: Penguin.

Maharishi Mahesh Yogi 1972. No title. Xerox copy of an internally circulated transcription of a lecture given in California.

Maharishi Mahesh Yogi 1968b. *The Divine Plan.* New York: Bantam.

Maharishi Mahesh Yogi 1968(1963). *The Science of Being and Art of Living.* New York: New American Library.

Maharishi Mahesh Yogi 1966(1963). *The Science of Being and Art of Living.* Rishikesh, India: International SRM Publications.

Maharishi Mahesh Yogi 1986. *Thirty Years Around the World — Dawn of the Age of Enlightenment,* vol. 1. 1957-64. Vlodrop, The Netherlands: MVU Press.

McCutchan, Robert 1977. The Social and the Celestial: Mary Douglas and Transcendental Meditation. *The Princeton Journal of the Arts and Sciences* 1, 2. pp. 130-63.

McGuire, Meredith B. 1987. *Religion: The Social Context* (2.ed.). Belmont: Wadsworth Publishing.
McMullin, Ernan 1987. The Impact of the Theory of Evolution on Western Religious Thought. In: Singh, D. pp. 75-85.
Melton, J. Gordon 1986. *Encyclopedic Handbook of Cults in America.* New York: Garland.
Melton, J. Gordon, Clarck, Jerome and Kelly, Adian A. 1991. *New Age Almanac.* New York: Visible Ink.
MERU Press 1977. *Scientific Research on the Transcendental Meditation Program*: Collected Papers, Volume 1. USA.
MIU Press (Maharishi International University Press) (publisher) 1988. *Scientific Research on The Maharishi Technology of the Unified Field: The Transcendental Meditation and TM-Sidhi Program. One Program to Develop All Areas of Life.* Fairfield, Iowa: MIU Press.
MIU Press (Maharishi International University Press) (publisher)1991. *MIU World. Documenting the Rise of Heaven on Earth Through Maharishi's Transcendental Meditation.* Vol. 1., No. 1. Fairfield, Iowa.
*Modern Science and Vedic Science; An Interdisciplinary Journal Devoted to Research on the Unified Field of All Laws of Nature.* Vol. 2, No. 1. 1988. Fairfield, Iowa: Maharishi International University.
*Modern Science and Vedic Science; An Interdisciplinary Journal Devoted to Research on the Unified Field of All Laws of Nature,* Vol. 3, No. 2. 1989. Fairfield, Iowa: Maharishi International University.
Morris, Richard 1990. *The Edges of Science; Crossing the Boundary — From Physics to Metaphysics.* Englewood Cliffs: Prentice-Hall.
MVU (Maharishi Vedic University) 1985. *Maharishi Vedic University Inauguration.* Washington: Age of Enlightenment Press.
Needleman, Jacob 1972(1970). *The New Religions; The Teachings of the East — their special meaning for young Americans* (Revised Edition). New York: Pocket Books.
Nelson, Geoffrey K. 1987. *Cults, New Religions & Religious Creativity.* London: Routledge & Kegan Paul.
Nørretranders, Tor 1988. *Det udelelige. Niels Bohrs aktualitet i fysik, mystik og politik.* Copenhagen: Gyldendal.
O'Flaherty, Wendy Doniger 1988. *Other Peoples' Myths. The Cave of Echoes.* New York: Macmillan.
Olson, Helena 1979. *Maharishi at '433'. The Story of Maharishi Mahesh Yogi's First Visit to the United States.* 2nd edition. Los Angeles: R.R. Donnelley.
Orme-Johnson, David W. Ph.D., and Farrow, John T. Ph.D. (eds.) 1977.

*Scientific Research on the Transcendental Meditation Program*: Collected Papers, Volume 1. New York: MERU Press.

Phelan, Michael 1979. *Transcendental Meditation. A Revitalization of the American Civil Religion.* Archives de Sciences Sociales des Religions, 48/1.

Polkinghorne, John 1987. *One World: The Interaction of Science and Theology.* Princeton: Princeton University Press.

Prabhupada, A.C. Bhaktivedanta Swami 1986. *Bhagavad-gita As It Is.* Complete Edition. Los Angeles: The Bhaktivedanta Book Trust.

Prabhupada, A.C. Bhaktivedanta Swami 1985. *Naturlig Glæde.* Copenhagen: The Bhaktivedanta Book Trust.

Prabhupada, A.C. Bhaktivedanta Swami 1990. *Liv kommer fra liv; moderne videnskab — fantasi eller virkelighed.* Copenhagen: The Bhaktivedanta Book Trust.

Prabhupada, A.C. Bhaktivedanta Swami 1981. *Perfektion i Stridens Tidsalder.* Copenhagen: The Bhaktivedanta Book Trust.

Prabhupada, A.C. Bhaktivedanta Swami 1984. *Teachings of Lord Caitanya. The Golden Avatara.* Los Angeles: The Bhaktivedanta Book Trust.

Prabhupada, A.C. Bhaktivedanta Swami 1972-85: *Srimad Bhagavatam 1-10 (34 vol.).* Los Angeles: The Bhaktivedanta Book Trust.

Prabhupada, A.C. Bhaktivedanta Swami 1987(1975). *The Nectar of Instruction. An Authorized English Presentation of Srila Rupa Gosvami's Sri Upadesamrita.* The Bhaktivedanta Book Trust.

Prime, Ranchor (Ranchor dasa) 1992. *Hinduism and Ecology. Seeds of Truth.* Godalming: WWF.

Rameswara Swami, Srila (ed.) 1984. *Origins — Higher Dimensions in Science.* The Bhaktivedanta Institute. The Bhaktivedanta Book Trust.

Richards, Steve 1985(1980). *Levitation. What it is — How it works — How to do it.* Wellingborough: The Aquarian Press.

Ringgren, Helmer 1969. The Problems of Syncretism. In: Hartman (ed.). p. 7-14.

Rochford, Burke E. Jr. Recruitment strategies, ideology and organization in the Hare Krishna movement. *'Social Problems'* 29 (4), pp. 399-410.

Rolston III, Holmes 1987. *Science and Religion — A Critical Survey.* New York: Random House.

Rose, Donna Sue, July 1976. The Transcendental Meditation Movement: Creation, Development and Institutionalization of a World View. Unpublished dissertation. Southern Illinois University.

Rothstein, Mikael 1991(a). *The Homecoming of ISKCON.* Preprint of the

papers delivered at the First Nordic Conference for South Asian Studies, vol. 1. NASA.
Rothstein, Mikael 1989(b). Transcendental Meditation og det naturvidenskabelige gudsbevis — Et eksempel på moderne synkretisme. *CHAOS*, nr. 12., pp. 58-69.
Rothstein, Mikael 1991(c). Mystik og ritual i Transcendental Meditation (with an English summary). *Religionsvidenskabeligt Tidsskrift* nr. 18., pp. 49-71.
Rothstein, Mikael 1991(d). Maharishi-effekten og Golf-krigen. *CHAOS Dansk-norsk tidsskrift for religionshistoriske studier*, nr. 15., pp. 96-116.
Rothstein, Mikael 1990. Naturen som en fejltagelse; Naturopfattelsen hos ISKCON. *CHAOS*, nr 14., pp. 77-102.
Rothstein, Mikael 1989. Selvforståelse og intern differentiering i Transcendental Meditation i Danmark. Unpublished dissertation. University of Copenhagen.
Rothstein, Mikael 1992. Videoer og Vismænd — Traditionel og moderne kanon i de nye religioner. *CHAOS Dansk-norsk tidsskrift for religionshistoriske studier*, nr. 18., pp. 83-112.
Russell, Peter 1978. *Transcendental Meditation og udviklingen af det indre menneske — En introduktion til Maharishi Mahesh Yogis teknik og lære*. Copenhagen: Borgen.
Sarva Jnana das (et al.) (eds.) 1991. *Vedic Science for The 21st Century. The Tradition Speaks for Itself*. Calcutta: Bhaktivedanta Gurukula.
Satsvarupa dasa Gosvami 1977. *Readings in Vedic Literature. The Tradition Speaks for Itself*. Los Angeles: The Bhaktivedanta Book Trust.
Scott, R.D. 1978. *Transcendental Misconceptions*. San Diego: Beta Books.
*Seeds of Truth — Lessons on Ecology and Planet Management from the Ancient Vedas of India*. 1989. Distributed by ICOREC, WWF-UK and 'The Network on Conservation and Religion', Great Britain.
Sheldrake, Rupert 1988. *The Presence of the Past*. London: Fontana.
Shinn, Larry D. 1987. *The Dark Lord: Cult Images and the Hare Krishna in America*. Philadelphia: Westminister Press.
Shinn, Larry D. 1987. The Future of an Old Man's Vision: ISKCON in the Twenty-First Century. In: Bromley and Hammond, pp. 123-40.
Sing, T. D. (ed.) 1987. *Synthesis of Science and Religion — Critical Essays and Dialogues*. San Francisco/Bombay: The Bhaktivedanta Institute.
Singh, T. D. 1987. Vedantic Views on Evolution. In: Sing (ed.), pp. 87-103.
Smith, Adrian B. (ed.) 1983. *TM: An Aid to Christian Growth*. Essex: Mayhew McCrimmon.

Stanesby, Derek 1985. *Science, Reason & Religion*. London: Routledge.
Stone, Donald 1976. The Human Potential Movement. In: Glock and Bellah, pp. 93-115.
Thompson, Richard L. (Sadaputa dasa) 1981. *Mechanistic and Nonmechanistic Science. An Investigation Into the Nature Of Consciousness and Form*. Los Angeles: The Bhaktivedanta Book Trust.
Thompson, Richard L. (Sadaputa dasa) 1989. *Vedic Cosmography and Astronomy*. Los Angeles: The Bhaktivedanta Book Trust.
Vishnupada, Harikesa. *En Tidløs Livsstil*. ISKCON i Danmark. Copenhagen s.a.
Vishnupada, Harikesa 1981. *Varnasrama Manifesto for Social Sanity*. The Bhaktivedanta Book Trust.
Wallace, Robert Kieth 1991. *The Neurophysiology of Enlightenment*. Fairfield, Iowa: MIU Press.
Wallis, Roy 1987. Hostage to Fortune: Thoughts on the Future of Scientology and the Children of God. In: Bromley and Hammond, pp. 80-90.
Wallis, Roy 1984. *The Elementary Forms of the New Religious Life*. London: Routledge & Kegan Paul.
Whaling, Frank 1987. The Hindu Tradition in Today's World. In: Whaling, Frank (ed.): *Religion in Today's World*. Edinburgh: Clark. pp. 128-73.
Woodrum, Eric 1975. A Sociological Study of the Transcendental Meditation Movement. M.A. thesis. Unpublished. University of Texas at Austin.
Woodrum, Eric 1977. The Development of the Transcendental Meditation Movement. *The Zetetic Scholar*, No. 1., pp. 38-48.
Woodrum, Eric 1985. Religious Belief Transformation; A Study of This Worldly Religion. *Sociological Inquiry*, Vol. 55. No. 1., pp. 16-35.
Woodrum, Eric 1982. Religious Organizational Change; An Analysis Based On the TM Movement. *Review of Religious Research*, Vol. 24. No. 2., pp. 89-103.

# Index

Acquaviva, S. S.  17
Ahlbäck, Tore  206
Aron, Arthur  75, 77, 161, 205
Aron, Elaine  75, 77, 161, 205
Atlan, Henri  22, 23, 197
Aurobindo  98

Bainbridge, William Simms  43-45, 68, 99, 103, 204, 215
Baird, Robert D.  20
Bancroft, Anne  202
Bang, Jens M.  201, 206
Barker, Eileen  136, 192, 202, 210
Basham, A. L.  98-99
Bastide, Roger  51
Beckford, James A.  25, 42, 107, 201-2
Bellah, Robert N.  25, 41
Bhaktisiddhanta Saraswati Thakura  108
Bhaktiswaroop Damodar  119, 151, 155, 159
Bhaktivadenta Swami Prabhupada, A. C.  108-11, 116, 119, 122-24, 135, 139-41, 144, 146-50, 152-53, 156, 161, 170, 174-76, 178-79, 181, 184-87, 195, 200, 207-8, 211
Bhaktivinoda Thakura  108
Bloomfield, Harold H.  69, 215
Bohr, Niels  122, 206
Boyer, Pascal  125

Brahmananda Saraswati  26-27, 30, 37, 47, 62-66, 76-77, 169, 202, 204
Bromley, David G.  107, 109
Burr, Angela  10, 147-48, 195, 208, 211

Campbell, Anthony  30, 54, 202
Capra, Fritjof  205
Caitanya Mahabrabhu,  14, 108-11, 113, 117, 135, 150, 172, 174, 179, 208  191
Chopra, Deepak  28, 72, 203
Colpe, Carsten  18, 21, 36, 50-51, 201
Copleston, Frederick  49-50, 168, 214

Dalai Lama  13, 135
Dam, Max  211, 214
Dammann, Erik  196
Dandekar, R. N.  99
Darwin, Charles  144-47, 150-53, 155-56, 163, 165
Davies, Paul  87-88, 99, 204
Deadwyler, William (see Ravindra-svarupa dasa)
Diehl, Carl Gustav  37-39
Dillbeck, Michael  56, 94
Dimmitt, Cornelia  211
Domash, Lawrence  88
Dumezil, Georges  128

Einstein, Albert  85
Eliade, Mircea  80-84, 179-80, 198, 205-6
Ellwood, Robert S.  14, 35

Flor, Margherita  26, 211
Forem, Jack  30-31, 41, 46, 68-69, 102, 177

Geertz, Armin W.  20-21, 57, 79
Gelberg, Steven  107, 172
Gilhus, Ingvild  196
Goldhaber, Nat  70, 166
Gomatam, Ravi  147
Goswami, Satsvarupa dasa  178, 108, 208

Hagelin, John S.  188-89, 215
Heiler, W.  208
Hinnells, John R.  26, 108
Hollings, Robert  166
Holm, Nils G.  98
Hridayananda dasa Goswami  209
Hubbard, Ron L.  43, 84

Jackson, Daniel H.  68, 204, 215
Jarvis, Jerry  40, 69
Jensen, Tim  109, 202, 211
Johnston, Hank  105, 207
Judah, J. Stillson  107, 109, 173

Kapila  175-76, 178
Kulkarni, S. D.  215
Kvastad, Nils Bjørn  95

Leibnitz, G.W.  120
Lincoln, Bruce  205
Lutes, Charles  41

Madhva  15, 166, 171-72
Maharishi Mahesh Yogi  25-32, 37-41, 44, 46-48, 50-51, 53-54, 56-57, 60-68, 70-79, 82, 85-86, 88-89, 92-95, 100-2, 104-6, 108, 115, 117, 126, 139, 148, 166-71, 173, 176-79, 181-82, 184-89, 195, 202-5, 207, 210, 212-14
McCutchan, Robert  69-71, 196, 205, 213, 214
McMullin, Ernan  146
Melton, J. Gordon  26-27, 34, 45, 202
Midgley, Mary  201
Morris, Richard  52, 86
Muhammad  37

Needleman, Jacob  68, 202
Nelson, Robert  136, 202
Newton, Isaac  120, 204
Nimbarka  15
Nørretranders, Tor  206

Olson, Helena  66-67
Orme-Johnson, David  215
Otto, Rudolph  81
O'Flaherty, Wendy Doniger  101-2

Partin, Harry B.  14, 35
Patanjali  32
Podemann Sørensen, Jørgen  203

Polkinghorne, John C.  209
Prime, Ranchor  211

Radhakrishnan  99
Ramakrishna  98
Ramanuja  15, 166, 171-72
Ramesvara  118-19, 142, 149, 164
Rameswara  122, 127, 147, 151
Ravindra-svarupa dasa  119-20, 130, 139-41, 173
Richards, Steve  202
Ringgren, Helmer  19-21, 37
Rochford, E. Burke  107
Rolston III , Holmes  14, 48-49, 76
Rose, Donna Sue  25, 66, 93
Rothstein, Mikael  33-34, 84, 87, 96, 109, 141, 152, 160, 182, 202-3, 207, 211, 214
Russell, Peter  26, 28, 96, 105, 166

Sadaputa dasa  118, 122, 125-34, 139, 145, 148, 188-89, 197, 208-10, 215
Sankara  14-15, 26-27, 49-50, 166, 168, 171-73, 186, 189, 213-15
Sarva Jnana das  211
Saunaka Rishi dasa  207
Schaeffler, Richard  205
Scott, R. D.  41
Sharma, Hari  154
Sheldrake, Rupert  88-89, 206
Shinn, Larry D.  107, 109, 113, 116, 208
Singh, T. D.  134-35, 153

Smith, Adrian B.  166
Stanesby, Derek  13
Stark, Rodney  43
Steiner, Rudolph  37
Stone, Donald  25, 34
Suhotra Swami  208

Thompson, Richard L. (see Sadaputa dasa)

Urmila Devi dasi  153

van der Leeuw, Geradus  82
van Buitenen, J.A.B.  211
Vishnupada, Harikesa  116, 161, 208
Vivekananda  98

Wallace, A. R.  72, 151
Wallis, Roy  25, 41, 107, 115, 138, 202, 205
Whaling, Frank  192-93
Wheeler, John  87
Widengren, Geo  82
Woodrum, Eric  11, 25, 65, 67, 69, 71-73, 75, 79, 81

STAFFORD LIBRARY
COLUMBIA COLLEGE
1001 ROGERS STREET
COLUMBIA, MO 65216